POST-TRAUMATIC STRESS DISORDER

POST-TRAUMATIC STRESS DISORDER

Diagnosis, Treatment, and Legal Issues

BY C. B. SCRIGNAR, M.D.
Clinical Professor of Psychiatry
Tulane University School of Medicine
New Orleans

PRAEGER SPECIAL STUDIES • PRAEGER SCIENTIFIC

New York • Philadelphia • Eastbourne, UK
Toronto • Hong Kong • Tokyo • Sydney

Library of Congress Cataloging in Publication Data

Scrignar, C. B. (Chester B.)
    Post-traumatic stress disorder.

    Bibliography: p.
    Includes index.
    1. Post-traumatic stress disorder. I. Title. [DNLM:
1. Stress disorders, Post-traumatic. WM 170 S434p]
RC552.P67S37   1984   616.85'21   84-6942
ISBN 0-03-071597-0 (alk. paper)

Credit: Frontispiece, entitled Trauma, *drawn by Mary Sue Roniger.*

Published in 1984 by Praeger Publishers
CBS Educational and Professional Publishing
a Division of CBS Inc.
521 Fifth Avenue, New York, NY 10175 USA

© 1984 by Praeger Publishers

All rights reserved

456789 052 9876545321

Printed in the United States of America
on acid-free paper

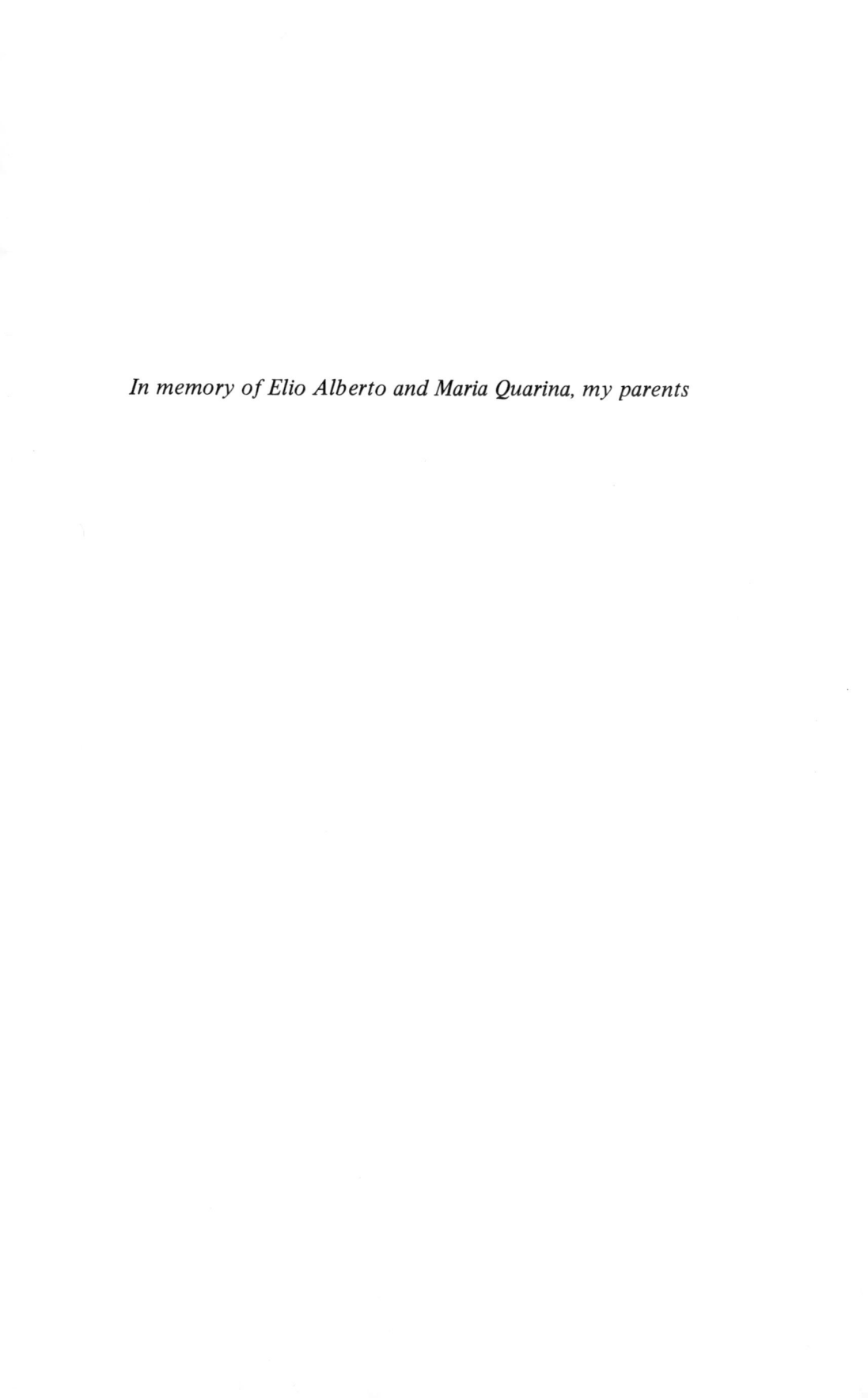

In memory of Elio Alberto and Maria Quarina, my parents

FOREWORD

Just what is a Post-Traumatic Stress Disorder, and what are its clinical and legal implications? It has long been known that traumatic events can produce serious emotional reactions. Indeed, the history of humankind is marked with trauma. When Chicago went up in flames, many people came down with PTSD, as it is now called. The victim of a mugging or a rape is left with psychological damage. As many as a million Vietnam combat veterans are claiming a Delayed PTSD.

To be sure, trauma has always been with us, yet the literature has been lean and the conceptualization poor. As recent as two generations ago, emotional distress of any kind was considered the result not of any environmental factors — social or psychological — but of such unsavory agents as witches, the devil, or "humors." Masturbation was frequently blamed.

There has been much progress in understanding trauma, but there is still a question of PTSD as a clinical entity, and how to deal with it. Until very recently, few mental health professionals, and even fewer attorneys, understood PTSD and its ramifications. Following World War II, professionals who endorsed the concept spoke about "traumatic neurosis" or "neurosis following trauma." It was not until 1980, with the publication of the American Psychiatric Association's third edition of its *Diagnostic and Statistical Manual (DSM-III)*, that PTSD entered the official nomenclature. The *DSM-III* describes PTSD as a constellation of characteristic symptoms that develop "following a psychologically traumatic event that is generally outside the range of usual human experience." Prior to 1980 the symptoms that are now grouped under PTSD were not included under a single diagnostic heading. The original edition of the *DSM*, published during the Korean war in 1952, included a diagnostic category for "Gross Stress Reaction" that referred to combat as one of a number of precipitating factors. The *DSM-II*, in 1968, dropped "Gross Stress Reaction," and categorized the symptoms under "Transient Situational Disturbances."

Is PTSD a valid or reliable concept? With the advent of PTSD as a diagnostic entity, some victims of severely stressful events are now regarded as suffering from a specific mental disorder etiologically related to a precipitating stressor. Some argue, however, that PTSD lacks clinical specificity and valid diagnostic criteria, or that it relies too heavily on a self-report of the individual, and that it can be readily abused as a legal defense in criminal cases or as an element of damages in negligence cases.

PTSD is among the few psychiatric disorders listed in the *DSM-III* that are defined in part by environment. The event context, described as "generally outside the range of usual human experience," poses the question of just what is included and excluded. Freud separated the war neurosis from the ordinary neurosis of peacetime, but he cautioned, "The war neurosis may proclaim too loudly the effects of mortal danger and may be silent or speak only in muffled tones of the effects of frustration in love." The *DSM-III* excludes from PTSD such common experiences as simple bereavement, chronic illness, business losses, and marital conflict; it includes rape, assault, military combat, floods, earthquakes, car accidents with serious physical injury, airplane crashes, large fires, bombing, torture, death camps, and other accidental human-made disasters.

Is a diagnosis in relation to a stressor event a distinction without a difference? The death of a loved one is an experience facing all of us, a common life event, leaving many in a pathological state. Is it any different from that resulting from events generally outside the range of usual human experience? What measure is to be taken of preexisting personality characteristics? What are the clinical and legal consequences of the disorder?

In this book Dr. C. B. Scrignar discusses the diagnosis, treatment, and legal issues of PTSD. Dr. Scrignar brings to the task a background of nearly 20 years of teaching and practical experience. In his career he has treated several hundred patients suffering with the disorder, and he has frequently been called upon as an expert witness in both criminal and civil cases. All too often, books written by academics have little practical value, whereas books by practitioners tend to be a mere telling of "war stories." This book is a wonderful integration of theory and practice. It is innovative. It is helpful to both clinician and lawyer and is, without doubt, the definitive work on the subject.

In both clinical and legal practice, PTSD is a relatively new way of describing and explaining behavior. The potential for creative and responsible applications of the concept is just being realized. Dr. Scrignar's pioneering text will educate, and his case examples will illuminate. He examines the diagnostic criteria for PTSD. He analyzes the legal issues. He discusses ways of testifying in court. He unravels the Delayed PTSD. And he does it all superbly, with utmost clarity. As lagniappe, he gives us witticisms we are not likely to forget.

Dr. Scrignar sets out, in a fascinating way, what he considers to be the sources for the production and maintenance of pathological anxiety — namely, the environment, encephalic events, and endogenous processes. They are called, for easy reference, the Three E's. The category Post-Traumatic Stress Disorder, Dr. Scrignar observes, could have been called Post-Traumatic Anxiety Disorder, since stress and anxiety involve the same psychophysiological systems and for all practical purposes are the same. Following a trauma the interaction of the Three E's determines whether or not a state of pathologic anxiety is maintained. Pathologic anxiety may be said to emanate from the Three E's — these factors interact to determine whether the anxiety will be maintained. Anxiety is described as pathologic when the autonomic nervous system discharges so quickly or unpredictably that the person is rendered seemingly incapable of thought or movement.

As Dr. Scrignar explains, the initial feature in determining whether a PTSD develops is the impact of the trauma on the individual's autonomic nervous system. Any outside stimulus, if perceived as dangerous, can be regarded as a trauma and precipitate a PTSD. A common misconception by lawyers and others is that a PTSD is dependent on physical injury, and that if no physical pathology is present, a PTSD is not valid. These days, however, litigation increasingly involves injuries having psychological components or claims that are based entirely on psychological harm. The courts, by and large, no longer require physical injury or impact in an action for negligent infliction of emotional distress, for instance.

Persistence in the habit of thinking and visualizing scenes directly and indirectly related to the traumatic event is one of the most important factors in maintaining a PTSD. These encephalic processes result in retraumatization of the patient when confronted with environmental stimuli that the patient associates with or that resemble the initial traumatic event. Dr. Scrignar describes this process as the Spiral Effect.

Because PTSD is a multifaceted disorder involving not only post-traumatic stress but disruptions in other areas of personal functioning as well, Dr. Scrignar has developed a broad range of appropriate treatment techniques. The goal of treatment is the gradual lessening and modification of stimuli from the Three E's through various antianxiety schemes. Usually a return to normal functioning is slow and tedious, but when the person begins to cope adequately with the stresses of everyday life, treatment is considered to be successful. As demonstrated through the case studies presented here and through his many other successes in private practice, Dr. Scrignar's treatment methods are worthy of critical acclaim.

It is an especial honor to introduce this book because Dr. Scrignar is a cherished friend. I met Chet, as he is affectionately known, in the early 1960s when I, though a law professor, was invited to do a residency in the Tulane University Department of Psychiatry and Neurology. Chet was a resident at the time. Even then, he was challenging old ideas and seeking new and more effective therapy. He was not afraid to look at the new for the sake of the old. He was imaginative then, always probing, as he is now. He was a pleasure to behold.

After a few years of practice, Dr. Scrignar found that traditional therapy was costly and ineffective for a considerable number of patients. His training in psychodynamics and psychoanalysis seemed inadequate for treating the types of patients discussed in this book. One is reminded of the characterization of psychotherapy as "an undefined technique applied to unspecified cases with unpredictable results – and for this technique, rigorous training is required." Dr. Scrignar turned his sights to behavior therapy. After studying under Dr. Joseph Wolpe in 1968, Dr. Scrignar began applying behavioral concepts to patients with "traumatic neurosis." He found behavior therapy best suited to conceptualize and to treat those involved in a traumatic incident. He has developed the therapy to a fine art. His behavior therapy center in New Orleans is a byword.

Dr. Scrignar is a prominent academic as well as practitioner. He excels in both word and deed. In fact, his academic achievements are so many that one might assume that he is fulltime in academia. He began teaching at Tulane University after finishing his residency, and currently he is Clinical Professor of Psychiatry in the Tulane University School of Medicine, Adjunct Professor of Law and Psychiatry in the School of Law, and Lecturer in the School of Social Work. In 1964 he initiated a course in forensic psychiatry in both the Tulane Department of Psychiatry and the then tradition-bound School of Law. At that time only a handful of law schools around the country offered a course in forensic psychiatry, and even those tended to focus primarily on issues of criminal reponsibility. Dr. Scrignar explored the psychological impact of trauma, and he turned it into a fascinating subject.

Dr. Scrignar is the author of more than 30 articles and an earlier book in the area, *Stress Strategies*. He has been active, giving generously of his time, in many professional and civic organizations. Friends love to have a coke or beer with Chet and to talk with him. He radiates with optimism and good cheer. He has been an inspiration. He has enriched my life, and for his friendship I am forever grateful. His wonderful spirit will be found in this book.

> Ralph Slovenko
> Professor of Law and Psychiatry
> Wayne State University School of Law

PREFACE

In 1964, when I first began teaching a course in forensic psychiatry at Tulane University School of Law/School of Medicine, the subject of personal injury and traumatic neurosis was pallid compared with the more intriguing and interesting aspects of criminal behavior and the law. The insanity defense, juvenile delinquency, adult crime, drug abuse, obscenity and pornography, prostitution, sexual perversion, and the places where miscreants dwell — jails, prisons, maximum security hospitals, and the streets — offered excitement and stimulation for the students and professors alike. During the decade of Tulane's "community- and action-oriented training program in law and psychiatry," convicted felons, drug dealers, pimps, prostitutes, and other sordid souls were invited to participate in class with such honorable guests as judges, criminal lawyers, prosecutors, police officers, jailers, politicians, and other members of the criminal justice system. The lively atmosphere of the classroom was peppered with salient questions, comments, and arguments as we all learned from one another. A lull occurred during the obligatory presentations on personal injury litigation and Traumatic Neurosis, as invited plaintiff and defense attorneys plodded through their ponderous presentations. The subject of the psychological impact of a trauma was unappealing to me at this time and nurtured nonaltruistic notions of fraud, fakery, and financial finagling.

As the years passed, former students, now attorneys, sought my assistance and advice for their "traumatized" clients. What was formerly somewhat of a bore became a fascinating puzzle — at times gin-clear, at other times mystifying. Unraveling the complexities of a patient's psychological response to trauma presented a challenge, and explaining my results in court became an exercise in pedagogy, debate, and persuasion, all of which were invigorating.

Treating traumatized patients proved to be a difficult endeavor. My personal analysis and training in psychodynamics seemed insufficient preparation for the perplexing task of reversing a "Traumatic Neurosis." Although supportive therapy and environmental manipulation were more potent than individual insight-oriented therapy, a framework for explaining and treating "traumatized" patients was lacking. Behavior therapy offered the theory and technology that appeared best suited to conceptualize and then to treat those who had been involved in a traumatic incident. Joseph Wolpe in 1948 had demonstrated that traumatic stimuli could elicit an anxiety response in the cat, similar to Neurosis in humans, and that these responses were largely learned and conditioned. After studying under Wolpe in 1968, I began applying behavioral concepts to patients with Traumatic Neurosis. The results proved to be superior to those from treatment methods I had formerly employed. As the years have passed, I have attempted to improve treatment, and the extent of my experience to date with several hundred patients is described within this book.

Although the concepts of stress and anxiety stem from different theoretical orientations (stress usually referring to an environmental stimulus and anxiety defined according to intrapsychic conflict), the terms are synonymous because they involve the same physiological axes and systems. In the context of this book, pathologic anxiety and stress can be interchanged, although in keeping with a clinical tradition, the terms anxiety and pathologic anxiety are used more frequently.

During the writing of this book, a colleague told me that he did not know whether he believed in the existence of the clinical entity Post-Traumatic Stress Disorder (PTSD). Such skepticism is not uncommon; clinicians often cast a suspicious glance at patients who appear unscathed following a trauma yet constantly complain of symptoms and sue for damages. The codification of PTSD in the third edition of the *Diagnostic and Statistical Manual of Mental Disorders*, the acceptance of PTSD in 1980 by the Veteran's Administration as a compensable, service-connected mental disorder, and the admissibility of PTSD in civil and criminal cases in most courts are realities that should persuade the nonbeliever. It is my hope that this book will contribute to a better understanding of PTSD and improve treatment for those suffering from this disorder.

ACKNOWLEDGMENTS

Many people have contributed to my knowledge of law and psychiatry and have given me support and encouragement during the writing of this book. Professor Ralph Slovenko of Wayne State University School of Law, a friend for more than 20 years, has freely given his time and talent over the years and was especially helpful during the writing of this volume. Ralph is one of those people who unselfishly give more than they receive, and I am thankful to count him as a special friend. I am indebted to Dr. William Bloom, Clinical Director at Southeast Louisiana State Hospital and Clinical Associate Professor of Psychiatry at Tulane University School of Medicine, for his thorough reading of the manuscript, which led to the inclusion of another chapter. Bill, an acquaintance since 1961, has become a close companion throughout the years and I thank him for his suggestions and continuing friendship. Drs. Daniel Winstead and Hugh Collins read the entire manuscript and made valuable suggestions for which I am grateful. I extend to both my sincere thanks. I wish to express my appreciation to Dr. Daniel Sprehe, an exceptional forensic psychiatrist, Clinical Associate Professor at the University of South Florida College of Medicine, and a close friend for almost a quarter-century, for sharing with me his extensive experience and knowledge in forensic psychiatry. Drs. Frank Silva, Aris Cox, Dennis Franklin and Judge Charles R. Ward of the Louisiana State Court of Appeals contributed to the writing of this book by their encouragement and sharing of knowledge of law and psychiatry. Michael Duffy and Vernon Crawford, colleagues and running companions, have read the first draft of this book and have made valuable comments for which I am most appreciative and I thank them. Over the years, in formal and informal discussions, Profs. Tom Andre, Harvey Couch, and Bob Force of Tulane University School of Law have helped guide my thinking about the law, and to them I give my thanks. Leslie Gervin, Visiting Professor at Tulane Law School, was especially helpful with the chapter on legal issues, as was C. Peter Erlinder, Assistant Professor at William Mitchell College of Law, and to both, recent acquaintances, I am thankful. My professional association with practicing attorneys has added a dimension of reality to my writing, and I wish to thank

Messrs. Danny Becnel, Paul Demarest, Mike Fenasci, Remy Fransen, Ed Golden, Henry Klein, Pete Lewis, Julian Murray, Evan Trestman, Fritz Wiedemann, and Larry Wiedemann.

During the creation of this book, my secretary, Mrs. Debbie Ely, devotedly gave of her nimble mind and fingers. She also has embarked on a creative endeavor, for coincident with the birth of this book is the birth of her first child. I wish you well, Debbie, and thanks.

Michael Fisher, Barbara Leffel, Rachel Burd, and Mary Ellen Brehm of Praeger also deserve thanks for the constructive comments and extremely valuable editorial assistance.

Finally, I wish to thank an old mentor, Dr. Robert G. Heath, former Chairperson of the Department of Psychiatry and Neurology at Tulane University School of Medicine, for asking me in 1964 to teach forensic psychiatry.

CONTENTS

Foreword *by Ralph Slovenko*   vii

Preface   xii

Acknowledgments   xiv

List of Tables   xviii

One
Historical Perspective: Trauma and Stress   1

Two
Trauma and Pathologic Anxiety   11

Three
Predisposition and Clinical Course   39

Four
Signs and Symptoms   57

Five
Differential Diagnosis   75

Six
Treatment   99

Seven
Legal Issues   137

Eight
Prevention   175

Nine
Case Histories   185

Ten
Summary and Conclusion 223

References 249

Index 263

About the Author 270

LIST OF TABLES

1-1	*DSM-III* Diagnostic Criteria for Post-Traumatic Stress Disorder	9
2-1	Levels of Anxiety Chart	13
2-2	Anxiety Source Profile I: Environmental Events	31
2-3	Anxiety Source Profile II: Encephalic Activities	33
2-4	Anxiety Source Profile III: Endogenous Sensations	34
4-1	Characteristics and Symptoms of Stage I	59
4-2	Characteristics and Symptoms of Stage II	62
4-3	Symptom Inventory Checklist	66
4-4	Characteristics and Symptoms of Stage III	70
5-1	*DSM-III* Diagnostic Criteria for Somatization Disorder	79
5-2	*DSM-III* Diagnostic Criteria for Conversion Disorder	80
5-3	*DSM-III* Diagnostic Criteria for Psychogenic Pain Disorder	82
5-4	*DSM-III* Diagnostic Criteria for Hypochondriasis	83
5-5	*DSM-III* Diagnostic Criteria for Chronic Factitious Disorder	84
5-6	Malingering as Listed in the *DSM-III*	86
5-7	*DSM-III* Diagnostic Criteria for Simple Phobia	89
5-8	*DSM-III* Diagnostic Criteria for Generalized Anxiety Disorder	89
5-9	*DSM-III* Diagnostic Criteria for Dysthmic Disorder	91
5-10	*DSM-III* Diagnostic Criteria for Antisocial Personality Disorder	94
6-1	Self-Assessment Form	104
6-2	Foods and Substances to Be Avoided When Taking Monoamine Oxidase Inhibitors	116
6-3	Treatment of Insomnia or Difficulty Falling Asleep	117
8-1	Cardinal Characteristics of Post-Traumatic Stress Disorder	179
8-2	Persons in Contact with Patient following Trauma	183

ONE
HISTORICAL PERSPECTIVE: TRAUMA AND STRESS

Behavioral abnormalities following a trauma are coeval with humanity itself. No less than modern humans, Peking and Cro-Magnon man unquestionably were exposed repeatedly to danger, both real and imagined, and experienced emotional reactions to trauma. Thunder, lightning, and other unexplained phenomena and more concrete threats from the environment, such as vicious animals and pugnacious fellow human beings, undoubtedly frightened, injured, or killed some of our primitive ancestors. One can only imagine what the reactions of our progenitors were to these life-threatening situations. However, it would seem probable that some of the survivors of these environmental traumas suffered what in modern times has been referred to as a Traumatic Neurosis and most recently codified as Post-Traumatic Stress Disorder (PTSD). From what we know of primitive humans, it is highly probable that the dysfunctional dependent behavior associated with a Stress Disorder would not have been tolerated. Members of a hunting group whose existence depended on success in their perpetual search for food to meet basic survival needs would most likely have banished, punished, or put to death unproductive members stricken by stress following a trauma, unless the victim were clever enough to claim a supernatural intervention and proclaim himself a shaman or medicine man.

As many millennia passed, civilization progressed to the agrarian and then to the industrial era. Population increased and hamlets grew into towns, towns into cities, and cities coalesced into nations.

With the increased concentration of people and especially with the development of machines, a person's opportunity for involvement in a traumatic incident also increased. However, attention focused on the physical effects of trauma and any emotional aftereffects were ignored. Prior to the nineteenth century, history leaves little recorded notice of the relationship between trauma and psychological reactions, even though the concepts of fault and negligence and the law of torts had begun to evolve before this time (Malone 1970).

Wars, the most intense, concentrated, destructive human activity, eventuate in trauma, both physical and psychological. Battlefields, the arena for broken covenants, are ghastly places of mayhem and trauma. The sounds of battle — the discharge of weapons, the fierce shrieks of attackers, the wailing of the wounded merging into the cacophony of combat — would terrify most people. The sights and smells of war are no less frightening. The maniacal looks on the faces of the enemy, together with the sight of broken, bloodied, dismembered, and disemboweled bodies of combatants and the pervasive stench of death, assail the eyes and nose of the living. Undeniably, thoughts of imminent death or injury must flood the minds of soldier and civilian alike, firmly embedding the trauma of war into consciousness.

There can be no question that some soldiers throughout history — to say nothing of the civilian victims of pillage and plunder — have been adversely affected emotionally, either temporarily or permanently, by war whether they received a physical injury or not. Yet, the relationship between war trauma and psychological sequelae received little attention until the late nineteenth century.

In the United States, Jacob Mendes DaCosta (1871) was the first to study the important physiological effects of the Civil War upon veterans, and his findings were published in the *American Journal of Medical Sciences*. DaCosta described symptoms, similar to those described earlier among British troops in India and during the Crimean War, of young Civil War veterans (two-thirds of his 300 patients were 16 to 25 years old) that included palpitations, increased pain in the cardiac region, tachycardia, cardiac uneasiness, headache, dimness of vision, and giddiness. He theorized that since there was no evidence of myocardial disease, the condition was due to a disturbance of the sympathetic nervous system. He labeled the condition "Irritable Heart," and it became known as DaCosta's Syndrome (Wooley 1982).

Sir Thomas Lewis (1919) observed symptoms of chest pain, breathlessness, palpitations, tachycardia, and fatigue in soldiers of World War I and called this "Soldier's Heart and the Effort Syndrome." Summing up, Lewis stated, "It is because these symptoms and signs are largely, in some cases wholly, the exaggerated physiological response to exercise . . . that I term the whole the 'Effort Syndrome'." While noting that nervous manifestations were "more or less prominent," Lewis wrote that "a proportion of the patients whom I include in the group, Effort Syndrome, sooner or later acquire a diagnosis of Neurasthenia." Oppenheimer (1918), a contemporary of Lewis, noted the psychoneurotic factor in Irritable Heart of soldiers, but concentrated on the cardiac manifestations of the disorder, preferring the term "Neurocirculatory Asthenia" (Dalessio 1978).

Nonpsychiatric physicians of the early twentieth century were usually internists who concentrated on the cardiac manifestations of soldiers exposed to combat during World War I. Nervousness was noted but not emphasized by these cardiac-oriented physicians. Indeed, even today, this tendency continues, as DaCosta's Syndrome has evolved into the Mitral Valve Prolapse Syndrome, which embraces most or all of the clinical criteria associated with the earlier diagnostic entities (Wooley 1976). As psychiatry and the other behavioral science began to develop, study of the effects of trauma upon an individual took three separate but related directions: psychoanalysis (Neurosis); stress ("flight or fight" and the "alarm reaction"); and behavioral psychology (learning theory).

PSYCHOANALYSIS AND NEUROSIS

Sigmund Freud (1895) wrote a paper entitled "On the Grounds for Detaching a Particular Syndrome from Neurasthenia Under the Description 'Anxiety Neurosis'." Freud's perspicacity led him to sort out anxiety from the mélange of symptoms found in patients suffering from neurasthenia. The concept of Anxiety Neurosis gained slow acceptance by many physicians, but psychiatrists quickly embraced this psychoanalytic explanation. By the 1940s psychiatrists rather than internists or other physicians studied and treated World War II veterans suffering from the traumatic effects of battle (Kardiner and Spiegel 1947). Although the soldiers' symptoms were the same as observed by DaCosta (1871) and Lewis (1919), the diagnostic labels "Irritable Heart" and "Effort Syndrome" were abandoned as emphasis changed from somatic symptoms to intrapsychic processes. The symptoms were considered to be manifestations of anxiety and neurotic in origin. Diagnostic labels such as "Traumatic War Neurosis" and "Combat Neurosis" suggested the relationship between environmental trauma and onset of symptoms, but the condition was conceptualized in terms of a neurotic reaction. Unanimity was not present, however, as some clinicians preferred the concept of stress and wrote about combat or battle stress, battle fatigue, combat exhaustion, and acute combat reaction (Grinker and Spiegel 1945).

Following World War II, theories of Neurosis held sway and were the conceptual framework within which the psychophysiological effects of war and later civilian trauma were viewed. The term "Traumatic Neurosis" came into popular usage (Kaiser 1968). Psychoanalytic theories of Neurosis leaned heavily on an intrapsychic origin of anxiety based on concepts of conflict and repression. They embraced mythological analogies (e.g., Oedipus, Electra, Narcissus) to explain intrapsychic phenomena. These interesting and mysterious formulations attracted intellectual attention, but psychophysiological and psychoendocrine events were either ignored or subordinated to speculation and theory. The symptoms induced by trauma, now labeled as "anxiety," were viewed as a result of neurotic conflicts. This resulted in minimizing the contribution of stress researchers in the formulation of the clinical entity Traumatic Neurosis. The unfortunate result was that stress and anxiety, which involve the same psychophysiological axis, became separated in the minds of researchers and clinicians alike.

Another major dilemma and a source of considerable confusion were the attempts to reconcile Neurosis with Traumatic Neurosis. Repressed and unresolved unconscious conflicts with parents or significant others during childhood are generally considered to be etiologically significant in the development of Neurosis. In Traumatic Neurosis an external event precipitates the disorder in persons whose premorbid personality may be normal or perhaps neurotic (Cohen 1970; Slovenko 1973). These two conditions sharing the label of "Neurosis" are obviously not comparable, since in Neurosis no environmentally induced trauma is recognized as necessary to produce neurotic symptoms, whereas in Traumatic Neurosis trauma induced by an environmental event is considered to be a sine qua non.

Clinicians observed that a high percentage of persons developing a Traumatic Neurosis had a past history of psychiatric symptoms that could qualify as a Neurosis. This raised the possibility that a latent neurotic illness was made manifest by the traumatic incident. Perplexingly, it was also observed that apparently healthy individuals with no neurotic predisposition also developed a Traumatic Neurosis. This conundrum was not solved, but merely restated by Robitscher (1966) who, summarizing an American Psychiatric Association (APA) round table discussion "Neurosis and Trauma" (1960), wrote that all categories of incapacity can be "boiled down to three main types":

1. Traumatic Neurosis: A healthy individual becomes mentally ill as a result of an overwhelming stress.
2. Compensation or Triggered Neurosis: The individual has a latent illness triggered or precipitated by trauma and held onto by the patient for largely unconscious reasons.
3. Malingering: The individual consciously deceives.

This classification fitted the facts as observed by clinicians, but it fitted poorly into the nosology of Neurosis. Only a healthy (non-neurotic) individual can become neurotic as a result of an overwhelming stress (trauma). Persons, presumably emotionally unstable, who have a latent illness can, following a trauma, have their Neuroses "triggered." Also, as the label suggests, patients hold onto the Neurosis for largely unconscious reasons related to monetary compensation. Implicit, but not clearly stated, in this classification is the element of quantification — both of the trauma and the degree of mental illness present in the individual prior to the trauma. However desirable it may be to objectify trauma and Neurosis into measurable units, this is not possible at present, and the classification scheme does not improve the understanding of trauma and stress.

Eschewing the term "Neurosis," Modlin (1967) proposed "Post-Accident Anxiety Syndrome" as a more suitable label to describe the effects of trauma owing to an accident. The grouping of symptoms into a syndrome under the rubric of anxiety added clarity to a post-traumatic clinical entity that was not to emerge again until 1980 (*DSM-III* 1980).

STRESS – FLIGHT-OR-FIGHT RESPONSE AND THE ALARM REACTION

While psychoanalysis was gaining momentum during the early part of the twentieth century, the psychophysiological aspects of trauma ("emergency situations") were being studied by Walter Cannon and Hans Selye. Cannon (1929) wrote about a phenomenon he termed "homeostasis" and the "flight-or-fight" response. When a living organism was confronted with a threat to its physical integrity, or homeostasis, it responded to the "traumatic stimuli" by an activation of the sympathetic nervous system and a stimulation of the neuroendocrine system, especially the adrenal medulla. The physiological response that ensued (increased heart rate and cardiac output, increased respiration, dilation of the arteries to the skeletal muscles, etc.) prepared the organism for flight or fight as an adaptation for survival. Selye (1946, 1950, 1956) described an organism's reaction when it was suddenly exposed to traumatic stimuli to which it had not adapted and termed this "the alarm reaction," the first stage of a response he called "General Adaptation Syndrome." Selye, who first introduced the term "stress" as a physiologic concept, described the alarm reaction as an endocrine response to emergency situations. Alterations in cardiovascular functioning, respiration, muscle tone, and other physiological systems are a part of the alarm reaction. Selye observed that if this system is driven too hard or too long (chronic stress), the arousal becomes a health hazard. The symptoms produced by Cannon's flight-or-fight response (1929) and Selye's alarm reaction (1946, 1950, 1956) were strikingly similar to those of the Civil War veterans described by DaCosta (1871). It is apparent today that both Cannon and Selye were pursuing parallel courses and were studying various aspects of the same psychophysiological response to trauma that later came to be known as stress.

Stress researchers concentrated their efforts on the study of environmental influences on the nervous and endocrine system as they affected various organ systems of the body. This proved to be a more pragmatic approach to the study of stress than that of most psychiatrists and psychologists who observed stress but called it "anxiety" and postulated intrapsychic theories of Neurosis. Stress thus stood apart from anxiety in the minds of researchers, clinicians, and the public, although both terms were used to explain the same psychophysiological response (Scrignar 1983). This divergence created considerable confusion in formulating a unified concept concerning the effects of trauma upon an individual. Even today, stress and anxiety, although physiologically identical, should be interchangeable terms, but they are not because they connote different frames of reference for clinicians and the public.

BEHAVIORAL PERSPECTIVE

From Pavlov (1927) to Skinner (1938), behaviorists, sharing a scientific orientation, had a natural kinship with stress researchers, since both delved into psychophysiological responses to environmental stimuli. Unlike stress investigators, behaviorists were more clinically oriented and developed a technology that could be applied toward the treatment of pathologic symptoms and behavior in humans. In the oft-quoted experiment on Little Albert, Watson and Rayner (1920) produced an animal phobia in the 11-month-old child. In this famous experiment, which would be viewed today with disapproval by many and probably would not be allowed, the investigators struck a large iron bar behind the child each time he touched a white rat. The aversive noise soon conditioned a fear of the animal, which later generalized to other furry objects. Mary Cover Jones (1924) added a therapeutic touch when she devised a method for reversing children's fears. In the case of a 3-year-old boy called Peter, Jones noted that if a phobic object was systematically presented while the hungry child was eating, the fear response gradually abated. These early case studies during the 1920s lay in obscurity for many years to be later resurrected when the history of behavior therapy was written.

In the late 1940s, Joseph Wolpe (1958, 1982), a most significant and persistent investigator and clinician who deserves the title of "father of modern behavior therapy," conducted animal experiments which could be viewed as inducing Traumatic Neuroses. Cats were placed in an experimental cage where they periodically received painful, but not tissue-damaging, electrical shocks to their paws. The cats responded to this trauma initially with surprise, but this was quickly followed by extreme fearfulness (anxiety). After a time electrical shocks were not needed to elicit the fearful (anxious) response, and placement of the animals in the experimental cage was sufficient to stimulate an agitated and anxious state. Eventually, even the sight of the animal handler or the room where the experiment took place elicited the anxiety response.

In the classic conditioning experiment, Wolpe clearly demonstrated that traumatic stimuli could elicit a response in the cat similar to anxiety in humans. Significantly, the same response could be elicited in the absence of the aversive stimulus by simply exposing the animals to various elements of the surroundings where the trauma took place. This Pavlovian experiment was not new, but the extrapolation of results to human beings led to a different way of conceptualizing Neurosis and, more importantly, opened new avenues of treatment. Wolpe hypothesized that neurotic habits in humans were largely learned and conditioned, and he pointed out that there were numerous opportunities in real life for humans to develop neurotic habits as a response to anxiety-evoking situations. The stimulus-response relationship between environment and anxiety symptoms, supported by Wolpe's work, sparked a trend toward a more objective analysis of Post-Traumatic Stress symptoms and a treatment method called "systematic desensitization." The veil of mysticism that shrouded previous concepts of Neurosis and locked clinicians into an unclear view of the relationship between trauma and anxiety was now lifted. The stimulus-response (trauma-anxiety) model offered a physiological as well as a behavioral explanation for the relationship between trauma and anxiety.

REVISION OF NOMENCLATURE

As behavioral and pharmacologic approaches to the treatment of anxiety made steady advances, a reevaluation of terminology was necessary. It became increasingly apparent that "Neurosis," a term wedded to psychoanalytic thinking, was inadequate, for under this diagnostic heading a conglomeration of disparate psychiatric disorders were grouped — anxiety, depression, hysteria, dissociative reaction, hypochondriasis, depersonalization, and even neurasthenia (*DSM-II* 1968). In 1974 the Council on Research and Development appointed an advisory committee on Anxiety and Dissociative Disorders. The committee labored for 5 years, eventually deciding that there was no consensus concerning the definition of Neurosis. The group noted that psychoanalytic, social learning, cognitive, behavioral, and biological models all attempt to explain the development of the various neurotic disorders. Rather than endorse any theoretical conceptualization, the task force wisely decided to eliminate the term "Neurosis" and employ the atheoretic heading "Anxiety Disorders." Most of the psychiatric disorders formerly subsumed under Neurosis were now included under this new generic heading. For the first time a category called Post-Traumatic Stress Disorder was included. PTSD supplanted "Traumatic Neurosis," a term that had been used extensively in the literature but had never been officially endorsed by the APA in its first two editions of the *Diagnostic and Statistical Manual of Mental Disorders (DSM)*. Divorced from the theoretic restraints and limitations of the concept of Neurosis, the signs and symptoms of a PTSD could be described in terms of an Anxiety Disorder (Table 1-1).

TABLE 1-1
DSM-III Diagnostic Criteria for Post-Traumatic Stress Disorder

A. Existence of a recognizable stressor that would evoke significant stress in almost everyone.
B. Reexperiencing of the trauma as evidenced by at least one of the following:
   (1) Recurrent and intrusive recollections of the event
   (2) Recurrent dreams of the event
   (3) Sudden acting or feeling as if the traumatic event were recurring, because of an association with an environmental or ideational stimulus
C. Numbing of responsiveness to or reduced involvement with the external world, beginning some time after the trauma, as shown by at least one of the following:
   (1) Markedly diminished interest in one or more significant activities
   (2) Feeling of detachment or estrangement from others
   (3) Constricted affect
D. At least two of the following symptoms that were not present before the trauma:
   (1) Hyperalertness or exaggerated startle response
   (2) Sleep disturbance
   (3) Guilt about surviving when others have not, or about behavior required for survival

Table 1-1, continued

---
(4) Memory impairment or trouble concentrating
(5) Avoidance of activities that arouse recollection of the traumatic event
(6) Intensification of symptoms by exposure to events that symbolize or resemble the traumatic event
---

Source: Diagnostic and Statistical Manual of Mental Disorders, third edition, 1980. Reprinted with permission of the American Psychiatric Association.

CURRENT STATUS – POST-TRAUMATIC STRESS AS AN ANXIETY DISORDER

In 1980, the third edition of the *DSM* (1980) was published by the APA. In this manual PTSD is listed under the heading of Anxiety Disorders. Since stress and anxiety involve the same psychophysiological systems and for all practical purposes are the same, Post-Traumatic Stress Disorder could easily have been called Post-Traumatic Anxiety Disorder. Medical tradition dies hard, however, and presumably stress, which is normally associated with an environmentally induced event, was chosen in lieu of anxiety. Confusion could have been avoided and consistency maintained if stress had been eliminated from the diagnostic label but mentioned in an explanatory note or in the descriptive text. Perhaps it is enough at present to have some unanimity of opinion within the official psychiatric community that a mental disorder can develop from exposure to a traumatic incident.

TWO
TRAUMA AND PATHOLOGIC ANXIETY

The patient, a 28-year-old iron worker for a shipbuilding company, had just emerged from the hold of a vessel and was walking on the port side of the ship toward the stern. Someone called him, and he stopped and turned toward the hold he had just vacated. He was about 25 to 30 feet from the hold when there was a sudden violent explosion. The blast knocked him aft and the iron worker stumbled backward, desperately trying to keep his balance. He landed on his back and as he looked upward he saw metal flying into the air and the decapitated figure of a man hurled upward into space. To one side he also saw the legless form of another man tossed into the air. The huge roar of the explosion permeated the scene, followed in a few seconds by copious clouds of dark suffocating smoke. The iron worker stumbled, crawled, and then ran from the scene onto the dry dock. He was very scared and experienced tachycardia, palpitations, dyspnea, a heavy feeling in his chest, shaking, nausea, and profuse sweating. He went back to the ship to check on his coworkers and he saw a huge hole in the side of the vessel. One coworker ran past him hysterically screaming and yelling. As he approached the ship he looked down and saw the decapitated body of a close friend. The iron worker was frantic and began crying as he was led away to the first aid station and later to a hospital. Physical examination and X-rays disclosed no serious injuries. He was discharged on admission and sent home. The iron worker developed a PTSD.

A 42-year-old married ticket agent for a travel agency was driving his car down a highway as he was returning home from work. The next thing he remembered was opening his eyes in an ambulance and the attendant telling him he was going to be okay. Then he again lapsed into unconsciousness. Several days later he was told that a large 18-wheel truck had run a red light and broadsided his car. His automobile was totaled and doctors told him that he was lucky to be alive. He sustained the following injuries: three broken ribs; fracture of the lower right arm; deep lacerations extending from the left wrist to the upper arm, involving muscles and nerves; hairline fracture of the pelvis; trauma to the left knee; multiple lacerations and bruises of the face and head; two broken teeth; and dislocation of the jaw. The ticket agent required surgery to reset bones and to sew up the lacerations. He remained in the hospital for three weeks and returned to work 6 months following the accident. He did not develop a PTSD.

THE NATURE OF THE TRAUMA

The nature of the environmentally induced trauma and especially its impact upon the physical functioning of an individual can vary. The traumatic event may result in no, slight, or moderate to severe physical injury. When moderate to severe injury results from a trauma, and particularly when surgery or medical treatment is required, clinicians and casual observers have no difficulty in discerning the relationship between trauma and injury as it relates to pain and mental suffering. Harder to comprehend are those cases that involve no or slight physical injury and in which persons continue to complain of incapacitating symptoms. This latter group in which emotional symptoms predominate appears enigmatic because the patient's complaints and symptomatic behavior seem out of proportion to the trauma that was experienced. Emphasis is one-sided, however, when one concentrates only on the nature of the trauma as it impacts on the physical structure of the body. The two contrasting vignettes at the beginning of this chapter illustrate what is frequently seen in clinical practice — the severity of the psychiatric symptoms is not necessarily correlated with the severity of the physical trauma. In order to appreciate why this is so, an understanding of the concept of pathologic anxiety as it relates to trauma is necessary. As will be seen later, trauma, whether it be mild or severe, may or may not precipitate pathologic anxiety and a PTSD.

PATHOLOGIC ANXIETY

A subjective interpretation of whether anxiety is pathologic or not can be avoided if anxiety is conceptualized strictly in terms of autonomic nervous system functioning. In this context anxiety is pathologic when the autonomic nervous system discharges: so intensely that it renders an individual incapable of speech, movement, or thought; unpredictably and frequently in an attacklike manner; or regularly for a long duration (Scrignar 1983). Although autonomic activity is but one of the many neurophysiological and endocrine events associated with anxiety, it correlates closely with phenomena that can be observed clinically and reported by patients. Imprecise labels that refer to anxiety as adaptive or maladaptive, appropriate or inappropriate, or realistic or unrealistic can be avoided if anxiety is considered to be pathologic when the autonomic nervous system discharges frequently, intensively, or for long duration. These three parameters of pathologic anxiety can be defined and described in terms of symptomatic behavior (Table 2-1).

TABLE 2-1
Levels of Anxiety Chart

Level	Symptoms of Anxiety
Level 5 (panic)	Acute, intense, dysphoric symptoms include feelings of impending loss of physical and mental integrity, depersonalization, derealization, and incorrect encephalic statements, e.g., thoughts of impending doom, going crazy, going out of control, dying, or other thoughts of a cataclysmic nature. Panic attacks occur suddenly, without apparent warning, and are followed by severe anxiety symptoms. Autonomic hyperactivity is a prerequisite for the development of a panic attack.
Level 4 (severe)	Acute, intense symptoms include palpitations, dyspnea, hyperventilation, tightness or pain in the chest, trembling or shaking, sweating, dizziness, vomiting, fainting, tingling sensations in hands and feet, cold, clammy feeling, and hot flashes or flushing. Symptoms usually occur abruptly and unpredictably in the form of an anxiety attack.
Level 3 (moderate)	Chronic, moderate anxiety includes somatic symptoms usually affecting the gastrointestinal, cardiovascular, respiratory,

Table 2-1, continued

Level	Symptoms of Anxiety
	genitourinary, or musculoskeletal systems. When persons are in this level for most of their waking state, they are suffering from a Generalized Anxiety Disorder.
Level 2 (mild)	Subclinical mild symptoms are characterized by statements from persons that they are uptight, edgy, high strung, tense, or nervous.
Level 1 (normal)	Nonsymptomatic.

Source: Reproduced with permission from *Stress Strategies: The Treatment of the Anxiety Disorders* (Scrignar, 1983).

The effect of trauma upon a person's autonomic nervous system determines whether or not a PTSD develops. When the trauma stimulates high levels of pathologic anxiety in a vulnerable person, a PTSD is likely to develop. Persistence of pathologic anxiety, a pathomnemonic feature, distinguishes PTSD from a normal response to a stressful event. In the latter case, a person may experience high levels of anxiety at the time of the trauma, but the anxiety quickly diminishes and does not materially affect the person's life. On the other hand, individuals who develop a PTSD may experience periodic intense anxiety symptoms or, more commonly, persistent moderate levels of anxiety subsequent to their trauma. In order to understand, then, why it is that for some victims of trauma pathologic anxiety is a sequela and for some it is not, it is essential to view and to distinguish carefully among the three sources of pathologic anxiety.

THE THREE E'S, TRAUMA, AND PATHOLOGIC ANXIETY

The *environment, encephalic* events, and *endogenous* processes, the three E's, are responsible for the production and maintenance of pathologic anxiety. The interplay among the stimuli from the external world, the cognitive activities of the brain, and the internal physiological processes of the body contribute to pathologic anxiety (stress). Following a trauma, the interaction of the Three E's determines whether or not a state of pathologic anxiety is maintained. An understanding of the Three E's and trauma, therefore, clarifies the mechanisms that exist between the trauma and a pathologic emotional condition, a PTSD.

Environment

Under the proper circumstances, any environmental stimulus may be regarded as a trauma. When the trauma impacts on one or more of the five sensory pathways to the brain, stimulation of the sympathetic nervous system, followed by anxiety, results. The environmental stimulus (trauma) may be of short duration and occur only once, as in the case of an accident. In other instances it may occur intermittently and be of longer duration, as in wars, imprisonment, or systematic torture.

The initial essential feature in the development of a PTSD is neither the type nor the duration of the environmental trauma, but rather the impact the trauma has upon the autonomic nervous system of the victim. A full awareness and perception that the immediate environmental trauma poses a definite threat to the life or limb of the victim is a prerequisite for the evolution of a PTSD. At the time of the impact or shortly thereafter, the perception of imminent danger must be impressed upon the mind of the traumatized person, along with the certain conclusion of death or serious injury. The trauma must result in intense and severe autonomic nervous system discharge and the pathologic anxiety that is generated must be remembered in order for a PTSD to develop.

Vehicular Trauma

Traumas caused by accidents involving vehicles such as automobiles, trucks, airplanes, or boats, frequently result in death or serious injury. Many survivors of these accidents later develop a PTSD, particularly if they were not rendered unconscious and were fully aware of the potential for danger to self. The awareness of danger may precede, occur concurrently, or follow exposure to the traumatic incident.

A middle-aged secretary encountered a severe thunderstorm with violent winds and torrents of rain while driving home from work. She was driving on an expressway when suddenly her car engine stalled. She had been driving very slowly owing to poor visibility, and thus her automobile did not have enough momentum to switch lanes. She was stranded in the middle of the expressway. Realizing the precariousness of her situation, the secretary turned on the flasher lights and also pumped the brake pedal, hoping that both would alert oncoming drivers and prevent a rear-end collision. At the same time, she frantically tried to restart her automobile. As she looked in the rearview mirror, she saw a car rapidly approaching, the driver apparently oblivious to her plight and not responsive to her signals of distress. With mounting fear she braced herself for the inevitable collision that occurred a few seconds later. Unhurt except for some strained mucles, the secretary experienced severe palpitations, labored breathing, and extreme trembling as she marveled that she was still alive. Following this experience she displayed the signs and symptoms of a PTSD with phobic anxiety about driving and a phobia about driving on expressways, especially at night in the rain.

A middle-aged businessman returning home from a meeting was a passenger on a commercial jet. The jet had taxied to the end of the runway and was commencing its takeoff when suddenly the landing gear collapsed and the airplane began skidding down the runway. The piercing sound of metal collapsing and rending and the frenzied screams of frightened passengers filled the air as the jet slid to a stop. Efficiently and calmly, the flight attendants opened all safety exits, prepared the exit chute, and authoritatively instructed all passengers to disembark. Escape from the damaged airplane was conducted without any loss of life or serious injury to anyone. As the passengers were herded into a nearby hanger, the disabled aircraft suddenly exploded and burst into flames. The businessman, shaken by the entire experience, looked upon the flaming wreckage with horror that escalated into panic when he considered that "but for the grace of God," he could have been inside the airplane at that time. The smoke and flames of the burning jet, suggesting Dante's *Inferno,* became etched in the mind of the man. He later accepted free drinks from the airline but declined the offer of a ticket on the next flight and returned home by train. He developed a PTSD with a phobia of flying.

Industrial Trauma

Industrial settings — manufacturing plants, oil refineries, construction sites, and many other blue-collar workplaces — are inherently dangerous places with the potential for trauma. Heavy equipment, moving machinery, flammable gases or solvents, chemicals, and the carelessness of others are environmental influences that can be harmful or deadly to workers. Although safety regulations and procedures are mandated by private and public monitoring agencies, accidents still occur with regularity. When a worker is seriously injured, ministration to physical needs generally supersedes attention to the psychological manifestations produced by the trauma. After the physical injuries have been attended to, however, it is not uncommon for the symptoms of pathologic anxiety to become manifest. Unfortunately, physicians or other clinicians who fail to appreciate the psychological aftereffects of trauma may grow disdainful of patients who complain of anxiety symptoms, especially when physical injuries have healed and patients claim inability to return to work.

> An oil refinery worker in his early twenties was told by his foreman to unbolt a valve cover on a pipeline that connected two large petroleum storage tanks. The young man proceeded to unscrew the bolts, and when the last bolt was removed, the valve cover blew off, narrowly missing him. A blast of hot, flammable gas struck him in the chest and arms. In shock, the worker looked down and saw his clothes on fire and the skin of his chest melting "like candle wax." He was a human torch, screaming in pain and fright, haphazardly running in circles. He was pursued by his fellow workers who corralled him, doused his flaming clothes, and called for medical assistance. Many months later, when he had recovered from his burns and was pronounced physically fit by his doctors, he was told he could return to work. Overlooked, however, was the patient's extreme anxiety and phobic avoidance of all fire. Even the sight of a burning cigarette or an unlit match caused tachycardia, hyperventilation, and hyperhidrosis. Work in an oil refinery was impossible since he had developed a PTSD with a severe phobia of fire and all things potentially flammable.

Criminal Assaults

The unlawful use of coercion or battery upon an individual is an odious act that precipitates anxiety and is capable of initiating a PTSD. A blow to the body by fist or bludgeon, the sight of a weapon aimed at one's head, and verbal threats portending injury or death constitute environmental traumas that are associated with criminal conduct. Burglars, armed robbers, rapists, and other miscreants who impose their will by force can precipitate pathologic anxiety in their victims. When perceived as a threat to life, assaults stimulate the victim's autonomic nervous system, and in a vulnerable person a PTSD may result.

Following a party late one night, a 23-year-old medical student was walking down a darkened street, attempting to locate his car, when he encountered a stranger. The man reached in his pocket, withdrew a handgun, pointed it at the medical student's chest, and excitedly demanded money. The frightened student desperately attempted to explain that he never carried much money and was merely trying to find his automobile in order to drive home. The gunman raised the pistol to the medical student's head and with choice expletives threatened death if he did not produce money. The medical student urinated in his pants as he helplessly pleaded with the armed robber, offering the keys to his car and an empty wallet. The gunman emphasized his demand for money by pulling back the hammer on the pistol. The medical student, now trembling violently, offered the hold-up man all of his possessions. The robber rifled through the student's pockets, extracting keys, coins, and a wallet. He then ordered the student to turn around and start running as fast as he could and not look back. The student complied and began running, fearing a bullet in his back. The medical student developed a PTSD.

Sometimes a criminal assault can result in physical injury.

A 32-year-old man was awakened late one night by the sound of a racing car engine. The man put on his bathrobe, told his wife to watch their two children, and left to investigate. His condominium was surrounded by a wall and a large, solid gate with a window at eye level. The man walked outside, went to the gate, peered through the window, and saw a shotgun protruding from the passenger window of a car. He heard the blast of the shotgun and felt stinging, burning sensations in his body. He turned and ran to the open door of his home and remaining outside slammed it to prevent the assailants from going into his house and harming his wife and children. Running to the side of the house, he heard the automobile accelerating and feared that his unknown assailants were tracking him. In response to the noise of the shotgun, a neighbor opened his side door and the wounded man hurried into that house. Although not seriously injured, the man was bleeding profusely from superficial wounds caused by shotgun pellets lodged within his body. The man developed a PTSD with a sensitivity to loud noises and a phobia of darkness and weapons.

Chemical Substances

The environment contains numerous chemical substances that can act as traumatic agents when inhaled, ingested, or injected. During accidents involving chemical spills, pungent and toxic gases may be inhaled by workers or passersby, causing irritation of the mucous membranes of the eyes and respiratory passages. Following exposure to the noxious fumes, and after physical symptoms have cleared, some persons exhibit emotional symptoms of a PTSD. Marijuana smoke can act as a traumatic stimulus especially when it is highly concentrated or laced with another psychoactive substance. Such smokers can develop a PTSD with a supersensitivity to the smell of marijuana smoke or even ordinary cigarette fumes and a phobia or phobic anxiety of surroundings identical or similar to the place where the marijuana was smoked. The oral consumption of certain medications or psychoactive substances, especially hallucinogens, can be associated with a severe emotional reaction and intense anxiety that can culminate in a PTSD. Indeed, "flashbacks" have been reported by users of LSD, psilocybin, and other hallucinogens, as well as phobias of all drugs. Any chemical substance that has the capacity for autonomic arousal is capable of precipitating an anxiety attack and a Stress Disorder.

> A 53-year-old nurse with a terminal illness developed renal failure that required kidney dialysis. The nurse accepted her illness philosophically and remained optimistic. Although her twice-weekly trips to the renal dialysis unit interfered with life to some extent, she managed to function as wife and mother to her family. One day while being dialyzed, the nurse noted a "formaldehyde taste" and reported this to clinical personnel at the unit. It was discovered that by mistake, formalin had been introduced into the dialysate solution. The dialysis was immediately terminated for that day. The nurse became extremely agitated and, upon hearing of the error, wondered how such a mistake could have been made. Her plight was such that she could not drive home and her husband was called. Following the incident, the nurse became gravely disturbed and was unable to carry on with her usual household duties. She complained of intense anxiety, insomnia, nightmares, and other symptoms related to her trauma. A "personality

change" was noted by members of her family, and she never functioned normally again. She could not drive her car, cook meals, or care for the house herself. With great difficulty and in a state of intense anxiety, the nurse was forced by necessity to continue dialysis. Her condition quickly deteriorated and she died within 2 months. She had developed a PTSD following the accidental addition of formalin into the dialysis solution. Although she was suffering from a terminal illness, one can deduce that the Stress Disorder probably hastened her death.

Chemical substances emanating from the environment can act as primary traumatic stimuli. These substances, of course, produce certain physiological changes within the body and can act directly on the nervous system to produce symptoms of pathologic anxiety. A combination of environmental and endogenous events better defines the traumatic stimulus. However, since chemicals from the environment must be inhaled, ingested, or injected, it seems appropriate to list environment as the primary source of the trauma.

Rescuers at a Disaster Site

Rescuers charged with the task of gathering and identifying the bodies of disaster victims are often confronted with horrible scenes of carnage. The environment, strewn with disfigured corpses and body parts, acts as a traumatic stimulus for many rescue workers. Even experienced rescuers under the proper circumstances can be traumatized by the sights, sounds, and smells of a disaster scene.

A coroner's assistant was told to report to the scene of a jet aircraft crash where more than 150 people were believed to have perished. Upon arriving at the scene of the disaster, he and others set up a makeshift morgue where the victims of the plane crash were taken for identification. As the black, zippered body bags arrived at the temporary morgue, the coroner's assistant was assigned the task of photographing the human remains with close-up shots of bodies and body parts to assist in identification. The body bags contained dismembered torsos, smashed skulls, an assortment of arms, legs, intestines, and fragments of human flesh. The coroner's assistant had viewed death and mutilated bodies before, but not on the magnitude presented by this tragic disaster. He did his job in a competent and professional manner until he viewed the corpse of a boy who reminded him of his grandson. Although he had been working steadily for 4 hours and was fatigued, he had had no symptoms until then. He hesitated in his work and began to feel extremely apprehensive and mildly nauseated. He managed to photograph the dead boy and went on with his work. The next body bag he opened was smoking and steaming, since the clothing on the body was still burning when it was put into the black bag. As the coroner's assistant bent over to take a close-up photograph, the stench of burning flesh assailed his nostrils, causing him to retch. Shortly afterward, he trembled, shook violently, felt his heart pounding, had difficulty breathing, and vomited. Feeling wretched, he asked to be excused from duty. The sights, sounds, and smells of the disaster stimulated intense autonomic activity and pathologic anxiety and precipitated a PTSD.

Minimal Environmental Trauma and PTSD

Sometimes patients present with the signs and symptoms of a PTSD following minimal environmental trauma, and at first glance the relationship between the trauma and PTSD seems ludicrous.

A 43-year-old computer operator was shopping at a supermarket when a 4-pound bag of carrots fell on her head as she was bending down to pick up some groceries. Stunned, she lost her balance and fell on her buttocks. Almost simultaneously, another bag of carrots fell on her head, further dazing her. A grocery store clerk, smiling at her predicament, came to assist her. Unamused, the woman became indignant, but was mollified by the store manager. Still shaken by the experience, the woman returned home where she developed intense headaches and increasing agitation. She experienced a severe anxiety attack with a dissociative reaction and was unable to sleep. Over the course of the next few days, she remained in bed and became fearful whenever she was left unattended. She experienced nightmares, flashbacks of the "carrot bag incident," and intense anxiety, nausea, and severe headaches. She consulted a doctor who hospitalized her, suspecting an organic brain syndrome. After 5 days of exhaustive examinations and numerous laboratory procedures, the doctor said that there was nothing physically wrong with her. The patient's anxiety continued for the next several months, and she sought treatment first with a psychologist, then with a psychiatrist. Over the course of the year, the patient remained disabled, exhibiting the typical signs and symptoms of a PTSD that had remained undiagnosed.

A 31-year-old secretary, went to a lunch counter and ordered a sandwich. When her food arrived, she took a large bite of the sandwich and was musing about the work she had to perform that afternoon.

When she began to take a second bite of the sandwich, she looked between the bread slices and saw one-half of the body of a dead cockroach. Knowing that she had just consumed the other half of the roach, she became extremely nauseated and vomited into the sandwich plate. The counter clerk, noting her distress, came to her assistance. When it was explained that she had just eaten a cockroach, he called the manager who graciously agreed to refund her money for the sandwich. The patient developed intense anxiety, insomnia, nightmares depicting giant bugs, and a phobia of roaches. She was tormented by the idea that she might get some dreadful disease, and she scrupulously avoided any possible contact with roaches. The secretary had her entire house fumigated and an insect exterminator was consulted to decontaminate her house on a more-than-regular basis. Her symptoms of anxiety, insomnia, nightmares, and phobia of roaches continued for over a year before she sought treatment for her PTSD.

When persons are involved in vehicular collisions, industrial accidents, or criminal assaults, it is easy for others to identify with the emotional sequelae of these encounters. It is more difficult to empathize with those persons who are involved in environmental traumas that at worst are distasteful and unpleasant and at best no trouble at all. In order to appreciate the incapacitating nature of minimal environmental trauma, one must understand the Traumatic Principle.

The Traumatic Principle

The Traumatic Principle is: Any environmental stimulus, whether it produces physical injury or not, if perceived as dangerous can be regarded as a trauma and can precipitate a PTSD. The preceding vignettes illustrate that the essential factor in the development of a PTSD is not the type or duration of the environmental trauma but rather whether the trauma intensely activates the person's autonomic nervous system. Also vital is a conscious awareness of the degree of danger connected with the traumatic event along with a full appreciation of the potential for serious injury or death to self and possibly others. The prerequisites — perception of potential danger and intense activation of the autonomic nervous system — may occur before, during, or after the environmental trauma. Sufficient time is necessary for the life-threatening nature of the traumatic event to be impressed upon the patient's mind;

sometimes only seconds of exposure, but more often longer, to the "dangerous" situation is required. The Traumatic Principle is borne out further in those instances where a PTSD develops in the absence of any discernible physical injury. Witnessing disasters can be trauma enough to stimulate the autonomic nervous system, produce pathologic anxiety, and a Stress Disorder. No physical injury need occur, but a physiological response to the trauma must eventuate in and be maintained by encephalic activity, as will be discussed below.

Encephalic Events

Encephalic events (thoughts, visual images, fantasies, assumptions, beliefs, perceptions of external events, and dreams) following a trauma play a major role in the development and especially in the sustentation of a PTSD. Thoughts and visual images related to the traumatic incident are stored in the mind, and these memories can be played back like a tape cassette in a video recorder. When these "video tapes of the mind" are played back repeatedly, portraying the trauma with frightening and grisly elaborations, they generate and sustain pathologic anxiety, thereby retraumatizing the victim. Patients tend to ruminate and speculate on the possibility that a more perilous or potentially fatal consequence could have resulted from the traumatic incident. Macabre visual images project dangerousness and, together with dour speculations of a more devastating outcome, morbidly preoccupy a patient. The fragility of life and the impermanence of existence become dominant thoughts during the waking hours, as elaboration of the traumatic theme includes such self-statements as "I could have been paralyzed, blinded, maimed, or killed" and "But for the grace of God or luck or both, I should be dead."

The woman whose automobile was stalled on the expressway on a rainy night had repeated and protracted, vivid visual images of a car traveling at high speed smashing into her vehicle. Each time she looked into the rearview mirror of her car, these thoughts became more manifest, especially while driving at night in the rain. Implacable images of the jet airliner exploding and bursting into flames and thoughts of being trapped inside and burning to death were indelibly etched on the mind of the businessman who survived the air crash. Every time he considered a journey by airplane, these morbid thoughts and images evoked such great anxiety that he avoided flying. The oil refinery worker, whenever he considered returning to work, looked at the burn scars on his arms and chest and recalled his skin "melting like wax." He relived the intense pain and nearness to death associated with his accident. The sounds and sights of jet airliners and certain cooking odors stimulated images in the mind of the coroner's assistant of carnage at the scene of the airplane disaster. For the first time, he was very anxious during autopsies and refused to travel by airplane.

Persistence in the encephalic habit of thinking and visualizing scenes directly or indirectly related to the trauma is one of the most important factors contributing to the chronicity of a PTSD. Persons inadvertently reexpose themselves in imagination to the traumatic event, thereby sensitizing themselves to various aspects of the original trauma and perpetuating the Stress Disorder. To a casual observer, the victim of a PTSD appears to be an irritable complainer or a moody, withdrawn ruminator overly concerned with a trauma long passed. In reality, however, the covert encephalic activity of thinking, visualizing, and elaborating on various elements of the traumatic incident keeps the trauma fresh and alive, and plays a major role in the maintenance of a PTSD.

As time passes, the affected person's encephalic processes may not dwell entirely upon the traumatic event but may switch emphasis to the current incapacity believed to be a consequence of the trauma. Anxiety-evoking thoughts now include reference to an inability to work, financial problems, marital conflicts, sexual dysfunction, disintegration of social relationships, diminished recreational activities, and generalized and vague self-statements contrasting life-style before and after the trauma. Often, preoccupation with somatic symptoms prevails, especially if pain and physical injury accompanied the original trauma. A feeling of dudgeon and a retributive attitude toward those deemed responsible for the traumatic incident pervade the person's mind. When thoughts of self-reproachment, remorse, and dismay take sway, depression becomes a common accompaniment to PTSD.

Endogenous Events

Another source of pathologic anxiety is the physiological sensations within the body — endogenous events. When these sensations are afferently perceived and interpreted pathologically, stimulation of the autonomic nervous system results in the production of pathologic anxiety. Persons who have experienced a trauma frequently become organically oriented, especially when pain or other uncomfortable physiological sensations result from the original trauma. In spite of repeated negative findings during medical examinations, patients cling obdurately and erroneously to the conclusion that there is something physically wrong with them. Such a conclusion is not entirely spurious or without substance, since the source of uncomfortable endogenous sensations can result from: residual soft tissue damage to muscles and ligaments, resulting from the original trauma, which cannot be detected by objective examination; motor tension; or visceral symptoms resulting from pathologic anxiety. In all cases pathologic anxiety either initiates or accentuates these uncomfortable somatic symptoms. An apprehensive expectation and increased vigilance and scanning, also characteristic of a Generalized Anxiety Disorder, together with a hyperawareness of endogenous sensations further increase pathologic anxiety, which in turn increases uncomfortable somatic sensations. Pain focuses patients' minds on the certainty of physical defect or disease, and they are loath to listen to alternative explanations for their physical discomfort. Not only are patients impervious to psychophysiologic discussions of pain, but they may also think that the physician believes that they are imagining their symptoms or malingering.

Sometimes patients fail to appreciate the consequences of a Stress Disorder and adhere to a belief of organic causality. In fact, as will be seen from the following case history, skepticism may lead to unsuccessful therapeutic outcome.

> A 38-year-old truck driver was involved in a traffic mishap that resulted in his ejection from the cab of his truck onto the pavement. Following the accident the truck driver was stunned but not hurt seriously. Complaints of back pain prompted medical attention, but examination including X-rays disclosed no serious physical injury. A diagnosis of sprained muscles was made, and the patient was sent home with prescriptions for an analgesic and a muscle relaxant. The truck driver's back pain persisted, and symptoms of headache, nausea, and malaise added to his discomfort. Insomnia, nightmares, nervousness, sexual problems, dizziness, lack of interest in life, and a phobia of driving a truck complicated the clinical course. Not reassured by repeated negative examinations, the truck driver sought organic verification

for his physical discomfort as he doctor-shopped, but no physical cause for his symptoms was ever discovered. As time passed family relations disintegrated and his wife divorced him, taking their three children with her. An inability to work led to financial insolvency, and the truck driver was forced to move into the house of his grandparents. Still complaining of pain, wearing a back brace, and using a walking stick, the truck driver continued to trek to doctors' offices, where X-rays, a myelogram, a discogram, and a computed axial tomographic scan failed to convince him that he was structurally sound. A recommendation to see a psychiatrist was greeted by skepticism and, as he predicted, psychological treatment proved ineffective. Even following a successful lawsuit, the patient continued to complain of somatic symptoms and remained disabled, firmly convinced that he had something physically wrong with him.

RETRAUMATIZATION

A perplexing question concerning PTSD is why and how pathologic anxiety is maintained following the acute trauma. The presence of acute and chronic anxiety symptoms seemingly in the absence of specific stimuli may puzzle a casual onlooker or clinician, especially when there are fluctuations of low and high anxiety for no apparent reason. A thorough analysis and appraisal of the patient's anxious state usually reveal retraumatization — encephalic replaying of the mental video tapes concerning the trauma. As the patient relives the trauma in imagination, the autonomic nervous system is stimulated and pathologic anxiety results. Encephalic retraumatization is usually put in motion by environmental stimuli. When the PTSD patient encounters any environmental stimulus that resembles and brings to mind the traumatic incident, encephalic activity portraying the original trauma or some similar variant usually occurs. For the victim of an automobile accident, screeching tires, traffic noises, the accident site, heavy traffic, the sight of other vehicles, or the smell of gasoline may elicit vivid images of the original accident. Similarly, the sights, sounds, and smells associated with a PTSD are environmental stimuli that are capable of initiating anxiety-evoking encephalic activity. Retraumatization constitutes the most important factor in the prolongation of symptomatic behavior and must be dealt with during the treatment of a PTSD.

THE SPIRAL EFFECT

Endogenous sensations also remind the patient of the traumatic incident and introduce the notion of physical impairment caused by the trauma. Following the perception of pain or physical discomfort, thoughts and visual images pertaining to the trauma stimulate the autonomic nervous system, increasing motor tension and producing more intense somatic manifestations of anxiety. This magnification of physical symptoms alarms the patient and stimulates additional encephalic activity concerning bodily damage, thus producing a cycle and the "Spiral Effect" (Figure 2-1). The cycle continues and the ensuing Spiral Effect of encephalic and endogenous events intensifies anxiety, the uncomfortable sensations of which confirm the unsoundness-of-the-body hypothesis that was related to the original trauma. In this manner, somatic symptoms can

**FIGURE 2-1.
The Spiral Effect.**

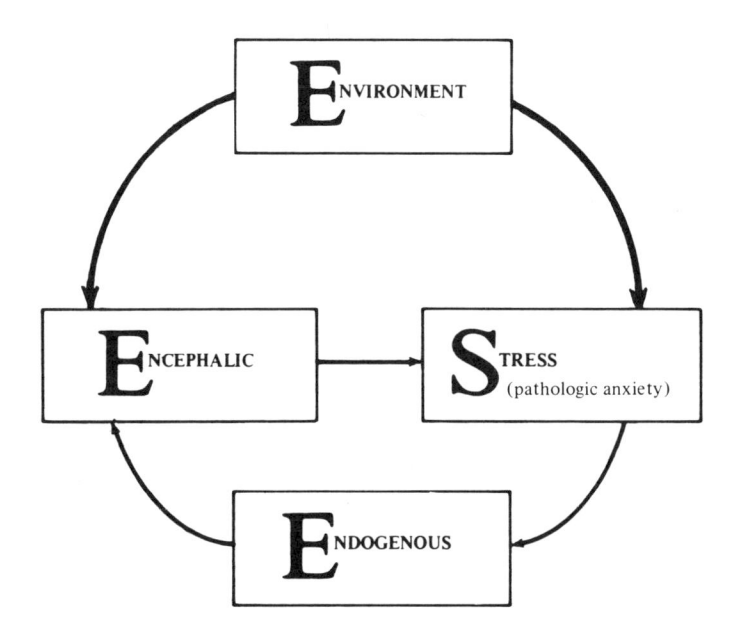

persist in the absence of organic disease or environmental stimuli for months and even years following the trauma. These patients may still believe that they are suffering from the residual physical effects of the traumatic incident rather than from the spiral effect.

CASE HISTORY

The Three E's — Interplay in a PTSD

The following case history typifies what is encountered in clinical practice and illustrates the application of the Three E's to PTSD.

> The patient, an attractive girl in her early twenties, was in an automobile driven by her boyfriend when she felt a slight bump, "like we had a blowout." She turned and looked out the rear window of the car and gasped with fright as the entire window was filled with the grill of a huge truck. Her fear turned to terror as the rear end of the car was lifted up by the huge truck and the car turned end over end. Her body was propelled forward and her face struck the dashboard of the car. She felt the crush and heard the crunch of her teeth loosening, followed almost immediately by "an explosion of pain" and the salty taste of blood. The car then careened against the expressway railing, and as she looked out the side window, she saw the ground about 30 feet below the elevated expressway. "I am going to die," she frantically said to herself while the car bounced off the railing and rolled over and over "as if it was in slow motion." The patient was thrown to her left against her boyfriend and her head slammed against the left window. As the car continued rolling, the patient was then thrown to the opposite side of the car, and she felt an awful pain in her scalp. The patient related later that she was wearing her hair, which was waist-length, in a ponytail, and somehow it got caught outside of the car. The car, now upside down, was sliding along the ground and the patient's ponytail was between the pavement and the top of the car. As the car continued to skid, she felt intense scalp pain as some of her hair was pulled out. Simultaneously, her head was pulled tightly against the door opening, and the patient was pinned by her hair. Not knowing her hair was tangled between the automobile and pavement, she thought she was paralyzed. Smelling gasoline and fearing that the car might explode, she tried desperately to extricate herself from the car; however, she was helplessly immobilized. As she looked out the car window, she saw the

enormous front wheels of the truck and believed erroneously that the truck, which had actually stopped, was moving toward her and would crush her. She screamed hysterically for several minutes, believing that she was paralyzed and dying. Later, when help arrived, she was reassured that her hair was tangled beneath the wreckage and that she would be freed momentarily. A passerby produced a hunting knife, and her hair was hacked away "in a sawing motion" and she was freed. During the rescue she looked about the interior of the car and noted blood splattered all over. She became panic stricken and felt that she must be seriously injured. Eventually, she was removed from the car, placed in an ambulance, and taken to a hospital.

Probably because she was young and athletic, the woman miraculously sustained no irreversible physical injuries. Examination at the hospital revealed that she was bruised and battered but not seriously injured. Her teeth were loosened, her jaw was dislocated, several large tufts of hair had been pulled from her scalp, and she had numerous small lacerations over her face, arms, and legs. After her wounds were tended to, the patient was sedated and remained in the hospital for 1 week.

She began experiencing nightly bad dreams in which she relived her awful accident or some variation of it. Often the patient would wake up screaming, struggling, and sweating profusely. After a while she began to fear sleep because of horrible nightmares. She became extremely anxious and obsessed about the possibility of another accident. These ruminations lasted for hours and occurred daily. Physical symptoms dominated her consciousness as she experienced backaches, joint pain, and a variety of muscular aches. A new malady, headaches, began to plague her along with dizzy feelings and a tendency to lose her balance. Although she had never had any problems with nocturnal teeth grinding, she experienced bruxism on a nightly basis. She was "jumpy," extremely sensitive to noise, and easily startled. Upon viewing television or movies portraying accidents, especially when humans or animals were involved in violence, she became anxious and agitated and experienced nausea. Her accident occurred in a compact-sized car, and she developed a phobia of driving or riding in small cars, which she considered unsafe. She also had phobic anxiety of expressways, heavily trafficked streets, and enclosed places, especially if exit from the small enclosure was impaired or blocked.

After the acute crisis had passed and the physical effects of the trauma had gradually subsided, the young woman continued to experience anxiety symptoms. During the day she was pathologically preoccupied with the accident and at night she had nightmares. The patient's memory for the details of the auto crash was remarkable, and she frequently fantasized the horrifying aspects of the entire traumatic incident, often elaborating and speculating upon a more devastating outcome. At the end of these rampant reveries, she often experienced an anxiety attack or intense discomfort. She was hypervigilant when encountering situations she thought dangerous, and for the first time in her life was cautious and restrained. Competition in gymnastics was discontinued since she felt weakened by her traumatic experience. She felt ugly and unattractive and was hypersensitive about minute scars on her face and body. Headaches, pains, and physical discomfort were a constant reminder of the traumatic incident, and she was puzzled by the persistence of these body aches. As time passed these physical symptoms attenuated to some extent, but they were still present in varying degrees 1.5 years following the accident. She was suffering from symptoms of anxiety and depression, though none of her physicians paid any attention to the psychiatric sequelae of her trauma. Indeed, the patient did not discuss any of the symptoms she was experiencing with them, fearing they would think her insane. She confided in her attorney who was familiar with PTSD and referred her for consultation.

After a discussion of the accident the patient was asked to fill out an Anxiety Source Profile (ASP; Tables 2-2 to 2-4) and to check only those items that caused anxiety following the accident. The ASP helped to identify those environmental, encephalic, and endogenous events that still served to stimulate and maintain pathologic anxiety.

Environmental Events

On the Environmental Section of the ASP (Table 2-2), the patient checked the following items that elicited much [4] or very much [5] anxiety: being alone; crossing streets; journeys by car, train, airplane, bus, or boat; weapons; sick people; being in an elevator; enclosed places; doctors; being seen unclothed; leaving home; physical examinations; heavy traffic; expressways; noises; courtrooms; and judges or lawyers (she was involved in a personal injury suit and frequently had to relate the history of her accident to her attorneys and others).

The trauma that the young woman experienced impacted on all five of her senses. Stimulation of proprioceptive pathways initiated her traumatic experience when she felt a slight bump, "like a tire

TABLE 2-2
Anxiety Source Profile I: Environmental Events

Check the appropriate column to indicate the degree of anxiety, nervousness, discomfort, or fear that the item caused you *before* the accident or traumatic incident (O) and has caused you *following* the accident or traumatic incident (X).

	1. Not at All	2. A Little	3. A Fair Amount	4. Much	5. Very Much

1. Being alone
2. Speaking in public
3. Urinating in public bathrooms
4. Eating in public
5. Writing in front of others
6. Crossing streets
7. People who seem insane
8. Taking a test
9. Dentists
10. Storms
11. Worms
12. Receiving injections
13. Strangers
14. Journeys by car
15. Journeys by train
16. Journeys by airplane
17. Journeys by bus
18. Journeys by boat
19. Crowds
20. Cats
21. Birds
22. Dogs
23. Harmless snakes
24. Mice or rats
25. Insects
26. Harmless spiders
27. Fish
28. Sight of deep water
29. Weapons
30. Dirt, germs
31. Fire
32. Sick people
33. Being criticized

Table 2-2, continued

	1. Not at All	2. A Little	3. A Fair Amount	4. Much	5. Very Much

34. Being touched by others
35. Being in an elevator
36. Angry people
37. Parting from friends
38. Enclosed places
39. Darkness
40. Nude men
41. Nude women
42. Doctors
43. Making decisions
44. Being with a member of the opposite sex
45. Large open spaces
46. Being seen unclothed
47. Taking medicine
48. Ministers or priests
49. Funerals
50. Police
51. Leaving home
52. Physical examinations
53. Marriage
54. Insecticides
55. Vomiting
56. Bridges
57. Lights
58. Heavy traffic
59. Expressways
60. Odors or fumes
61. Static electricity
62. Being in public places
63. Attending meetings
64. Waiting in lines
65. Swimming
66. Courtrooms
67. Judges or lawyers
68. Body excretions (mucus, urine, feces)
69. Telephones

Table 2-2, continued

	1. Not at All	2. A Little	3. A Fair Amount	4. Much	5. Very Much
70. Procrastination					
71. Food					
72. Failure					
73. Noises					
74. Poisons					
75. Masturbation					
76. Heights					

Source: Adapted from *Stress Strategies: The Treatment of the Anxiety Disorders* (Scrignar 1983). Reproduced with permission.

TABLE 2-3
Anxiety Source Profile II: Encephalic Activities

Check the column that most frequently indicates the *time* you spent thinking or visualizing about the following subjects *before* the accident or traumatic incident (O) and that you spend *following* the accident or traumatic incident (X).

	1. Not at All	2. A Little	3. A Fair Amount	4. Much	5. Very Much
1. Dying					
2. Disease or illness					
3. Insanity					
4. Homosexuality					
5. Being out of control					
6. Panic					
7. Injury					
8. Being contaminated					
9. Violence					
10. Making mistakes					
11. Being trapped					
12. Embarrassment or humiliation					
13. Making decisions					
14. Being unworthy					
15. Explosions					
16. Being assaulted (or raped)					
17. Being victimized by a criminal					
18. Rejection or disapproval					

Table 2-3, continued

	1. Not at All	2. A Little	3. A Fair Amount	4. Much	5. Very Much
19. Sexual performance					
20. Evil					
21. Accidents					
22. Going crazy					
23. Impending doom					

Source: Adapted from *Stress Strategies: The Treatment of the Anxiety Disorders* (Scrignar 1983). Reproduced with permission.

TABLE 2-4
Anxiety Source Profile III: Endogenous Sensations

Check the appropriate column to indicate the *frequency* with which you experienced the following sensations or feelings *before* the accident or traumatic incident (O) and with which you have experienced them *following* the accident or traumatic incident (X).

	1. Not at All	2. A Little	3. A Fair Amount	4. Much	5. Very Much
1. Smothering					
2. Choking					
3. Nausea and vomiting					
4. Heart beating fast					
5. Tightness of chest					
6. Headaches					
7. Pain					
8. Dizziness					
9. Tingly feelings					
10. Feelings of fainting					
11. Trembling					
12. Blurry vision					
13. Buzzing or ringing in ears					
14. Feeling hot or cold					
15. Crawling sensations on skin					
16. Feeling dirty					
17. Feeling unreal or like another person					

Table 2-4, continued

	1. Not at All	2. A Little	3. A Fair Amount	4. Very Much	5. Very Much
18. Sweating					
19. Urinating unpredictably					
20. Defecating unpredictably					
21. Feeling angry					
22. Light-headedness					

Source: Adapted from *Stress Strategies: The Treatment of the Anxiety Disorders* (Scrignar 1983). Reproduced with permission.

blowing out." Visual impressions impacted traumatically when she turned and looked out the rear window of the car and saw huge headlights within an enormous truck grill. Proprioceptive pathways were again stimulated when the truck hit the vehicle, tumbling it end over end. Pain and the taste of blood suffused her mind when her body and face violently struck the dashboard of the car. As the car careened against the guardrail of the elevated expressway, more visual impressions increased her fear as she saw the ground 30 feet below and presaged the car plummeting through the railing, killing her. As the car bounced off the railing and began to roll over and over, she was tossed "like a rag doll" from one side of the automobile to the other, further aggravating her proprioceptive trauma. The environment begot more proprioceptive trauma when her hair became tangled beneath the wreckage of the car, causing intense scalp pain and immobilization. Olfaction, the smell of gasoline, contributed to the trauma as the overturned car began leaking fuel and she feared an explosion and fire. Finally, the sight of the enormous front wheels of the truck and the automobile interior splattered with blood caused her to scream hysterically. During the accident the rending and scraping of metal and the sound of glass breaking were auditory sensations associated with the trauma. Visual, auditory, olfactory, taste, and proprioceptive stimuli impacted greatly upon the patient during the course of her accident. Although the accident lasted only about a minute, all five of her senses were stimulated in such a manner as to panic her.

Encephalic Events

On the Encephalic Section of the ASP (Table 2-3), the patient checked that she spent much [4] or very much [5] time thinking about or visualizing the following subjects: dying, death or illness, being out of control, panic, injury, violence, being trapped, explosions, accidents, and impending doom.

Although the accident lasted only a minute or so, the patient related that "the entire incident appeared to be in slow motion." The temporal sequence and the minute details of the accident were firmly and almost indelibly impressed upon her mind. Each day she spent considerable time thinking about and visualizing various aspects of the trauma, with the addendum that she might have been more seriously injured or killed. Like the replaying of a video tape, she reexperienced the trauma many times in her imagination. Retraumatization, the constant replaying of the video tapes in her mind, resulted in a hyperactive autonomic nervous system and a chronic state of anxiousness. Her encephalic activity served to perpetuate the effects of her trauma, thereby maintaining high levels of pathologic anxiety. Even her sleep was plagued by negative encephalic activity (nightmares) that reflected her preoccupation with the trauma during the waking state. As the young woman visualized, talked, and thought about the accident or various aspects of it, anxiety was generated. The patient, however, did not make this correlation. Like a moth attracted to a flame, the patient, it seemed, could not escape from her obsessions about the accident. Many things reminded her of the trauma. The sight of large trucks or small automobiles, expressways, sudden noises, the screech of tires, the sight of blood, television programs or movies portraying accidents or violent action, and many other associations to the surroundings where the accident took place elicited negative encephalic activity. Like a cat in an experimental cage, the young woman responded predictably and adversely to these stimuli and, as if on cue, played the video tapes of her mind repeating the traumatic experience. As retraumatization occurred, replete with the signs and symptoms of pathologic anxiety, her PTSD was sustained.

Endogenous Sensations

On the Endogenous Sensations Section of the ASP (Table 2-4), the patient checked that she experienced the following sensations or feelings much [4] or very much [5] of the time: nausea, heart beating fast, tightness of the chest, headaches, pain, dizziness, feelings of fainting, trembling, crawling sensations on the skin, feeling unreal or like another person, feeling angry, and light-headedness.

Immediately following the accident, pain and discomfort were significant sequelae. The young woman suffered from numerous cuts, bruises, and puncture wounds. Her jaw was dislocated, teeth were loosened, one hip joint was extremely tender, and muscles throughout her body were extremely sore. With the passage of time, headaches and nausea were an almost daily occurrence and joint and muscular pain continued. Any experience of pain or discomfort in any part of her body acted as a pernicious reminder of disability owing to the accident. Endogenous events, even normal physiological sensations, were misinterpreted as residual, perhaps permanent, injuries sustained in the accident. Pain augured thoughts and images of her trauma and permanent disablement. The uncomfortable endogenous sensations, whether due to soft tissue damage or to anxiety, stimulated encephalic activity that resulted in more anxiety and additional physical discomfort. The interplay between endogenous and encephalic events served to heighten and maintain anxiety, thus setting up a vicious Spiral Effect. The patient's symptoms became chronic, as did her PTSD.

SUMMARY

The severity and type of trauma are not necessarily correlated with the development of a PTSD; rather the effect of a trauma upon a person's autonomic nervous system determines whether or not a PTSD develops. When a trauma stimulates high levels of anxiety in a predisposed person and the anxiety persists, a PTSD develops. In contrast, in a normal response to a stressful event, anxiety quickly diminishes and does not materially affect a person's life. In PTSD the sources for the initiation and maintenance of pathologic anxiety are the environment, encephalic events, and endogenous processes — the Three E's. The principle that any environmental stimulus under the proper circumstances can precipitate a PTSD is essential to an understanding of trauma. The trauma impacting on one or more of the five sensory pathways to the brain is perceived as dangerous and results in the stimulation of the autonomic nervous system, producing the symptoms of pathologic anxiety. Encephalic events play a major role in the development and especially the sustentation of a PTSD. Thoughts and visual images related to the traumatic incident are stored in the mind as memories that can be retrieved and played back like the tape cassette in a video recorder. When a patient encounters any environmental stimulus that brings to mind the traumatic incident, the video tapes of the mind are repeatedly replayed, thus retraumatizing the person. Encephalic retraumatization plays an important role in sustaining a PTSD. Endogenous sensations also remind the patient of the traumatic incident and, most importantly, maintain the notion of organic impairment caused by the trauma. The Spiral Effect of endogenous and encephalic events intensifies anxiety and reinforces the idea of physical disability.

THREE

PREDISPOSITION AND CLINICAL COURSE

An individual's predisposition to PTSD or traumatic neurosis has intrigued clinicians over the years. Not all soldiers in the same battle, persons in the same automobile accident, or workers exposed to an identical explosion in an industrial plant develop a PTSD. Why similar traumas impact differently is not known with certainty, but clearly there must be differences between the individual who develops a PTSD and the one who does not.

A common clinical conclusion of traumatologists, whether studying the effects of war or of civilian stress, is that persons who develop and maintain symptoms following exposure to a traumatic incident seem to be predisposed or vulnerable. Various investigators have noted premorbid personality characteristics and a pretraumatic history of neurotic traits and temperament and recorded psychiatric illness (Brend 1939; Brill and Beebe 1951; Lewy 1941; Slater 1943). Some investigators have studied the hereditary predisposition of traumatized persons and have felt that when this tendency was present, little stress was necessary to precipitate a disorder, whereas considerable stress was needed to produce a breakdown in nonsusceptible persons (Robitscher 1966; Cohen 1970). Correspondingly, persons who are anxious and insecure cope less adequately than more emotionally healthy persons, and hence are more susceptible to the effects of trauma.

Although there is a paucity of reliable statistics relating to the incidence, prevalence, and predisposing factors of PTSD, there are data concerning these factors for anxiety disorders. Since the hypothesis offered here is that persons with an Anxiety Disorder appear predisposed to the development of a PTSD, information concerning the prevalence, incidence, family history, and twin studies of anxious persons are relevant.

PREVALENCE

Under various definitions of Anxiety Disorders, the prevalence in the general population varies from 2 to 5 percent (Marks and Lader 1973). Crowe et al. (1980) and Noyes et al. (1978a) estimate the lifetime risks at 4 and 21 percent, respectively. Investigators have found that the prevalence of Anxiety Disorders in the general medical population varies. One study (Glass et al. 1978) utilizing a self-report inventory reported a prevalence of 27 percent in patients. Other studies indicate that 14 percent of patients in a cardiology practice (Marks and Lader 1973) and 22 percent of surgical patients (Noyes et al. 1978b) suffer from significant anxiety. In a review of the health problems of consecutive adult patients in an inner-city primary care setting, 8 percent of the patients were diagnosed as suffering from an Anxiety Disorder (Freidin 1980). Obviously, there are numerous variables and subjective assessments associated with the statistics related to the prevalence of Anxiety Disorders in the general population and in medical practice. These variables affect interpretation. In the absence of an objective test quantifying the incidence of anxiety, establishing its prevalence will be fraught with difficulties (Cloninger et al. 1981).

FAMILIAL INCIDENCE

Over the years the increased incidence of anxiety among family members has been noted, stirring speculation regarding heredity and genetics. One study (McInnes 1937) reported the prevalence of affected siblings of probands where no parent was involved to be 8.3 percent; if one parent was affected, the prevalence rate rose to 26.5 percent. Subsequent studies in 1951 (Cohen et al.) and 1978a (Noyes) reported that if neither parent had an Anxiety Disorder, the rate among siblings of probands was 15.6 and 9.4 percent, respectively. When one parent was affected, the rate was 2.2 and

24.1 percent, and if both parents had diagnosable anxiety, the rate rose to 34.6 and 44.4 percent, respectively. A 1948 study (Wheeler et al.) examined the children of probands and discovered a rate of 49 percent — a significantly greater risk than the 6 percent rate of a control group. More recently, these results were corroborated in a comprehensive family study of Anxiety Disorders (Crowe et al. 1980), which reported the risks of interviewed relatives to be 41 percent compared with the 8 percent risk among relatives of controls. The high correlations between family members and siblings are very significant, but a separation of genetic and environmental effects cannot be made on the basis of these data.

TWIN STUDIES

A 1969 study (Slater and Shields) of 17 monozygotic twins found the concordance rate for Anxiety Neurosis to be 41 percent. In contrast, the concordance rate for 28 dizygotic twins was only 4 percent. A more recent study in Norway (Torgersen 1978) found the concordance rate of Anxiety Neurosis in monozygotic twins to be 30 percent, whereas the rate of 56 dizygotic twins was only 9 percent. Support for genetic factors primary over environment came from a study (Shields 1962) of three pairs of monozygotic twins who were reared apart and were all found to be concordant for anxiety symptoms. Although these studies strongly suggest a genetic predisposition for an Anxiety Disorder, the hereditary evidence is not yet as strong as it is for schizophrenia. More studies of this type will be necessary to sort out the genetic and environmental factors responsible for Anxiety Disorders.

PTSD AND PREDISPOSITION

Whether interpreted genetically or environmentally, the data from familial and twin studies of persons with an Anxiety Disorder or Anxiety Neurosis have relevance to a PTSD. Observations made by traumatologists over the course of years clearly reflect the conclusion that most persons who develop persistent mental symptoms following a trauma appear to be predisposed. Evidence for a pretraumatic personality predisposition abounds in the literature, especially in the analysis of combat soldiers. Clinicians studying the effects of trauma on civilians have also noted pretraumatic personality traits and have written about "unstable, labile, latent, nervous, immature, dependent, neurotic" personality characteristics, all of which could be subsumed under the heading "Anxiety Disorder" or "Anxiety Neurosis." It is the impression of the author that the individuals who are susceptible and predisposed toward developing a PTSD are essentially those persons who have a past history of anxiousness whether it has come to clinical attention or not. The data on Anxiety Disorders cited previously therefore have relevance to a PTSD. Persons with an anxiety level of 2 (mild) or 3 (moderate) who have been exposed to a trauma would understandably respond in a more pathological manner. The symptomatic behavior and clinical course of a PTSD, in this light, become more understandable.

The author has examined 10 patients, all of whom were subjected to the same traumatic experience. The nine men and one woman were working in an industrial plant when an explosion occurred at a chemical manufacturing plant located about a quarter mile away. Toxic gas fumes dispersed into the area surrounding the industrial plant. Following the explosion, confusion and uncertainty concerning the dangerousness of the accident delayed immediate evacuation although the smell of gas was pungent and pervasive. The explosion was heard clearly by everyone, and emergency sirens warned of danger, but there was no official order to evacuate the area until several hours later. Workers in the industrial plant therefore were exposed to the noxious fumes of the toxic chemicals, developing respiratory symptoms and tearing of the eyes. Finally, without adequate explanation, the workers were sent home and told that they would be recalled when the danger had passed. Each of the ten persons were examined by physicians, including psychiatrists. Physical examinations, chemical analyses of body fluids, and pulmonary function tests revealed no evidence of permanent physical injury, and all were expected to recover from the irritating effects of the gas within a few weeks. The ten workers filed a personal injury suit and were referred for psychiatric evaluation by their attorneys. Evaluations of the workers revealed that six displayed no significant mental disorder, whereas four continued to have respiratory symptoms, insomnia, nightmares, anxiety related to the plant premises, and generalized apprehensiveness and had developed a PTSD. The family and personal histories of the six nonsymptomatic workers were stable and indicated no evidence of an Anxiety Disorder. The four workers who later developed a PTSD described one or more of their close (first-degree) relatives as being nervous, anxious, or worriers. During early developmental years, each member of the PTSD group reported a disruption of family life and a history of death, divorce, or chronic illness of parents. The PTSD group had a previous history of either treatment for psychiatric disorder or for psychophysiological illness during childhood or as adults. All persons in the PTSD group admitted that they were "worriers," and interviews with spouses confirmed their self-observation. It was concluded that the workers who had developed a PTSD were suffering from pathologic anxiety prior to the trauma. Although the group was small, the observations and results are consistent with the aforementioned studies and tend to support the hypothesis that an anxious premorbid state predisposes a person to the development of a PTSD.

CLINICAL COURSE

Stage I — Response to Trauma

Phlegmatism is seldom a response to trauma. Most persons subjected to situations that have the potential for causing injury or even death react with alarm or fear. Following impact with the incursive trauma, irrespective of any physical injury, one or more of the five senses are stimulated, which activates the autonomic nervous system and related stress mechanisms, producing symptoms of pathologic anxiety. In nonanxious persons with a favorable genetic and environmental background, anxiety symptoms usually dissipate within an hour. The nonsusceptible person may shake, tremble, and experience tachycardia, palpitations, nausea, vomiting, or even physical injury. After the acute crisis has passed, the symptoms are followed by a philosophical and thankful frame of mind. Persons who do not develop a PTSD do not dwell or speculate on the more dire consequences of the trauma. Instead, they thank God or fate for their survival and move on with the business of life. Over the course of years, the traumatic incident may intrude in imagination or in dreams, but this is not a frequent or recurrent pattern and, more importantly does not disrupt everyday living.

During treatment or hospitalization for a physical injury resulting from the trauma, optimism, acceptance, and adaptation to any disability, together with compliance with treatment and acquisition of a successful coping style, improve prognosis and diminish future disability. Resort to psychiatric treatment seldom occurs unless the physical injury is very severe and irreversible. Organic mental disorder, dismemberment, loss of sight, or other serious injury such as severe burns or multiple fractures requiring long periods of convalescence may necessitate psychiatric consultation or treatment, but the mental disorder is more likely to be depression rather than PTSD.

Persons predisposed to the development of PTSD respond differently to trauma during Stage I. The susceptible person's baseline of anxiety is above normal (see Table 2-1). Therefore, the response to trauma is exaggerated and results in more severe symptoms. In part, this explains why an identical trauma with quantitatively equivalent amounts of stress produces a higher degree of anxiety in the susceptible than in the nonsusceptible person. For example, the "normative anxiety level" for a nonsusceptible person is at Level 1, whereas a vulnerable person prone to a PTSD has a normative anxiety level at Level 2 or 3 prior to the trauma (Figures 3-1 and 3-2). Furthermore, susceptible individuals invariably perceive the trauma in an exaggerated fashion and overreact to all real or imagined dangers inherent in the trauma. The wheels of rumination are set in motion as vulnerable persons obsess about their trauma and presage danger. Overreaction coupled with obsessive preoccupation differentiate a normal response to trauma from a pathologic one and lead to the development of PTSD.

Stage II – Acute PTSD

If symptoms related to the trauma intensify or persist beyond 4 to 6 weeks, the patient is in the acute phase of a PTSD. When predisposed patients reflect back to the time of their trauma, they admit to a feeling of powerlessness and an inability to control or influence events leading up to the trauma. Symptoms reflecting an intense autonomic nervous system discharge and a "state of shock" are most commonly reported, and patients concluded just before the impact of the trauma that they were about to die. Following

FIGURE 3-1
Acute Post-Traumatic Stress Disorder (PTSD). Predisposed persons are at Level 2 prior to the impact of the environmental trauma (ET). The trauma, perceived as dangerous, causes intense activation of the autonomic nervous system and a rise in anxiety. The traumatized person experiences severe anxiety that gradually diminishes after the trauma is over. In those persons who develop a PTSD, anxiety does not return to a pretraumatic baseline but remains elevated at the moderate range (Level 3).

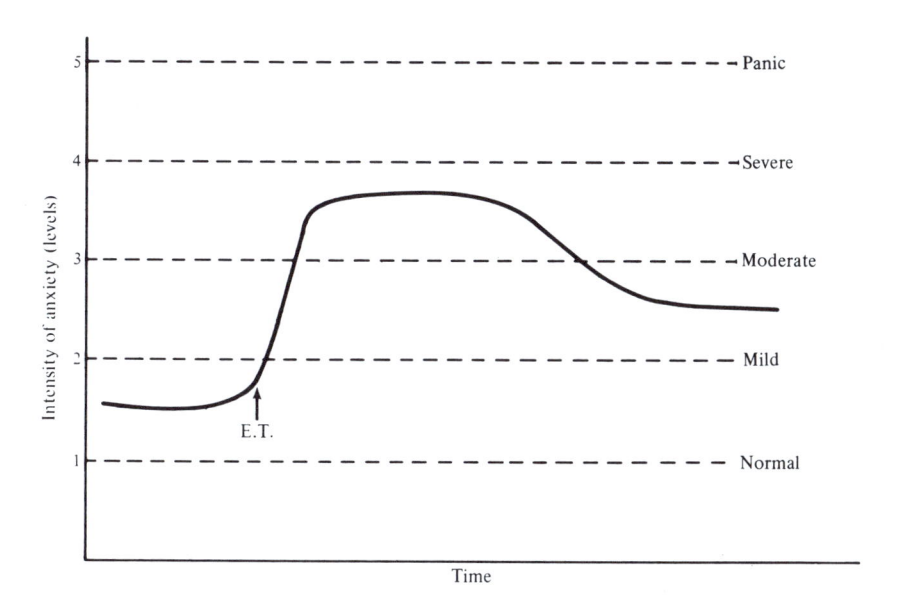

the trauma they exhibit surprise but not much relief as they contemplate how they could have been killed or seriously injured.

The trauma becomes the focal point of the patient's existence. During the day patients relive the trauma in their imagination. They talk informally and inordinately about it with relatives, friends, and acquaintances and more formally, usually in greater detail, with their lawyers and doctors. At night, sleep is interrupted by nightmares that portray the traumatic incident or a more macabre or grisly variant. Patients often awaken abruptly, screaming and thrashing about, their nightclothes drenched with sweat. Upon awakening, there is little relief as they ponder their bad dreams, rendering further sleep impossible. As daylight approaches patients are not

FIGURE 3-2
Acute Post-Traumatic Stress Disorder (PTSD) — Prolonged Trauma.
The environmental trauma (ET) impacts on a vulnerable person and is perceived as dangerous. The autonomic nervous system is stimulated, causing anxiety to rise into the intense range (Level 4). When the trauma is continuous (CT), such as innatural catastrophes or war, anxiety slowly escalates to Level 5, where it may remain for a period of time. At this point persons seem "numb" and in a "state of shock." Anxiety diminishes over time but does not return to pretraumatic levels, remaining instead at the high range of moderate anxiety (Level 3).

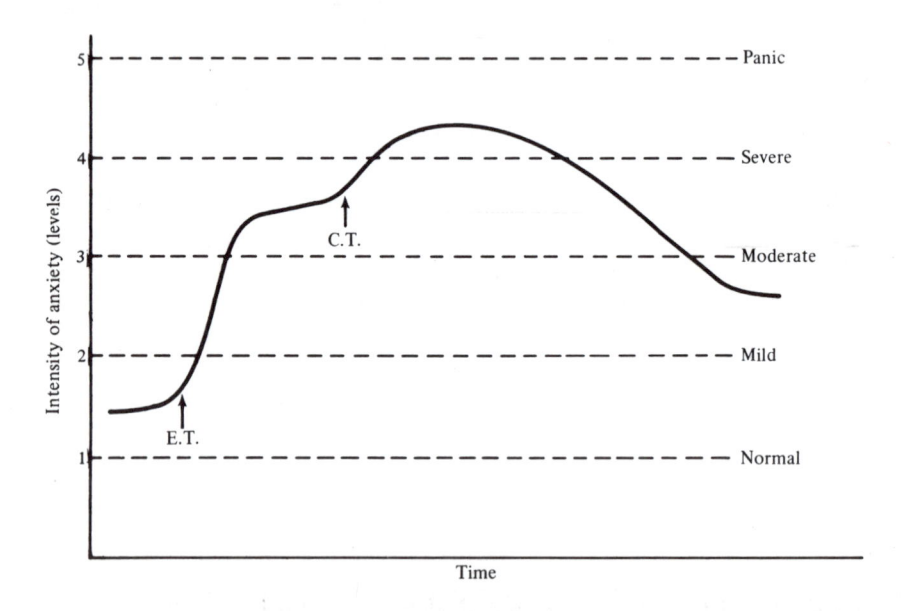

rested but remain frightened and fatigued and they begin envisaging the trauma. Imaginal retraumatization takes place, and this encephalic activity reexposes and sensitizes the patient to various aspects of the trauma. In this manner retraumatization continues unchecked over the course of months and years unless interrupted by treatment.

A state of anxiousness continues throughout the day, and autonomic hyperactivity and increased motor tension produce psychosomatic symptoms or aggravate existing pain. The mind's eye turns inward, and patients attribute their physical symptoms to some organic process. The endogenous sensations of pain and physical discomfort also stimulate negative encephalic statements and remind patients of their trauma. The Spiral Effect of endogenous and encephalic events is set in motion, further intensifying anxiety and at times producing feelings of unreality, depersonalization, and/or derealization.

During Stage II, patients' lives become centered around the traumatic incident and all else is subordinated to the concern that the trauma may have ended their life or caused more serious injury. Family and friends are relegated to a position of lesser importance as patients' self-centeredness contributes toward an alienation from other people. Patients become preoccupied, introspective, and withdrawn; this change of behavior is noted by friends and relatives who conclude that the patient has experienced a "personality change." Life-style alters as anxiety intrudes and interferes with usual activities. An inability to return to work is a bad omen, as occupational impairment frequently entails a role reversal within the family and a restructuring of life-style not conducive to harmonious family relationships. Lack of money and uncongenial conjugality result when a breadwinner is out of work. Unemployed persons with a PTSD do not leave for work each morning, but remain home with the spouse. This increased togetherness does not lead to enhanced intimacy, but rather to increased opportunity for unpleasant confrontations. As marital satisfaction wanes, so does the frequency of sexual interaction, along with a decline of shared pleasure from recreational and social activities.

Surges of higher anxiety occur when patients encounter environmental stimuli closely resembling the scene of the trauma. Depictions of accidents, injury, or death on television and in movies cause agitation and anxiety. For example, persons involved in an automobile accident become highly agitated and anxious when viewing and hearing on television automobile crashes or chase scenes that involve the screeching of tires and the sounds of police sirens. Some patients develop a phobia and avoid surroundings similar to the traumatic scene. For instance, patients may avoid going to work if that is where the trauma took place, or may avoid driving or riding in automobiles following an accident. Phobic behavior is often viewed by others as peculiar and contributes to the observation that a personality change has occurred. Persons are high-strung and overly sensitive to quick, unpredictable stimuli such as sudden noises, fast-moving objects, and commotion of any type.

Fear and frustration are intermittently replaced by anger, irritability, and ill humor. An unpleasant disposition increases social isolation, for people who dwell on the unpleasant side of life tend to be poor companions. A negativistic attitude concerning treatment also develops, since numerous visits to different doctors have provided no permanent succor. A retributive attitude soon solidifies, and a visit to an attorney results in a personal injury lawsuit or other form of legal action.

Stage III – Chronic PTSD

Disability, demoralization, and despondency characterize Stage III, Chronic PTSD, which, according to the *DSM-III* (1980), must have a duration of symptoms for six months or more. Actually, there is no sharp delineation between Acute and Chronic PTSD (Figure 3-3). As time passes, however, the patient's emphasis and orientation gradually change from a preoccupation with the actual trauma to an obsessive concern with physical disability attributable to the trauma. Disablement lies at the center of the patient's thoughts and actions. Somatic preoccupation and obsessions relating to injury dominate the patient's waking hours. Patients dolorously declare as they complain of physical symptoms in their trek from doctor to doctor that they want only to be the way they were before the trauma. In many cases a comparison of life-style before and after the trauma is quite striking. Changes from employed to unemployed, physically active to dormant, good natured to grouchy, fun loving to depressed, solvent to in debt, self-sufficient to dependent, and potent to impotent reflect but a few unpleasant extremes in life-style and status experienced by patients during the chronic stage.

Clinically, patients complain of many of the symptoms referable to autonomic hyperactivity, motor tension, apprehensive expectation, vigilance, and scanning, which are characteristic of a Generalized Anxiety Disorder. The history of a precipitating trauma at onset distinguishes a PTSD from Generalized Anxiety Disorder. Surges of higher anxiety sometimes occur and occasionally are associated with feelings of unreality, but these episodes of depersonalization and/or derealization generally disappear as pathologic anxiety diminishes. Depression secondary to chronic anxiety, and

FIGURE 3-3
Chronic Post-Traumatic Stress Disorder (PTSD). Patients with Chronic PTSD are at the moderate level of anxiety (Level 3) throughout most of their waking hours. Environmental stressors (ES) not necessarily related to the original trauma may elevate anxiety to the severe range (Level 4). Persons suffering from a Chronic PTSD are extremely vulnerable and sensitive to environmental stressors, since quantitatively fewer stimuli are required to elevate anxiety into the severe range. Patients or clinicians may incorrectly ascribe symptomatic behavior to the original trauma when current life stressors are responsible for the elevation of anxiety.

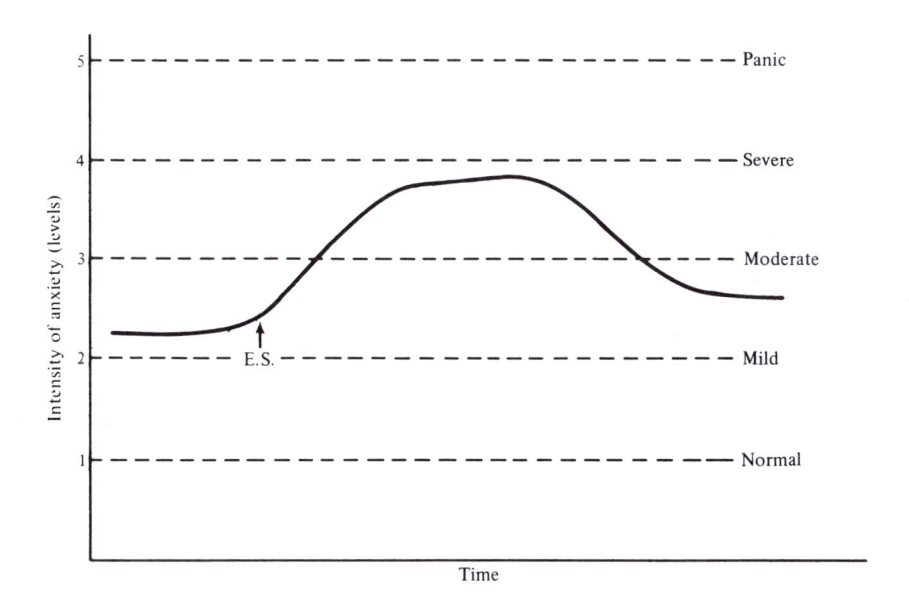

disablement are commonly manifest during Stage III; despair and a pessimistic mood can cloud and dominate other symptoms (Bromberg 1979). Sometimes suicidal ideas emerge and coalesce into half-hearted gestures and infrequently into death. Some patients seek solace by resorting to alcohol or other drugs. Chemical substances, however, offer only short-term relief and severely complicate the course of PTSD. Breakdown in family relations, financial problems, inability to work, and all of the other issues mentioned in Stage II continue and worsen with time.

Although disability is the hallmark of Stage III, litigiousness does not lag far behind. Frustration and irritability build to a choleric mood, which eventually erupts into anger and a retributive attitude aimed toward those believed to be primarily responsible for the individual's trauma and subsequent disability. Civil lawsuits, although prompted by anger and reprisal, are seldom specious, for in most cases a well-documented trauma preceded disability. The legal action once filed becomes the hub of patients' lives, and they frequently vilify their traumatizers, feeling completely justified in a bid to seek compensation for injuries incurred. Some patients become quasi lawyers, familiarizing themselves with pertinent laws and legal procedures. Still others become impatient with the slowness of the legal process and phone their lawyers frequently in an attempt to hasten civil proceedings. Although patients who are involved in litigation may embellish and exaggerate their symptoms, it is the experience of the author that most malingerers have been weeded out by lawyers and doctors before cases come to court.

Many physicians and jurists are of the opinion that traumatized patients with significant psychiatric illness will recover following successful litigation. However, Sprehe (1982) in a follow-up of 108 patients over a 10-year period has reported that 78 percent of his patients with significant psychiatric illness were "no better" and 58 percent were not working following successful adjudication of their cases. The "greenback poultice" is more fantasy than fact. As Valliant (1981) has pointed out, continuing psychiatric therapy following settlement of the legal issues is required if traumatized patients are ever to return to the workplace.

During Stage III patients become notoriously resistant to usual medical treatment and begin to believe that their condition is beyond the comprehension and therapeutic skills of their physicians. Disenchantment with medical therapy grows until patients become convinced that they are incurable and chronically disabled and have reached an end-stage in their illness. Lack of response to medical treatment reinforces and confirms this belief, and patients tend to shun a psychiatric referral because of the implication of "craziness." The notion of disablement owing primarily to a psychiatric disorder has important consequences for prognosis, and PTSD must be defined in concepts involving treatment and rehabilitation if patients are ever to resume a productive life.

It is interesting to note and speculate about how attorney and physician attitudes contribute to the patient's self-image as a disabled person. Lawyers, of course, see advantage in manifest pathology at the time of the trial and may indicate this to patients either directly or indirectly. Physicians, frustrated by patients who turn plaintiff and whose emphasis seems more on tort than therapy, may dismiss such recalcitrants and label them laggards or malingerers who appear more motivated by money than cure. The treatment of patients with Chronic PTSD offers an unusual challenge to physicians. Patience, understanding, and tenacity can be rewarding when patients are rescued from a possible lifetime of uselessness and unproductiveness.

DELAYED PTSD

The reporting by patients or the observation by clinicians of stress symptoms many months or even several years following the original trauma has been called Delayed PTSD. According to the *DSM-III* (1980), in Delayed PTSD the onset of symptoms occurs at least 6 months after the trauma. Although patients may not make the connection between the trauma and subsequent symptoms, retrospective analysis suggests a causal relationship. At times, when symptomatic behavior follows a flashback of the original trauma or nightmares vivify old memories of the traumatic incident, patients and clinicians conclude that the emotional effects of the original trauma had remained latent or dormant, only to surface at this time (Kolb and Mutalipassi 1982). Why and how this should occur and the mechanisms underlying a delayed response to trauma are never made clear by commentators. Lack of clarity, however, has not modulated interest in Delayed PTSD, perhaps because the concept fits well into traditional psychiatric beliefs of conflict, repression, and defense mechanisms.

In the experience of the author, a Delayed PTSD is actually an Acute Stress Disorder that has become chronic and later is identified possibly because symptoms have been made more manifest by subsequent stress. The delay, therefore, has been in recognizing, diagnosing, and treating the Chronic PTSD. An analysis of the Three E's usually reveals that an increment of anxiety at a later time is due to environmental stressors not directly related to the original trauma. Patients with inadequate personal resources or coping skills fail to deal effectively with the additional stress and develop symptoms of pathologic anxiety, often taking on the coloring of the original trauma. To an untrained eye, it appears that the patient is having a delayed response to the original trauma rather than symptom intensification owing to additional stress.

Most patients labeled as having Delayed PTSD are suffering from the chronic symptoms characteristic of Stage III of a PTSD. Low-grade or sporadic spurts of pathologic anxiety have been present since the original trauma, incapacitating them sometimes severely. The Chronic PTSD patient's normative anxiety level is at Level 3, and it can be seen that only a small environmental stressor is required for a patient to reach Level 4, the severe range, where symptoms of pathologic anxiety are very intense. Patients become perplexed when memories of their original trauma become mixed with current environmental stressors and often place primary responsibility for symptoms and troublesome behavior on the original precipitating trauma.

The diagnosis of Delayed PTSD can also be misapplied when a person has encountered two separate and distinct traumas at two discrete periods of time. Just as a person may fracture the same arm twice or contract the same illness on two or more occasions, an individual subjected to two different traumas at different times can develop a PTSD on each occasion.

A 59-year-old World War II combat veteran was driving his truck down a narrow highway that was shrouded with fog. Visibility was poor and the man slowed his truck. Suddenly, through the fog, he saw the dim outlines of headlights coming straight toward him. He slammed on the brakes and attempted to swerve away from the oncoming headlights, but a collision was inevitable; he braced himself for the impact. At the last second, the oncoming vehicle swerved, too late, to the right, and the truck driver hit the other vehicle on the side, knocking it off the road and head on into a tree. Unhurt but shaken, the truck driver got out of his cab and hurried to assist the stricken driver of the other vehicle. Looking into the wrecked automobile, he saw the battered face and broken body of the driver, apparently lifeless. Attempts to open the door of the car to rescue the driver were fruitless, and the truck driver went back to his vehicle and radioed for assistance. The state police arrived, conducted an investigation, and concluded that the dead man had been intoxicated, thereby exonerating the truck driver. Subsequently, the truck driver developed the typical signs and symptoms of a PTSD.

Past history revealed that in 1943, when he was a 19-year-old Marine Corps private serving in the South Pacific, he was involved in fierce combat. Under constant fire from the Japanese, the young soldier and his platoon were pinned down and had to remain in a foxhole for a day and a long night. Frightened but fatigued, he fell into a deep sleep later that night as the fire lessened. Upon awakening the next morning, he tried to rouse his best friend who lay huddled against him. When he shook his friend by the shoulders, his head lolled back, revealing a large, bloodied cavity where the face had been. Panic stricken, the young private leapt out of his foxhole and ran to the rear to find a medic. Sobbing hysterically and speaking almost incoherently, he told the medics where to find his friend. He then was given an injection that induced somnolence. Later, he was shipped back to the United States and placed in the psychiatric ward of a military hospital. He received an honorable discharge for medical reasons from the U.S. Marine Corps and reentered civilian life. During the next 3 years he was in and out of Veteran's Administration (VA) Hospitals because of extreme nervousness, sleep disturbance, incessant nightmares about war, and an inability to adjust to civilian life. Finally his symptoms subsided and he returned to activities he had enjoyed prior to the service. Over the course of the next 30 years, he did not require any further psychiatric treatment. Occasionally, memories of war intruded upon his consciousness and on rare occasions he dreamed about his combat experiences, but his war trauma never interfered with daily living.

Following the accident, which occurred 35 years after his last psychiatric hospitalization, the truck driver again developed nervousness, sleep disturbance, nightmares, and other symptoms of a PTSD. Ruminations and dream content were primarily related to his vehicular accident and the death of the driver. The second trauma did remind him of his combat experiences and another physician made the diagnosis of Delayed PTSD, but the previous war trauma remained at the periphery of the driver's thoughts. The second trauma precipitated a second PTSD and was not a delayed response to stress.

When persons display stress symptoms long after the time of the traumatic incident, it is appropriate to delve into any relationship between the past trauma and current symptoms. One can discover an untreated Chronic PTSD, symptoms of pathologic anxiety not directly related to a PTSD, or, if another trauma has occurred, a second PTSD unrelated to the first. Delayed PTSD seems a poor choice as diagnostic label because of the implication that all subsequent stress symptoms are directly related to the original trauma.

Survivors of major catastrophes, rather than victims of ordinary accidents, are more likely to be diagnosed as having Delayed PTSD (Brend 1939; Lewy 1941; *DSM-III* 1980). Wars, natural disasters, explosions, fires, and aircraft or train crashes involving a huge loss of life make larger impressions upon the minds of survivors and observers than do everyday traumas (Figure 3-2). Patient and physician may connect any subsequent symptom or pathologic behavior to the disaster. This automatic assumption, of course, is not necessarily true, but it reinforces the idea that the effects of a trauma can be delayed or appear at any time in the future.

Combat veterans of all wars carry within their minds terrible memories of death and destruction. When recalling the disturbing trauma, most veterans may experience momentary anxiety, but not the persistent anxiety characteristic of a PTSD. The celebrated author William Manchester, (1980) described in his book *Goodbye Darkness: A Memoir of the Pacific War* scenes of World War II violence that included accounts of how he killed a Japanese soldier and how he was wounded. Manchester reported that the mental images related to his killing of the Japanese soldier remained forever fixed in his mind and that occasionally he still dreams about this incident. He required no psychiatric treatment and his subsequent life, judging from his success as an author, has not been adversely affected.

Veterans of the Vietnam conflict epitomize sufferers of what is called Delayed PTSD, but the real delay was the acceptance by the government of the traumatic effects of an unpopular war on the combat soldier and prisoner of war. Undeniably, if veterans, especially combat soldiers, had been examined prior to being returned to the United States, a significant number of them would have displayed signs and symptoms of an Acute PTSD. However, upon return to the States, many Vietnam-era veterans with a PTSD were processed and discharged from the armed services, their Stress Disorder undetected, minimized or ignored. The affected veterans, upon returning home, were plagued with memories and nightmares of wanton death and needless destruction. Ashamed and afraid, many of these veterans of the early post-Vietnam era neither sought treatment nor considered their symptoms and behavior to be pathologic. Biased emotionalism had distorted the effect of the Vietnam conflict on combat veterans, but as time passed it became increasingly obvious that this conflict, like any other war, had left its mark on certain veterans. Symptoms typical of Stages II and III of PTSD experienced by veterans were endured or self-treated with alcohol or sedative-type drugs. In Vietnam many combat soldiers had easy access to unlimited quantities of inexpensive alcohol, opium, and hashish. Upon discharge self-tranquilization learned in Vietnam was simply transferred to the United States, only at home many of the drugs had to be obtained illicitly, forcing veterans to resort to antisocial behavior (Friedman 1981). Substance abuse disrupts family life, increases suicidal risk, affects job performance, facilitates antisocial behavior, and together with the debilitating effects of PTSD severely incapacitates the veteran (Figley 1978; Goodwin 1980; Walker 1981). Statistical studies indicate that Vietnam combat veterans had more difficulties in readjustment than would be expected in a comparable population of veterans not exposed to combat (Fischer et al. 1980; Wilson 1980; Keane and Fairbank 1983). Later, when the Vietnam conflict was placed in proper perspective and the combat veteran received appropriate recognition for service to the country, PTSD was also recognized as a legitimate psychiatric sequela to an unpopular war. The condition is, of course, service related and can be treated by the methods outlined in this book.

SUMMARY

All people react emotionally when exposed to a trauma, but only predisposed persons develop and maintain symptoms characteristic of a PTSD. Although the evidence is not definitive, it suggests that a predisposition to a PTSD may result from genetic influences similar in many respects to predisposition in persons suffering from an Anxiety Disorder (Anxiety Neurosis). Individuals who develop a PTSD go through various stages of the disorder. During Stage I, impact and reaction to the trauma, anxiety symptoms do not subside. Rather, symptoms are maintained beyond 4 to 6 weeks or even are heightened and begin to affect many areas of life. Excessive concern with the traumatic incident and obsessive preoccupation with death or more serious injury characterize Stage II — Acute PTSD. As PTSD progresses beyond 6 months, the condition becomes chronic, Stage III. The patient's emphasis changes from preoccupation with the actual trauma to overconcern with disability attributable to the trauma. Demoralization, depression, and disillusionment with medical treatment predominate during Stage III. A retributive attitude and extreme hostility develop, particularly when a legal suit is filed and depositions and court appearances focus the patient's attention to matters of fault. Successful litigation usually does not resolve a PTSD; studies indicate that symptoms, unresolved psychiatric conflicts, and unemployment continue in the majority of cases in spite of a monetary award.

The concept of the diagnostic term "Delayed PTSD" can be challenged. Although the idea of a delayed response to trauma may fit well into psychological concepts of conflict, repression, and defense mechanisms, it does not mesh well with clinical observations. At least three possibilities exist to explain what has been called a Delayed PTSD: (1) Persons from the time of the original trauma display the symptoms of a Chronic PTSD that has remained unreported, undiagnosed, and untreated. (2) Persons who have been marginally coping with a Chronic PTSD are subsequently exposed to environmental stressors unrelated to the original trauma, and the intensification of symptoms may take on the coloring of the original trauma. (3) Persons may experience two totally unrelated traumas at two different periods of time and develop a PTSD following each trauma. Delayed PTSD seems a poor choice as a diagnostic label because of the implication that all subsequent stress symptoms are directly related to the original trauma.

FOUR
SIGNS AND SYMPTOMS

In PTSD what appears to be a potpourri of symptoms is really a complex and well-organized set of pathologic behaviors interlaced with multiple issues occurring at different periods of time. At the onset immediately following the trauma, the clinician's chief concern may consist of sorting out symptoms and determining whether the cause is physical, mental, or fraudulent. When physical factors are ruled out, the clinician must make a judgment about whether the symptoms are genuine (a mental disorder) or fake (malingered). As time passes even the relatedness of symptoms to trauma may be subject to question or forgotten. Issues of laziness versus sickness enter the clinical picture when a worker's compensation claim is initiated by the patient. When a financial reward is tied to symptomatic behavior, the sincerity of the patient comes under scrutiny, as questions of primary and secondary gain are raised during a personal injury suit. Depending upon the paradigmatic proclivities of the clinician, value judgments concerning the patient's symptoms confuse the clinical picture and may result in the withholding of treatment. In truth, pejorative adjectives describe many of the patient's attempts to cope; clinicians must be aware of their own attitudes toward patients who claim disability following a trauma because these views influence an objective appraisal of symptoms.

The stage of the disorder and hence the time when an evaluation for treatment commences determine which set of symptoms is clinically more manifest. PTSD is a multifaceted disorder, but pathologic anxiety always lies at the core. Anxiety symptoms persist throughout all three stages of PTSD, but they are most obvious during Stage I and during the earlier part of Stage II. Concern with physical symptoms and depression, on the other hand, are more likely to occur during Stage III. Litigation and a tendency toward overexaggeration of symptoms, however, occur during the height of legal action, and a misdiagnosis of Malingering may be made. Addiction to alcohol or other drugs begins in Stage II but may become malignant during Stage III, completely obscuring other signs and symptoms of PTSD. Patients obsessively preoccupied with pain or other physical discomfort may orient the clinician toward a somatic etiology or a Psychogenic Pain Disorder. Despondency and depression may be misinterpreted as an affective disorder unrelated to the original trauma. Disillusionment with medical treatment often found in patients during Stage III may be shared by physicians who have become upset with patients who do not respond to treatment, resulting in a referral or refusal to continue therapy. These are some of the pitfalls that await clinicians who evaluate and treat traumatized patients. An appreciation of the signs and symptoms present in each of the three stages of PTSD adds clarity and gives perspective to the disorder.

STAGES AND SYMPTOMS

Stage I — Response to Trauma

Most everyone would respond emotionally to situations perceived as a potential threat to life or limb. A narrow miss or collision with an oncoming automobile or an actual encounter with an armed robber would produce similar physiological reactions in most people. The trauma impacts on a single or a combination of the five senses and must be perceived and interpreted as a danger to self in order for autonomic arousal to occur. Sudden stimulation of the autonomic nervous system produces symptoms characteristic of an acute anxiety reaction, as can be seen in Table 4-1. Patients describe the experience as a "spurt of adrenaline throughout my entire body." Feelings of fear are accompanied by an accelerated heartbeat, exaggerated and increased breathing, nausea (sometimes accompanied by vomiting), shakiness, trembling of the entire body, dizziness, and a feeling of "shock." The number and intensity of anxiety symptoms

TABLE 4-1
Characteristics and Symptoms of Stage I

Characteristics

History of a specific trauma from the environment has impacted on one or more of the five senses, has been interpreted and perceived as dangerous, and has resulted in a sudden discharge of the autonomic nervous system.

Almost everybody who is involved in a traumatic incident will respond in the fashion described above. For most persons these symptoms subside within a few weeks, and there is no impairment of family, vocational, recreational, or social life. Treatment is not required and time usually heals. Stage I is not an Anxiety Disorder but a reaction to environmental stress. Pathologic behavior becomes manifest during Stage II.

Sources of Stress

Environmental

The environmental stimulus, the trauma, impacts on one or more of a person's five senses. The environs where the trauma took place frequently become a phobic stimulus, and, depending upon the nature of the trauma, vehicles, industrial plants, or similar settings may elicit anxiety. Any environmental event that is identical to or resembles any part of the traumatic incident may also stimulate anxiety.

Encephalic

The patient's central encephalic activities are visualizing and thinking about the traumatic incident. Intrusive thoughts (flashbacks) of the trauma, highlighting closeness to death or serious injury, may occur. Dreams portraying the actual traumatic incident, some variant of it, or any situation involving danger are also frequent.

Endogenous

Endogenous events consist of pain or physical discomfort in any part of the body. The uncomfortable endogenous feelings were not present before the trauma, and the perception of them stimulates and triggers encephalic activity related to the initial trauma. Endogenous sensations may also be the result of chronic anxiety.

Symptoms

Helplessness, powerlessness
Increased heart rate
Dyspnea

Table 4-1, continued

Hyperventilation
Nausea
Vomiting
Extreme trembling or shaking
Excessive sweating
Dizziness
Feeling faint (light-headedness and unsteadiness)
Blurry vision
Hot flashes or flushing
Tingling sensations in the arms or hands (parasthesias)
Diarrhea
Urinary or fecal incontinence
Nervousness
Ringing in the ears
Outbursts of anger
Inability to remember recent events
Headaches
Pain
Restlessness
Hypersensitivity to sudden or rapidly changing stimuli (noise, light)
Sleep disturbance
Nightmares
Irritability
Difficulties in concentration
Feelings that familiar things are strange or unreal

Source: Compiled by author.

vary with the trauma and individual. Sometimes persons experience a dissociative reaction with feelings of unreality or depersonalization. Subsequent to the trauma patients may complain of sleep irregularities, bad dreams, pain if physical injury was part of the trauma, nervousness, and irritability. Patients may ponder the accident and speculate that they could have been more seriously injured or even killed. These encephalic actions increase anxiety. Exposure to environments similar to or resembling the surroundings in which the original trauma took place also evokes anxiety. Loud noises, sudden kaleidoscopic visual phenomena, and abrupt changes in almost any stimulus irritate and make patients "jumpy" and apprehensive.

Interestingly, amnesia seems to protect persons from the unpleasant emotional effects of a trauma. If persons are unaware of a trauma because of inattentiveness, a failure to perceive impending danger correlates with diminished psychiatric morbidity. Similarly, when persons are rendered unconscious as a result of the trauma and are amnesic about it, symptoms of anxiety are much less. Perhaps this is because there are no video tapes of the mind portraying the traumatic incident to stimulate pathologic anxiety.

For most persons a trauma produces only temporary discomfort. Even if the trauma was severe, persons who are not predisposed to a PTSD usually overcome their psychological reaction within 4 to 6 weeks. Memories of the traumatic incident may persist for years or even for the lifetime of the person, but they do not intrude significantly on daily functioning. Transient symptoms of anxiety, sleeplessness, and even nightmares may occur infrequently, but no major disruption of life results. Stage I is the endpoint for most individuals who have encountered an environmental trauma. Vulnerable persons predisposed to a PTSD move on to Stage II.

Stage II — Acute PTSD

From the onset persons who develop a PTSD exhibit pathologic anxiety (Linn 1975; Horowitz et al. 1980; see Table 4-2). Like a person reprieved from death, a look of fear is seen upon the patient's face when relating the history of the trauma, especially when detailing the moments before impact. Invariably, patients believed that they would be killed. Because it is emotionally painful to discuss the details of the trauma, some patients gloss over anxiety-laden material when relating the history. Often, it becomes necessary to direct the patient's attention to events just prior to and shortly following impact. Questions regarding what the patient was thinking and feeling at that time usually reveal an anxiety-associated content. As patients recall and relate thoughts about death, anxiety increases and talk becomes animated. Patients remember the actual trauma very well, and some will report that the entire traumatic episode seemed as if it were in slow motion. Patients report symptoms relative to the thorax, including tachycardia, palpitations, dyspnea, tightness or pain in the chest, and at times hyperventilation. Trembling of the hands and arms is an almost universal symptom, which

TABLE 4-2
Characteristics and Symptoms of Stage II

Characteristics

Morbid preoccupation with the trauma marks this stage. Patients are obsessed with all aspects of their trauma and constantly speculate upon more dour consequences that could have resulted. Symptoms from Stage I are maintained beyond 4 to 6 weeks, and there is definite impairment of family, vocational, social, and recreational life.

Sources of Stress

Environmental

Environmental stimuli that are identical to or closely resemble the surroundings where the trauma took place may elicit pathologic anxiety even after a considerable amount of time has elapsed since the original trauma. The environs of the trauma frequently become a phobic stimulus, and, depending upon the nature and place of the trauma, vehicles, industrial plants, or similar settings may be avoided. Environmental settings that the patient considers to be dangerous may also elicit pathologic anxiety and may be avoided even though there is no similarity to the initial traumatic situation.

Encephalic

The hallmark of Stage II is a total preoccupation with the trauma. Patients spend endless hours daydreaming, fantasizing, thinking, or talking about various aspects of their traumatic experience. Frequently, speculation and elaboration include a more devastating trauma than the one experienced. Nightmares depicting the trauma or some variant of it cause patients to awaken suddenly in a state of alarm. Because of the noxious nature of nightmares, patients may dread sleep. Encephalic activity (obsessions and ruminations) generates and sustains pathologic anxiety, so that patients remain in a very uncomfortable state throughout most of their waking hours. Retraumatization, whereby the patient repeatedly visualizes the traumatic incident, is a pernicious part of a Post-Traumatic Stress Disorder (PTSD) and helps explain why patients remain symptomatic long after the trauma has passed.

Endogenous

Pain or any uncomfortable physical sensation is a common concomitant of a PTSD and reminds patients of the original trauma. Endogenous sensations that were not present before the trauma focus the patient's mind on danger to self and stimulate encephalic activity in which the traumatic

Table 4-2, continued

incident is replayed back in the mind, further increasing pathologic anxiety. The Spiral Effect is set in motion, contributing to more anxiety and more physiological sensations that are interpreted erroneously, thus completing the cycle.

Symptoms

Patients experience a generalized feeling of nervousness with occasional surges of higher anxiety. Any of the symptoms listed in Stage I may be noted in patients during Stage II. In addition, the following symptoms may also be present.

Phobic anxiety
Phobic avoidance
Physical discomfort
Disinterest in sex
Fatigue, weakness
Ruminations about the traumatic incident
Marital problems
Inability to work
Retributive attitude
Litigiousness
Feeling that personality has changed
Feeling detached from others
Not being able to express or show feelings
Thoughts of death
Thoughts about accidents, injury
Guilt feelings for or about the trauma
Feelings as if the accident were happening again
Feelings of discouragement (subclinical depression)
Disinterest in life (family, recreational activities, work)
Feeling of unreality (depersonalization, derealization)
Episodes of terror or panic
Difficulties in making decisions

Source: Compiled by author.

may be accompanied by nausea or vomiting. Dizziness and unsteadiness of gait frequently force patients to sit immediately after the trauma because they fear locomotion would be impossible. Hot flashes or flushing may be accompanied by excessive sweating, blurred vision, and ringing in the ears. Patients invariably report that they felt extremely nervous and fearful following the trauma.

A trip by ambulance to the emergency room of a hospital or a ride home generally ensues after the trauma has passed. If physical injuries require hospitalization, the PTSD process is put "on hold" since the patient's mind may be distracted by physical pain or blunted by analgesic medication. When the patient is discharged from the hospital, a thread common to all patients with a PTSD emerges, regardless of whether physical injury occurred as a result of the original trauma. Predisposed patients become preoccupied and have an overwhelming obsession with their traumatic encounter. Vivid recollections of the trauma engender thoughts that they could have been killed, but downplay the fact that they have survived. Retraumatization takes place when the video tapes of the mind play back the entire traumatic incident while the high levels of anxiety generated sensitize the patients to various elements of the traumatic scene. The propensity to ruminate, visualize, and talk about the trauma encephalically maintains pathologic anxiety and sustains the disorder.

With time anxiety does not diminish but is heightened and maintained by the action and interplay of the Three E's. Patients continuously feel on edge, tense, and jumpy and look unwell. Commonly, patients complain of frontal or occipital headaches, tightness of the chest, nausea, and difficulties in concentration. Feelings of dizziness and unsteadiness are coupled with thoughts about fainting or abruptly losing consciousness and as a result incurring injury. Episodes of depersonalization or derealization may occur during these periods of increased stress.

Disturbed sleep invariably occurs at the onset of a PTSD. At night, while attempting sleep, patients ruminate over their trauma and related worrisome subjects. Relaxation leading to sleep becomes impossible, and patients tumble restlessly throughout most of the night, awakening the next day in a state of fatigue and ill temper. Nightmares depicting the traumatic event or a similar frightening situation frequently awaken patients from a shallow sleep. They may begin to dread sleep because disturbing dreams may erupt unpredictably, reawakening unpleasant memories of the trauma. Following a night of broken and inadequate sleep, the patient is frazzled and the ability to cope is adversely affected.

When patients are exposed to the traumatic site or environmental surroundings that closely resemble it, anxiety becomes more intense, at times escalating into a panic attack. The sudden appearance of palpitations, tachycardia, shortness of breath, as well as other acute anxiety symptoms terrifies patients and reinforces the idea that something is terribly wrong with them. Even scenes of accidents, death, or injury on television or movie screens evoke high anxiety, frequently leading patients to close their eyes, turn off their television sets, or leave the theatre. Phobic avoidance of situations resembling the traumatic setting prevents a return to usual life activities and helps sustain an apprehensive expectation.

Although patients feel anxious and irritable, they seldom complain of psychiatric symptoms and may feel offended if their physician or friends suggest that they consult a psychiatrist. Instead, the somatic manifestations of anxiety are interpreted by the patient as an indication of bodily damage or ongoing disease. An organic orientation blocks any insight into the psychological manifestations of PTSD, and patients relentlessly continue their trek from doctor to doctor in search of a remedy. If the physical symptoms persist in spite of medical treatment, patients gradually conclude that the trauma they have endured has resulted in a condition that is incurable and that has rendered them permanently disabled.

At some point during Stage II, some patients dwell on culpability for their trauma. Thoughts about negligence and carelessness of others spur anger and incite legal action. Clinicians must sort out exaggeration of the patient's complaints when litigation is pending. The Symptom Inventory Checklist (SIC; Table 4-3) and the ASP help to assess the extent to which the patient is embellishing symptoms. Interviews with family members or friends also help to place the patient's symptoms in perspective. Past medical or psychiatric records will give some indication of preexisting illness and pretraumatic personality and will shed light on symptoms that may have been present prior to the trauma. There is no question that litigation colors the symptomatic picture of PTSD, but in the author's experience outright conspiracy or Malingering is rare. A retributive attitude may inspire litigation, but it usually results from an honest assessment that the patient has been wronged and should receive

TABLE 4-3
Symptom Inventory Checklist

In the following list, please mark an X to show the degree to which you have experienced each item listed *following* the accident or traumatic incident. Also, please mark with an O to show to what degree you experienced that item *before* the accident or traumatic event.

	1. Not at All	2. Sometimes	3. Often	4. Very Often	5. Practically All of the Time

1. Heart beating fast
2. Difficulties in breathing
3. Trembling or shaking of the hands or body
4. Nausea
5. Vomiting
6. Diarrhea
7. Dizziness
8. Light-headedness or unsteadiness
9. Hot flashes or flushing
10. Tingling sensations in the arms or legs
11. Headaches
12. Physical pain
13. Nervousness (stress, anxiety)
14. Blurred vision
15. Ringing in the ears
16. Problems sleeping
17. Nightmares
18. Extreme sensitivity to noise
19. Irritability
20. Outbursts of anger
21. Lack of interest in sex
22. Excessive sweating
23. Feeling that my personality has changed
24. Marriage problems
25. Lack of interest in life (family, social/recreational activities)

Table 4-3, continued

	1. Not at All	2. Sometimes	3. Often	4. Very Often	5. Practically All of the Time
26. Feeling detached from others					
27. Depression					
28. Feeling faint					
29. Being told by others that I have changed					
30. Crying spells					
31. Not able to express or show my feelings					
32. Unable to remember recent events					
33. Thoughts of death					
34. Thoughts of suicide					
35. Thoughts about accidents					
36. Thoughts about injury					
37. Feelings of worthlessness					
38. Low energy level					
39. Slowness in thought or movements					
40. Difficulties in concentrating					
41. Tiredness, fatigue, weakness					
42. Restlessness					
43. Muscle aches					
44. Problems at work					
45. Feelings that familiar things seem strange or unreal					
46. Difficulties in making decisions					
47. Feeling "blue" or "down in the dumps"					
48. Feelings of terror or panic					
49. Feeling unreal or like another person					

Table 4-3, continued

On the following items, please mark an X *only* to show the degree to which you have experienced each item listed *following* the accident or traumatic incident.

	1. Not at All	2. Sometimes	3. Often	4. Very Often	5. Practically All of the Time
50. Avoidance of places that are not related to but remind me of the accident place					
51. Avoidance of places related to the accident or traumatic incident					
52. Thinking about the accident					
53. Anger toward self or others for their part in the accident					
54. Guilt feelings for or about the accident					
55. Having such feelings as if the accident were happening again (flashbacks)					

Source: Compiled by author.

compensation for injuries sustained because of the carelessness of others.

In summary, patients who reach Stage II have developed an Acute PTSD. Anxiety does not recede but is maintained by a combination of the Three E's. Obsessive concern for the traumatic incident characterizes Stage II, and as patients relive the trauma during conversation, in imagination, and in dreams, this process of retraumatization helps sustain the disorder. Environmental settings closely resembling the scene of the trauma also stimulate pathologic anxiety, and patients frequently develop a phobic avoidance of these situations. The somatic manifestations of anxiety, along with any symptoms owing to physical trauma, focus patients' attention on their bodily processes and increase anxiety vis-à-vis the Spiral Effect. If physical symptoms persist, patients tend to attribute them to organic factors even if there is no objective evidence to support this conclusion. Toward the end of Stage II, patients become concerned with chronic disability and litigation.

Stage III – Chronic PTSD

Emphasis shifts during Stage III from a preoccupation with the actual traumatic incident to an overzealous fixation on the consequences believed to have resulted from the trauma (Table 4-4). Patients frequently are somatically preoccupied and focus on disability. Pain, physical discomfort, fatigue, and a generalized feeling of malaise are likely chief complaints. Various aches and pains are described in minute detail, and patients tend selectively to glean ambiguous statements from their previous physicians in combination with the results of inconclusive laboratory procedures to support the notion that there might be something physically wrong. The patient is not easily dissuaded from the belief that organic pathology is causing the physical disability. If the physician dismisses symptoms cursorily without explanation, this is often interpreted by patients as a lack of understanding or disbelief. The issue of the cause of physical symptoms must be resolved at the onset, for it is often a pivotal point upon which success or failure in treatment may well be determined (Chapter six).

Beneath the somatic preoccupation and concern for disablement, a mental status examination will reveal chronic anxiety. Moist hands, apprehensive faces, and a fidgeting figure frequently greet the clinician during the initial examination. During the recitation of the history, patients become more anxious and exhibit signs of agitation as they relate details of the trauma at the time of impact. Symptoms similar to those of a Generalized Anxiety Disorder become evident during the examination. Signs and symptoms from the following categories are present: motor tension; autonomic hyperactivity; apprehensive expectation; and vigilance and scanning. Without a history of onset related to a specific traumatic event, PTSD might easily be mistaken for a Generalized Anxiety Disorder. The SIC and ASP quickly reveal the type and severity of additional anxiety symptoms. Generalized feelings of nervousness, irritability, restlessness, inability to relax, tension headaches, upset stomach, worrying, and fatigue are symptoms often related by patients.

TABLE 4-4
Characteristics and Symptoms of Stage III

Characteristics

During this stage the patient's preoccupation with the actual trauma recedes, being replaced by an obsessive preoccupation with the adverse consequences attributed to the trauma. Disability becomes the focus of the patient's life and all pain, physical discomfort, and deficits of behavior are attributed directly to the traumatic incident. Changes in life-style and status result from impaired functioning and affect family, work, social, and recreational activities. In this stage patients feel that a personality change has transpired because of the trauma. Chronic anxiety and problems attributed to disablement frequently lead to a secondary depression. During periods of stress, flashbacks can be associated with episodes of disassociation and feelings of unreality. A legal settlement of the patient's tort action occurs during Stage III but in most instances this has little effect on the course of the Stress Disorder.

Sources of Stress

Environmental

A wide variety of environmental stimuli perceived as dangerous may produce pathologic anxiety. Phobic anxiety or a phobia of the surroundings and situations related to the trauma may still exist. The patient's perceived disablement may adversely affect interpersonal relationships, participation in work, and social and recreational activities. Withdrawal from the environment is associated with depression.

Encephalic

The patient's central encephalic concern consists of disablement believed to have been caused by the original trauma. Although from time to time thoughts about the actual trauma cross the patient's mind, the traumatic incident no longer occupies a central place in thinking. The persistence of physical symptoms, nonresponse to treatment, incurability, permanent disablement, litigation, and the inability to resume usual life activities are themes that overshadow the actual trauma during Stage III. Depression is abetted by self-statements that impugn one's self-worth. Thoughts about death and suicide are not common but if present are indicative of depression. Patients become very self-centered and think excessively about their disability.

Table 4-4, continued

Endogenous
> Inordinate attention to pain, physical discomfort, and normal physiological processes of the body reaches a zenith during Stage III. Sickness becomes a dominant theme and incurability a constant thought as patients concentrate on their bodily sensations. The presence of pain and physical discomfort reinforces the belief that something is terribly wrong with them. Shortcomings, failures, and inability to cope are blamed on the "trauma-produced physical injury." Patients have little appreciation of the ability of pathologic anxiety to initiate or intensify somatic symptoms. The Spiral Effect between endogenous and encephalic events contributes to increasing anxiety and is operative throughout the chronic stage of Post-Traumatic Stress Disorder.

Symptoms

Anxiety Symptoms
> Any of the anxiety symptoms listed in Tables 4-1 and 4-2 can be found during Stage III; however, the intensity of anxiety is usually lower and less obvious. Patients are more likely to complain of generalized anxiety and irritability. Occasionally, surges of high anxiety occur in response to environmental stimuli, and patients may report a dissociative state with episodes of depersonalization and/or derealization.

Somatic Symptoms
> Headaches
> Musculoskeletal pain in almost any part of the body
> Weakness
> Epigastric pain
> Chest pain
> Pain in that part of the body injured during the traumatic incident

Encephalic Symptoms (Intrusive Thoughts)
> Thoughts about permanent disablement and incurability
> Thoughts about pain
> Thoughts about the carelessness and lack of concern of others
> Thoughts about litigation
> Thoughts about accidents and injury
> Thoughts about the disruption of life caused by the trauma
> Thoughts about economic problems
> Thoughts about work
> Thoughts about powerlessness

Table 4-4, continued

Depressive Symptoms
    Crying spells
    Low energy level
    Feelings of worthlessness
    Thoughts about death
    Thoughts about suicide
    Sleep disturbance
    Social withdrawal, isolation, loneliness
    Loss of interest in pleasurable activities
    Pessimistic attitude
    Psychomotor retardation
    Loss of appetite
    Feeling "blue" or "down in the dumps"

Source: Compiled by author.

Feelings of unreality (depersonalization/derealization) may occur as anxiety increases. Less prominent, intermittent anxiety symptoms such as dizziness, blurred vision, ringing in the ears, tingling sensations in the hands or feet, and vague physical sensations in almost any part of the body are usually not interpreted by patients as an indication of a psychiatric disorder but as a physical one. A phobia or phobic anxiety of places or settings closely resembling the scene of the trauma is not uncommon. Sleep disturbance is often present, but the frequency of nightmares usually diminishes during Stage III. Some patients resort to alcohol or other drugs as a form of self-treatment to allay anxiety, but a Substance Use Disorder only camouflages PTSD and complicates treatment.

Pessimistic ruminations permeate the patient's outlook during Stage III, and depression is often a secondary manifestation. In the chronic stage of PTSD, patients look unhappy and commonly relate that they are "down in the dumps." They may report any of the following dysthymic symptoms: feelings of worthlessness, crying spells, thoughts of death and suicide, low energy level, lack of enjoyment, and psychomotor retardation (feeling slow in thought and action). An emotional detachment and withdrawal from family and friends together with a lack of interest in activities formerly found to be pleasurable accentuate a depressed state. Most Chronic

PTSD patients are somewhat depressed. In some, however, the symptoms are most severe, and clinicians must be alerted to the possibility of a major depressive episode and suicide. A depressed state also interferes markedly with marital relations, especially interest in sex, and performance at work.

Patients normally do not seek consultation or treatment for a Stress Disorder, but are referred by their treating physician or lawyer. During initial sessions suspiciousness causes the patient to be guarded, and some resent the referral as an implication of mental illness. The clinician is therefore likely to be confronted with a patient who is irritable and ill-tempered and who may exhibit abruptness of manner and occasional outbursts of anger. A paranoid attitude may be evident when patients relate their symptoms and blame all of their problems on the trauma and the carelessness of others. Hostility may mount as patients give illustrations of a lack of concern or an uncaring attitude on the part of their employers, relatives, friends, or doctors. Occasionally during Stage III the patient's choleric mood intensifies and erupts into overt violent behavior toward others, usually the spouse or some other member of the family. These rageful episodes are more likely to occur when the patient is under the influence of alcohol or other drugs. Verbal threats toward physicians or lawyers occasionally occur, but physical violence is rare.

A retributive attitude toward those believed to be responsible for their trauma and hence their disability evolves into litigiousness. A monetary receipt for injuries sustained as a result of the trauma helps to salve the mind as litigation becomes a way for the patient to strike back. Although patients involved in litigation tend to overexaggerate their symptoms, outright deception or Malingering occurs infrequently. Treatment is retarded when patients begin to concentrate on forensic matters. The resolution of legal issues does not mean treatment should be terminated, for successful litigation does not lead to a cure in the majority of cases.

Thus, in Stage III the patient's preoccupation with the traumatic incident recedes, and an obsessive concern with the disablity attributable to the trauma predominates. Although the patient's chief complaint at this stage may be pain or physical discomfort, anxiety and anger are evident upon examination. Anxiety symptoms in PTSD are similar to those of a Generalized Anxiety Disorder, but the onset of symptoms coinciding with a trauma distinguishes the two. A phobia or phobic anxiety of places or situations identical or similar to the surroundings where the trauma took place is not uncommon. Sleep disturbance continues, but nightmares become less frequent. Chronic PTSD is often associated with a secondary depression and in some cases the dysthymic disorder may be quite severe. The somatic manifestations of anxiety when misinterpreted by patients hinder treatment and lead to frustration and irritability. Anger and a desire to be compensated for the negligence of others motivate legal action and preoccupy patients during Stage III.

SUMMARY

When one views PTSD in terms of a process moving from stage to stage, the symptoms and overt behavior of patients can be more easily understood. PTSD is basically an Anxiety Disorder precipitated by an environmental event. For reasons yet unclear, some persons cannot cope with the stress of a trauma and manifest symptoms attributable to a hyperactive autonomic nervous system. Pathologic anxiety is a central feature of a PTSD, but secondary manifestations complicate the course of the disorder. Depression, somatization, litigation, family conflicts, marital disharmony, vocational impairment, and insolvency all affect the patient's mental state and life-style. Patients prefer to expatiate on the secondary issues of a PTSD, frequently rationalizing that all symptoms and deficits of behavior are due to a permanent disability caused by the original trauma. Clinicians must unravel the tangled maze of symptomatic behavior and place in perspective for the patient's consideration the basic elements of pathologic anxiety caused by a pathologic reaction to trauma. In this manner, a treatment plan that has the maximal possibility of succeeding can be conceived.

FIVE
DIFFERENTIAL DIAGNOSIS

Diagnosis is easy when the clinician is oriented to the concept that trauma, whether it produces physical injury or not, can precipitate a Stress Disorder. A thorough history will reveal exposure to a traumatic event, acute stimulation of the autonomic nervous system, and symptoms characteristic of intense anxiety. Continuation of relatively undiminished levels of anxiety beyond 4 to 6 weeks with the presence of symptoms as mentioned in Chapter four indicates a pathologic reaction to trauma and the development of a PTSD. As time passes, the relationship between the trauma and symptomatic behavior becomes less obvious, and misdiagnoses can occur when the clinician or patient either overlooks or deemphasizes the connection between the two.

Depending upon the stage of PTSD, a plethora of symptoms confront the clinician: anxiety, depression, phobias, pain, vague physical complaints, sleep disturbance, sexual dysfunction, fatigue, and irritability. Further examination may reveal marital discord, financial problems, an unresolved personal injury lawsuit, inability to work, lack of interest in life, and other problem behaviors. If the patient presents with an alcohol or drug abuse problem, this may deflect the clinician from a PTSD, focusing attention instead on the antisocial personality characteristics of substance abusers. At times, deep depression mutes some symptoms of the PTSD, making diagnosis difficult. Clinicians must ferret through the maze of diagnostic possibilities, keeping in mind that trauma followed by pathologic anxiety lies at the core of PTSD.

Following a trauma, of course, organic factors must be taken into consideration during the evaluation of the patient (Trimble 1981). Head trauma may especially affect brain functioning and behavior. Correct diagnosis of organic brain syndrome influences subsequent treatment and prognosis.

> One patient, a 42-year-old married woman, was crossing a street when she was hit by an automobile and rendered unconscious. She was in a coma for 10 days and upon regaining consciousness could not remember the accident. Her recuperation was slow, and initially she was in great pain owing to fractures of two ribs and the right upper arm. Although the signs and symptoms of PTSD were not present, the patient experienced emotional lability, impairment in impulse control, mild apathy and indifference, and suspiciousness. The patient's mental symptoms were a result of trauma but caused by an organic personality syndrome and not a PTSD.

Persons can exhibit emotional symptoms following noncranial physical injury that may or may not be associated with a PTSD. The psychological effects of physical trauma, depression or another psychiatric disorder, may coexist with physical disability, especially if recovery is protracted or not forthcoming. There appears to be no relationship between the extent and severity of physical injury and the genesis of a PTSD. A pretraumatic personality predisposition and a full appreciation of the possibility for injury or death to self at the time of the trauma are two factors that are more important than physical injury for development of a PTSD.

Sometimes a trauma is associated with the presence of a psychotic mental disorder such as schizophrenia, paranoia, or Affective Disorder. Although stress related to trauma may aggravate these major mental disorders, a careful history and mental status examination usually reveal that they preexisted the trauma. Evidence of psychotic symptoms in the mental status examination or psychiatric records documenting psychosis prior to the trauma preclude the diagnosis of a PTSD. Although legal questions may arise when, as rarely occurs, the trauma seems to precipitate a psychotic disorder in the absence of any previous psychiatric history, no diagnostic dilemma presents itself. Medical and legal experts may wish to debate the causal relationship between trauma and psychosis, but the link is at best tenuous. In the absence of Organic Brain Syndrome, psychosis is widely believed to be a genetically determined biological illness that may be aggravated but not caused by environmental stress. There are some exceptions to this general rule, e.g., brief reactive psychosis, but this condition is relatively rare.

Disagreement among physicians concerning the presence or absence of a psychiatric disorder following trauma can be attributed to the following: (1) Lack of knowledge relating to the possible effects of trauma on the mental mechanisms, or simply lack of experience or insight into how patients can continue to complain of symptoms long after the expected time of healing. Mistakenly, Malingering is chosen as the best explanation to describe the person's condition. (2) A deep moralistic notion based on the protestant work ethic that all persons, even those who have been involved in a severe trauma, should make a genuine and determined effort to return to a productive life, however limited, within a reasonable time following the trauma. Some physicians get impatient, incredulous, and angry with traumatized persons who fail to comply with this expectation. Although these clinicians may be quite knowledgeable about the signs and symptoms of a PTSD, they are likely to state that they "don't believe" in the disorder, as if the clinical entity required faith and not objectivity for diagnosis. These physicians support their positions with conviction and fervor and are naturally eagerly solicited by defendants in personal injury suits. (3) Less commonly, the "Charlie McCarthy" or "Howdy Doody" phenomenon, in which some physicians will state in court or writing anything that those who pull the monetary strings want to hear. There is no question that attitude and orientation of the clinician toward trauma, litigation, and chronic illness play an important role in forming conclusions concerning a psychiatric disorder following trauma (Zusman and Simon 1983).

SOMATOFORM DISORDERS

Complaints of pain or physical discomfort dominate many patients' verbalizations. Therefore, mental disorders in which somatic symptoms play a prominent role should be ruled out before a diagnosis of PTSD is made. Of course, organic pathology must be assessed by appropriate physical and laboratory examinations before any psychiatric disorder is considered. When no physical disorder appears to be responsible for the patient's somatic complaints, one possibility that should be considered is Somatoform Disorder. Since any of the Somatoform Disorders – Somatization, Conversion, Psychogenic Pain, and Hypochondriasis – can be mistaken for a PTSD, the important differences among all of these disorders will be highlighted.

Somatization Disorder

Table 5-1 illustrates that any of the symptoms listed in the *DSM-III* (1980) for Somatization Disorder can also be found in patients with a PTSD. Pain and cardiopulmonary, psychosexual, gastrointestinal, and pseudoneurological symptoms may be present in patients with a PTSD who also appear to be quite sickly during the chronic stage of the disorder.

Important differences, however, exist between Somatization Disorder and PTSD. In PTSD, the onset of symptoms follows a specific environmental trauma and may occur at any age. During the acute stages, the traumatic incident is a dominant and intrusive feature of PTSD. The patient's ruminations, fantasies, and dreams about the trauma also differentiate PTSD from Somatization Disorder. An exaggerated startle response, sleep disturbance, nightmares, a phobia or phobic anxiety related to the trauma, or a disinterest or withdrawal from significant activities beginning soon after the trauma further distinguish PTSD from Somatization Disorder. PTSD patients may exhibit a wide range of symptoms that are usually anxiety based and do not reflect an almost lifelong, polysymptomatic disorder as listed in the diagnostic criteria.

Conversion Disorder

As in PTSD there is a relationship between an environmental stimulus and the onset of a Conversion Disorder (Table 5-2). Unlike in PTSD, patients suffering from a conversion reaction often exhibit "la belle indifference," an attitude of unconcern for their physical disability, which is discordant with the severity of the impairment. Issues of primary and secondary gain are of prime importance and are present from the onset in a Conversion Disorder, whereas in PTSD the onset is associated with the "existence of a recognizable

TABLE 5-1
DSM-III Diagnostic Criteria for Somatization Disorder

A. A history of physical symptoms of several years' duration beginning before the age of 30.

B. Complaints of at least 14 symptoms for women and 12 for men from the 37 symptoms listed below. To count a symptom as present, the individual must report that the symptom caused him or her to take medicine (other than aspirin), alter his or her life pattern, or see a physician. The symptoms, in the judgment of the clinician, are not adequately explained by physical disorder or physical injury, and are not side effects of medication, drugs, or alcohol. The clinician need not be convinced that the symptom was actually present, e.g., that the individual actually vomited throughout her entire pregnancy; report of the symptom by the individual is sufficient.

Sickly: Believes that he or she has been sickly for a good part of his or her life.

Conversion of pseudoneurological symptoms: Difficulty swallowing, loss of voice, deafness, double vision, blurred vision, blindness, fainting or loss of consciousness, memory loss, seizures or convulsions, trouble walking, paralysis or muscle weakness, urinary retention or difficulty urinating.

Gastrointestinal symptoms: Abdominal pain, nausea, vomiting spells (other than during pregnancy), bloating (gassy), intolerance (e.g., gets sick) of a variety of foods, diarrhea.

Female reproductive symptoms: Judged by the individual as occurring more frequently or severely than in most women: painful menstruation, menstrual irregularity, excessive bleeding, severe vomiting throughout pregnancy or causing hospitalization during pregnancy.

Psychosexual symptoms: For the major part of the individual's life after opportunities for sexual activity: sexual indifference, lack of pleasure during intercourse, pain during intercourse.

Pain: Pain in back, joints, extremities, genital area (other than during intercourse); pain on urination; other pain (other than headaches).

Cardiopulmonary symptoms: Shortness of breath, palpitations, chest pain, dizziness.

Source: *Diagnostic and Statistical Manual of Mental Disorders*, third edition, 1980.

TABLE 5-2
***DSM-III* Diagnostic Criteria for Conversion Disorder**

A. The predominant disturbance is a loss of or alteration in physical functioning, suggesting a physical disorder.

B. Psychological factors are judged to be etiologically involved in the symptom, as evidenced by one of the following:

   (1) There is a temporal relationship between an environmental stimulus that is apparently related to a psychological conflict or need and the initiation or exacerbation of the symptom.
   (2) The symptom enables the individual to avoid some activity that is noxious to him or her.
   (3) The symptom enables the individual to get support from the environment that otherwise might not be forthcoming.

C. It has been determined that the symptom is *not* under voluntary control.

D. The symptom cannot, after appropriate investigation, be explained by a known physical disorder or pathophysiological mechanism.

E. The symptom is not limited to pain or to a disturbance in sexual functioning.

F. Not due to Sòmatization Disorder or Schizophrenia.

Source: *Diagnostic and Statistical Manual of Mental Disorders*, third edition, 1980.

stressor that would evoke significant symptoms of stress in almost everyone" (*DSM-III* 1980).

Acute anxiety symptoms are evident from the onset in a PTSD, and chronic anxiety is commonplace during the latter stages. Anxiety, an important feature of PTSD, is absent or not prominent in a Conversion Disorder. If "la belle indifference" characterizes a Conversion Disorder, "la belle *d*ifference" marks PTSD patients, who are irritable, ill tempered, and fearful, frequently exhibiting a belligerent attitude toward those believed to be responsible for their trauma. Litigious PTSD patients may have a "secondary gain" in mind when they sue for monetary compensation, but self-righteousness, a belief that they should be compensated for damages caused by another's negligence, motivates this action. The primary and secondary gain of patients with a Conversion Disorder reflects more subtle needs based on a psychological conflict. The PTSD patient's somatic symptoms are usually anxiety related, whereas the physical disturbance of patients with a Conversion Disorder cannot be explained by any physical disorder or pathophysiological mechanism.

Psychogenic Pain Disorder

In both Psychogenic Pain Disorder and Conversion Disorder, psychological factors are judged to be etiologically important, and motivation for the maintenance of symptoms involves primary and secondary gain. Psychogenic Pain Disorder, therefore, could be considered a Conversion Disorder with pain as the most prominent symptom. According to the *DSM-III* (1980), owing to the different course and treatment implications, pain that can be conceptualized as a conversion symptom should instead be coded separately as Psychogenic Pain Disorder.

Pain following trauma can be a clinical characterization common to PTSD and PPD. In the absence of any organic cause, complaints of pain in PTSD are usually related to fluctuations in the level of anxiety. The source of the patient's pain can usually be traced to pathologic anxiety emanating from any combination of the Three E's, whereas in Psychogenic Pain Disorder no pathophysiological mechanism can be found to account for the pain. Additionally, pain in PTSD, unlike in Psychogenic Pain Disorder, is not the primary disturbance, but at times it may be the most prominent symptom. The onset, course, signs, and symptoms of PTSD clearly indicate an Anxiety Disorder with pain as one possible feature within a constellation of other symptoms. The decisive differentiating criteria between PTSD and Psychogenic Pain Disorder are to be found in Table 5-3, Section D: "not due to another mental disorder."

Hypochondriasis

The common features shared by Hypochondriasis and PTSD are preoccupation with physical symptoms and a belief in the existence

TABLE 5-3
DSM-III Diagnostic Criteria for Psychogenic Pain Disorder

A. Severe and prolonged pain is the predominant disturbance.

B. The pain presented as a symptom is inconsistent with the anatomic distribution of the nervous system; after extensive evaluation, no organic pathology or pathophysiological mechanism can be found to account for the pain; or, when there is some related organic pathology, the complaint of pain is grossly in excess of what would be expected from the physical findings.

C. Psychological factors are judged to be etiologically involved in the pain, as evidenced by at least one of the following:

   (1) A temporal relationship between an environmental stimulus that is apparently related to a psychological conflict or need and the initiation or exacerbation of the pain.
   (2) The pain's enabling the individual to avoid some activity that is noxious to him or her.
   (3) The pain's enabling the individual to get support from the environment that otherwise might not be forthcoming.

D. Not due to another mental disorder.

Source: Diagnostic and Statistical Manual of Mental Disorders, third edition, 1980.

of an organic etiology. Onset following an identifiable trauma and obsessive preoccupation with the traumatic incident characterize PTSD and distinguish it from Hypochondriasis. Physical defect caused by the injurious effects of a trauma captures the concern of the PTSD patient, whereas fear of having a dreaded disease occupies the mind of a hypochondriacal patient. Complaints fluctuate with hypochondriacal patients, involving various organ systems and diseases, but in PTSD the somatic complaint, usually pain, is steadfast and focuses on the part of the body believed to have been damaged by the trauma. As can be seen from Table 5-4, the diagnostic criteria for Hypochondriasis correspond in many respects to Stage III — Chronic PTSD. The onset and markedly different clinical course separate PTSD from Hypochondriasis.

TABLE 5-4
DSM-III **Diagnostic Criteria for Hypochondriasis**

A. The predominant disturbance is an unrealistic interpretation of physical signs or sensations as abnormal, leading to preoccupation with the fear or belief of having a serious disease.

B. Thorough physical evaluation does not support the diagnosis of any physical disorder that can account for the physical signs or sensations or for the individual's unrealistic interpretation of them.

C. The unrealistic fear or belief of having a disease persists despite medical reassurance and causes impairment in social or occupational functioning.

D. Not due to any other mental disorder such as Schizophrenia, Affective Disorder, or Somatization Disorder.

Source: Diagnostic and Statistical Manual of Mental Disorders, third edition, 1980.

FACTITIOUS DISORDER AND MALINGERING

The voluntary feigning, pretending, and masquerading of illness constitute an interesting clinical problem, perhaps more suited for a detective or police officer. Assessment of the credibility of statements by patients runs contrary to a physician's usual role of supplying succor and solace to suffering patients. Detection and correct diagnosis of a Factitious Disorder, however, ensure that inappropriate treatment will not be rendered. Uncovering a Malingering hoax also precludes unnecessary therapy and prevents a criminal act if the deception was designed to extort or finagle money from unsuspecting persons. Both Factitious Disorder and Malingering involve conscious deception, although the motivation for each condition differs (Table 5-5).

Factitious Disorder

Factitious Disorder falls into two categories depending upon whether a psychological or physical symptom is present. According to the *DSM-III* (1980), the feigning of symptoms is apparently under the individual's voluntary control and is motivated by the desire for the patient to assume the "patient" role. Factitious Disorder with psychological symptoms, also known as Ganser's Syndrome (Ganser 1898; Golden and MacDonald 1955; Auerbach 1982; Ford 1982), Pseudopsychosis, and Pseudodementia, is characterized by a voluntary production of severe symptoms, often psychotic, suggesting a mental disorder that is rarely confused with a PTSD. Chronic Factitious Disorder with physical symptoms, however, must be differentiated from PTSD. The reason for feigning physical disorder tends to be obscure but results in many visits to doctors, frequently leading to hospitalization and surgical intervention. Some patients become experts in their masquerade, often presenting elaborate and

TABLE 5-5
***DSM-III* Diagnostic Criteria for Chronic Factitious Disorder**

With Physical Symptoms

A. Plausible presentation of physical symptoms that are apparently under the individual's voluntary control to such a degree that there are multiple hospitalizations.

B. The individual's goal is apparently to assume the "patient" role and is not otherwise understandable in light of the individual's environmental circumstances (as is the case in Malingering).

With Psychological Symptoms

A. The production of psychological symptoms is apparently under the individual's voluntary control.

B. The symptoms produced are not explained by any other mental disorder (although they may be superimposed on one).

C. The individual's goal is apparently to assume the "patient" role and is not otherwise understandable in light of the individual's environmental circumstances (as is the case in Malingering).

Source: Diagnostic and Statistical Manual of Mental Disorders, third edition, 1980.

well-rehearsed medical histories. Chronic Factitious Disorder with physical symptoms has captured the imagination of medical practitioners (Asher 1951; Spiro 1968). This syndrome was named after Munchhausen, a German baron who lived in the eighteenth century and was reputed to have traveled from tavern to tavern telling tall tales about fantastic travels and adventures (Zusman and Simon 1983). Falsification and fabrication of the symptoms of physical illness understandably confound clinicians as well as the public. Factitious Disorder must be differentiated from Malingering, which, as will be discussed later, has the more understandable goal of achieving a definite objective that is of value, e.g., money or property.

PTSD is distinctly different from Factitious Disorder (Sparr and Pankratz 1983). Whereas PTSD patients may elaborate or exaggerate symptoms, fabrication is uncommon. In addition, the onset following a specific trauma, predictable clinical symptoms, the course of the disorder, together with the absence of a bizarre pretraumatic medical history including numerous visits to doctors and multiple hospitalizations and surgeries further distinguish PTSD from Factitious Disorder.

Malingering

The conscious, voluntary fabrication of an injury or illness for the purpose of achieving a definite goal characterizes the malingerer (Robitscher 1966; Cohen 1970; Slovenko 1973; Rosner 1982). The goal may vary, but it is usually something of value (Bromberg 1979; Trimble 1981), a tangible asset such as money, property, or some concrete advantage. Falsification of facts and lack of veracity when relating the history of injury or illness may be done naively or cleverly, rendering a clinician's task more or less difficult (Holland and Ward 1966).

In differentiating between the pretender and a genuinely traumatized person, interviews with malingerers will usually reveal an inconsistent history of the present illness and a lack of conformity to the usual symptom cluster of known physical or mental disorders. Clinicians should be alerted to the possibility of Malingering when any of the following antedate the trauma: antisocial behavior, litigation, poor work history, Substance Use Disorder, arrest or conviction for a serious misdemeanor or felony, and a chaotic life-style. If Malingering is suspected, it is wise to verify the history from other sources. Objective data from medical records, police reports, military service file, payroll record from previous employers, and even income tax returns give some indication of a person's coping behavior and life-style. With the patient's permission, interviews with relatives, friends, former employers, and other acquaintances may illuminate the character and veracity of the patient. The decision to treat or not evolves from the history and diagnostic procedures. Since the appellation of "Malingering" means no treatment will be administered, utmost care must be taken to avoid error. It is not the physician's responsibility to report malingerers to authorities, but only to refrain from treating patients who fake a medical or mental disorder. When physicians are subpoenaed into the courtroom for expert testimony, it then becomes appropriate for them to render an opinion regarding the authenticity of the patient's complaints.

In a section of the *DSM-III* (1980) entitled "For Conditions Not Attributable to a Mental Disorder That Are a Focus of Attention or Treatment," it is noted that a high degree of suspicion of Malingering should be aroused if any of the four items listed in Table 5-6 are present. Items 1 and 3 are to be found in many cases of a PTSD and, contrary to the manual, should not in themselves necessarily

TABLE 5-6
Malingering as Listed in the *DSM-III*

A high index of suspicion of Malingering should be aroused if any combination of the following is noted:

(1) Medicolegal context of presentation, e.g., the person's being referred by his attorney to the physician for examination.
(2) Marked discrepancy between the person's claimed distress or disability and the objective findings.
(3) Lack of cooperation with the diagnostic evaluation and prescribed treatment regimen.
(4) The presence of Antisocial Personality Disorder.

Source: Diagnostic and Statistical Manual of Mental Disorders, third edition, 1980.

raise a high index of suspicion for Malingering. It is true that some clinicians may suspect Malingering when patients fail to respond to treatment following a trauma and file a lawsuit. A certain amount of self-interest seems to be served when patients maintain symptoms in spite of vigorous treatment, but it is rash to assume that all such patients are malingerers. Patients with a PTSD seldom consider their conditions to be mental and generally do not voluntarily seek the services of a psychiatrist or psychologist. Furthermore, persons injured in accidents often consult lawyers to obtain advice concerning avenues of redress for injuries sustained. Lawyers conversant with the concept of PTSD are therefore a natural conduit for the referral of patients, though their motivations may not be entirely altruistic. The self-interest of patient and lawyer is of course served by litigation, but the medicolegal context of presentation should not in itself indicate a high level of suspiciousness for Malingering.

Contrariness and contentiousness are qualities found in many persons who are chronically ill. Physicians with little appreciation or toleration for traumatized patients with chronic mental disorders may mistake anger and ill temper as a sign of uncooperativeness. Instead, the ill humor and hostility frequently found in Stage III of a PTSD emanate from the chronic course of the disorder and the failure of previous treatment. Because chronic patients have usually consulted many physicians, they are familiar with and often disdainful of medical practitioners. After their anger has subsided, discontented patients can usually be persuaded to cooperate with a diagnostic evaluation and treatment. Malingerers, if they are fearful that diagnostic tests may uncover their pretense and thwart their objective of material gain, may steadfastly refuse to cooperate with any diagnostic evaluation.

PHOBIC AND GENERALIZED ANXIETY DISORDERS

Clinicians unfamiliar with the concept of stress following trauma might mistakenly conclude that the anxiety that they observe and that patients report reflects a Generalized Anxiety or Phobic Disorder unrelated to the trauma. Simple Phobia and Generalized Anxiety Disorders may be diagnosed by an unsuspecting or unsophisticated clinician not knowledgeable about concepts of traumatology. The ubiquity of anxiety in many clinical conditions necessitates closer scrutiny and comparison with criteria for PTSD.

Simple Phobia

At the time of the traumatic incident, patients may be conditioned adversely to the surroundings where the trauma took place. Depending upon the circumstances, patients may subsequently develop a Simple Phobia of situations, surroundings, or objects identical or similar to those present at the time of the trauma. It is not uncommon for patients who have been involved in automobile accidents to avoid driving or riding in cars, or for workers who have been injured in industrial accidents to avoid the accident site and to refuse to return to work. Seamen who have been involved in a marine accident may avoid ships and the sea. The avoidance may not be limited to the site of the trauma, but may extend to the performance of activities related to the original trauma. For example, the young man who was seriously burned during an explosion in an oil refinery avoided lighting matches, cooking on an open gas burner, barbecuing steaks, and handling solvents or any potentially flammable materials.

Phobic patients experience pathologic anxiety while they are in surroundings identical to or resembling those where the trauma took place. Any avoidance of such places is accompanied by anxiety reduction, and the amelioration of anxiety reinforces avoidance behavior, as is true in all Phobic Disorders. In PTSD the phobia that was precipitated by the acute trauma is symptomatically indistinguishable from a Simple Phobia (see Table 5-7). The post-traumatic onset of the phobia and the presence of the symptom cluster of PTSD place the phobia in the context of a broader disorder, thus disgtinguishing it from a Simple Phobia.

Generalized Anxiety Disorder

Even a brief glance at Table 5-8 will reveal that the diagnostic criteria for a Generalized Anxiety Disorder have striking similarities to symptoms found in a PTSD. This is not strange, however, because during Stages II and III of a PTSD, chronic anxiety is clinically manifest. The onset, however, of these disorders is markedly different. In Generalized Anxiety Disorder the history reveals no clear-cut beginning; rather the onset is gradual and insidious, the course of the disorder fluctuating with environmental stressors. In contrast,

TABLE 5-7
DSM-III Diagnostic Criteria for Simple Phobia

A. A persistent irrational fear of, and compelling desire to avoid, an object or a situation other than being alone, or in public places away from home (Agoraphobia), or of humiliation or embarrassment in certain social situations (Social Phobia). Phobic objects are often animals, and phobic situations frequently involve heights or closed spaces.

B. Significant distress from the disturbance and recognition by the individual that his or her fear is excessive or unreasonable.

C. Not due to another mental disorder, such as Schizophrenia or Obsessive Compulsive Disorder.

Source: Diagnostic and Statistical Manual of Mental Disorders, third edition, 1980.

TABLE 5-8
DSM-III Diagnostic Criteria for Generalized Anxiety Disorder

A. Generalized, persistent anxiety is manifested by symptoms from three of the following four categories:

   (1) *Motor tension*: Shakiness, jitteriness, jumpiness, trembling, tension, muscle aches, fatigability, inability to relax, eyelid twitch, furrowed brow, strained face, fidgeting, restlessness, easy startle.
   (2) *Autonomic hyperactivity*: Sweating, heart pounding or racing, cold and clammy hands, dry mouth, dizziness, light-headedness, paresthesias (tingling in hands or feet), upset stomach, hot or cold spells, frequent urination, diarrhea, discomfort in the pit of the stomach, lump in the throat, flushing, pallor, high resting pulse and respiration rate.
   (3) *Apprehensive expectation*: Anxiety, worry, fear, rumination, anticipation of misfortune to self or others.
   (4) *Vigilance and scanning*: Hyperattentiveness resulting in distractibility, difficulty in concentrating, insomnia, feeling "on edge," irritability, impatience.

B. The anxious mood has been continuous for at least one month.

Table 5-8, continued

C. Not due to another mental disorder, such as a Depressive Disorder or Schizophrenia.

D. At least 18 years of age.

Source: Diagnostic and Statistical Manual of Mental Disorders, third edition, 1980.

the onset of a PTSD is acute and well defined, and during Stage I anxiety symptoms are intense. During Stages II and III, when anxiety becomes chronic and less obvious, PTSD and Generalized Anxiety Disorder share common characteristics.

In addition to obsessive concern and preoccupation with an identifiable traumatic event, PTSD patients frequently report a phobia or phobic anxiety and complain of pain or physical discomfort. Whereas worry and physical discomfort may also be complaints of Generalized Anxiety Disorder patients, the history reveals no relationship to a traumatic event. An absence of phobic symptoms in Generalized Anxiety Disorder also helps to differentiate it from PTSD. It is both interesting and puzzling to note that the section on differential diagnosis of a PTSD in *DSM-III* (1980) states that if Anxiety Disorder develops following the trauma, this diagnosis should also be made.

DEPRESSION

Dysthmic Disorder

Sleep disturbance, chronic fatigue, lack of interest in work, impaired family relationships, social withdrawal, irritability and anger, concern with physical health, and a pessimistic attitude toward life are frequent complaints of a PTSD patient. As can be seen from Table 5-9, these characteristics fulfill many of the criteria for a Dysthymic Disorder. Depression, as has been noted earlier, is a common secondary manifestation of PTSD and may mask its signs and symptoms. Sometimes the depressive symptoms are severe, as in

TABLE 5-9
DSM-III Diagnostic Criteria for Dysthymic Disorder

A. During the past two years (or one year for children and adolescents), the individual has been bothered most or all of the time by symptoms characteristic of the Depressive Syndrome but that are not of sufficient severity and duration to meet the criteria for a Major Depressive Episode.

B. The manifestations of the Depressive Syndrome may be relatively persistent or separated by periods of normal mood lasting a few days to a few weeks, but no more than a few months at a time.

C. During the depressive periods there is either prominent depressed mood (e.g., sad, blue, down in the dumps, low) or marked loss of interest or pleasure in all, or almost all, usual activities and pastimes.

D. During the depressive periods at least three of the following symptoms are present:

   (1) Insomnia or hypersomnia
   (2) Low energy level or chronic tiredness
   (3) Feelings of inadequacy, loss of self-esteem, or self-deprecation
   (4) Decreased effectiveness or productivity at school, work, or home
   (5) Decreased attention, concentration, or ability to think clearly
   (6) Social withdrawal
   (7) Loss of interest in or enjoyment of pleasurable activities
   (8) Irritability or excessive anger (in children, expressed toward parents or caretakers)
   (9) Inability to respond with apparent pleasure to praise or rewards
   (10) Less active or talkative than usual, or feels slowed down or restless
   (11) Pessimistic attitude toward the future, brooding about past events, or feeling sorry for self
   (12) Tearfulness or crying
   (13) Recurrent thoughts of death or suicide

E. Absence of psychotic features, such as delusions, hallucinations, or incoherence, or loosening of associations.

F. If the disturbance is superimposed on a preexisting mental disorder, such as Obsessive Compulsive Disorder or Alcohol Dependence, the depressed mood, by virtue of its intensity or effect on functioning, can be clearly distinguished from the individual's usual mood.

Source: Diagnostic and Statistical Manual of Mental Disorders, third edition, 1980.

a major depressive episode, and suicide is a real possibility. At other times the dysthymic symptoms are less intense, and clinicians, unless alert, can fail to make the proper diagnosis. Recognition of depression is a prerequisite for treatment, but the dysthymic symptoms must be seen in a context secondary to the primary disorder of PTSD. Incapacity and demoralization due to the debilitating effects of a traumatic incident with a failure of coping mechanisms and medical treatment generally fuel despondency and depression. In those PTSD patients in whom depression is severe and definitely interferes with the person's functioning, the additional diagnosis of a Major Depressive Episode or a Dysthymic Disorder should also be made.

PERSONALITY AND SUBSTANCE USE DISORDERS

Studies indicate that there is a high incidence of alcoholism, drug abuse, and antisocial behavior among Vietnam-era veterans (Mace et al. 1978; Wilson 1980). The issues of criminal conduct, alcohol abuse, and illicit drug use are particularly relevant for the estimated 500,000 to 1.5 million Vietnam-era veterans believed to suffer from a PTSD (Walker 1981a, b). Although the relationship between Antisocial Personality/Substance Use Disorder and PTSD is unclear, at least two explanations can be advanced. The first is that antisocial conduct and/or substance abuse is related to the veteran's experience in Vietnam and is one of the manifestations of a PTSD. A second explanation is that antisocial behavior and substance abuse antedated service in Vietnam and continued post-Vietnam, having no relationship to experiences in Southeast Asia. A corollary to this proposition might be that even if a veteran had a preexisting disorder, a PTSD might coexist with it and be directly related to war experiences in Vietnam (Sierles et al. 1983). The correct conceptualization of a Vietnam-era veteran's or a civilian's psychiatric disorder preceding and following trauma has important considerations concerning disability payments, criminal responsibility, personal injury litigation, and treatment.

Antisocial Personality Disorder

As can be seen from Table 5-10, the essential feature of an Antisocial Personality Disorder is a history of continuous and chronic antisocial behavior that began before the age of 15 and persists into adult life. Patterns of truancy or expulsion from school, delinquency, and lying begin early in life and may be complemented by vandalism, theft, and aggressive behavior. Irresponsible behavior continues as a person matures and is manifest by erratic and poor work performance, nonacceptance of a parenting role, rejection of social norms, sexual promiscuity, aggressiveness, financial irresponsibility, lack of goal-directedness, prevarication, drunkenness, and drug abuse.

In addition to a life-style that includes habitual lying, involvement in illegal activities and frequently periodic incarceration in a penal institution, antisocial persons have difficulties maintaining personal relationships. As stated in the *DSM-III* (1980), "almost invariably, there is markedly impaired capacity to sustain lasting, close, warm, and responsible relationships with family, friends, or sexual partners." This observation is very important, since the Personality Disorder includes not only criminal behavior but also extends to deficits in interpersonal relationships, a critical point when differentiating an antisocial personality from a person who is only intermittently involved in criminal activities.

Veracity is at question when patients who have a history of criminal conduct claim a PTSD. Antisocial persons may malinger a PTSD for personal advantage. If a veteran fakes a PTSD and convinces others that it is service connected, disability payments from the VA can be collected. Following a trauma antisocial civilians may malinger a PTSD in order to collect worker's compensation payments or during a personal injury suit to collect damages. Defendants who are antisocial can claim a PTSD to avoid criminal prosecution or to support a plea of not guilty because of insanity.

When establishing a diagnosis of Antisocial Personality Disorder or PTSD, a detailed chronologic history must be taken and verified. Interviews with members of the patient's family and friends along with a review of all pertinent records help sort out falsehoods. The absence or presence of preexisting patterns of antisocial behavior, beginning as a child and continuing into adulthood, has great significance in interpreting "post-traumatic" behavior. Sources

TABLE 5-10
DSM-III Diagnostic Criteria for Antisocial Personality Disorder

A. Current age at least 18.

B. Onset before age 15 as indicated by a history of three or more of the following before that age:

  (1) Truancy (positive if it amounted to at least five days per year for at least two years, not including the last year of school)
  (2) Expulsion or suspension from school for misbehavior
  (3) Delinquency (arrested or referred to juvenile court because of behavior)
  (4) Running away from home overnight at least twice while living in parental or parental surrogate home
  (5) Persistent lying
  (6) Repeated sexual intercourse in a casual relationship
  (7) Repeated drunkenness or substance abuse
  (8) Thefts
  (9) Vandalism
  (10) School grades markedly below expectations in relation to estimated or known IQ (may have resulted in repeating a year)
  (11) Chronic violations of rules at home and/or at school (other than truancy)
  (12) Initiation of fights

C. At least four of the following manifestations of the disorder since age 18:

  (1) Inability to sustain consistent work behavior, as indicated by any of the following: (a) too frequent job changes (e.g., three or more jobs in five years not accounted for by nature of job or economic or seasonal fluctuation); (b) significant unemployment (e.g., six months or more in five years when expected to work); (c) serious absenteeism from work (e.g., average three days or more of lateness or absence per month), (d) walking off several jobs without other jobs in sight (Note: Similar behavior in an academic setting during the last few years of school may substitute for this criterion in individuals who by reason of their age or circumstances have not had an opportunity to demonstrate occupational adjustment).
  (2) Lack of ability to function as a responsible parent as evidenced by one or more of the following: (a) child's malnutrition; (b) child's illness resulting from lack of minimal hygiene standards; (c) failure to obtain medical care for a seriously ill child; (d) child's dependence on neighbors or nonresident relatives for food or shelter; (e) failure to arrange

Table 5-10, continued

for a caretaker for a child under six when parent is away from home; (f) repeated squandering, on personal items, of money required for household necessities.

(3) Failure to accept social norms with respect to lawful behavior, as indicated by any of the following: repeated thefts, illegal occupation (pimping, prostitution, fencing, selling drugs), multiple arrests, a felony conviction.

(4) Inability to maintain enduring attachment to a sexual partner as indicated by two or more divorces and/or separations (whether legally married or not), desertion of spouse, promiscuity (ten or more sexual partners within one year).

(5) Irritability and aggressiveness as indicated by repeated physical fights or assault (not required by one's job or to defend someone or oneself), including spouse or child beating.

(6) Failure to honor financial obligations as indicated by repeated defaulting on debts, failure to provide child support, failure to support other dependents on a regular basis.

(7) Failure to plan ahead, or impulsivity, as indicated by traveling from place to place without a prearranged job or clear goal for the period of travel or clear idea about when the travel would terminate, or lack of fixed address for a month or more.

(8) Disregard for the truth as indicated by repeated lying, use of aliases, "conning" others for personal profit.

(9) Recklessness as indicated by driving while intoxicated or recurrent speeding.

D. A pattern of continuous antisocial behavior in which the rights of others are violated, with an intervening period of at least five years without antisocial behavior between age 15 and the present time (except when the individual was bedridden or confined in a hospital or penal institution).

E. Antisocial behavior is not due to either Severe Mental Retardation, Schizophrenia, or manic episodes.

Source: *Diagnostic and Statistical Manual for Mental Disorders*, third edition, 1980.

of information other than the patient's verbal reports can confirm or negate a diagnosis of antisocial personality. The quality and duration of interpersonal relationships as evidenced by interviews with the patient's parents, spouse, friends, employers, and peers must be determined to support a diagnosis of either Antisocial Personality Disorder or PTSD.

Information concerning three different time periods must be gathered and contrasted in order to establish with reasonable certainty a diagnosis of PTSD. First, the pretraumatic personality and behavior of the individual should disclose no or minimal antisocial characteristics. Second, the trauma should be documented in detail and the person's presence at the time of the trauma verified; and the signs and symptoms following impact should be consistent with Stage I of a PTSD (Chapter four). Finally, post-traumatically the signs and symptoms of Stage II or III of a PTSD must be present. One cannot malinger personal past history, which can be substantiated; however, current symptoms can be more easily falsified without fear of detection. Inconsistencies and fabrications can be discovered when data concerning a person's pretraumatic, traumatic, and post-traumatic behavior are compiled and evaluated.

Substance Use Disorder

Substance abuse is defined as a pathologic use of substances that results in an impairment of social or occupational functioning, whereas substance dependence, a more severe condition, requires evidence of either tolerance or withdrawal. The *DSM-III* (1980) lists five classes of substances associated with both abuse and dependence: alcohol; barbiturates or similarly acting sedatives or hypnotics; opioids; amphetamines or similarly acting sympathomimetics; and cannabis. Substance Use Disorder may occur independently or coexist with another psychiatric disorder. It is not uncommon for persons with PTSD to self-treat their pathologic anxiety with alcohol or a sedative or hypnotic drug. Occasionally, marijuana (cannabis), or less commonly heroin, or other opioid substances also serve to ameliorate anxiety in the PTSD patient.

When the history reveals substance abuse or dependence only following a traumatic incident, one should be alerted to Substance Use Disorder secondary to PTSD. Clinicians who focus only on a patient's Substance Use Disorder may fail to recognize the signs and symptoms of PTSD, which would then go untreated. Lifelong abuse or dependence on substances related to Antisocial Personality Disorder has a different significance in terms of diagnosis and treatment.

SIX

TREATMENT

A complex array of psychosocial factors together with its chronic course places PTSD among those disorders that elude quick resolution. PTSD is a multifaceted disorder involving not only post-traumatic stress, but also disordered family relationships, problems of physical disability, inability to work, disruption of social and recreational life, worker's compensation claims, personal injury litigation, impaired interpersonal relationships, Substance Use Disorder, and, at times, criminal conduct. Since personal, interpersonal, and social factors interact pathologically in PTSD, the formulation of a comprehensive treatment regimen requires the inclusion of a broad spectrum of approaches. In addition, patient attitudes reflecting pessimism, demoralization, hostility, anxiousness, and disablement demand and require the special skills and sensitivity of the clinician.

Specific treatment for PTSD involves a correct conceptualization of the disorder with an accurate analysis of the sources of stress or pathologic anxiety. The impact and continuance of certain stimuli from environmental, encephalic, and endogenous sources — the Three E's — maintain the pathologic features of this disorder. The goal of treatment therefore consists of modifying selective stimuli from the external world, physiological processes, and cognitive activities of the brain. Clinicians may choose from a variety of therapeutic interventions to assist traumatized patients. The systematic and persistent application of appropriate antianxiety interventions as related in this chapter maximizes the success of treatment.

Depending upon the patient's mental status, family and personal relationships, and social support systems, a number of therapeutic interventions may be indicated during treatment. Before proceeding to interpersonal and social dimensions, the lowering of the patient's personal discomfort merits initial attention. Explanation-education, training in relaxation, encephalic reconditioning, and medication – four antianxiety interventions – afford the patient immediate relief from pathologic anxiety and warrant implementation as quickly as possible. As treatment proceeds the prescription of additional treatment depends upon the needs and progress of the patient.

Perhaps the clinician's attitude toward chronic illness presents the largest obstacle to successful outcome of treatment. Unattractive and unbeguiling characteristics of patients who complain constantly, show slow progress in treatment, and seem unappreciative of their therapist's best efforts generate negative attitudes in the clinician. If hostility is reciprocated, effective treatment cannot take place. Forbearance and tolerance for slow progress become necessary attributes and personal prerequisites for clinicians in order to maximize success in treatment. Ultimately, however, the barometer that indicates success is the diminishment or disappearance of pathologic anxiety and problem behavior with the restoration to a useful, productive, and satisfying life.

THERAPEUTIC INTERVENTIONS

Explanation-Education

Before patients are referred to psychiatrists or other clinicians from the behavioral sciences, they usually have undergone a mélange of tests and diagnostic procedures. Orthopedic surgeons and neurosurgeons have exhaustively examined the bony and neural structures of traumatized patients who continue to complain of pain or physical discomfort. In addition, other physicians are likely to have been consulted concerning an assortment of continuing complaints, and the patient has usually been subjected to other diagnostic tests and numerous examinations. Unfortunately, many patients do not receive a complete explanation or a clear-cut conclusion regarding their physical condition. Instead, vague statements that can easily be misinterpreted are given. Patients, therefore, are often confused regarding the results of many medical examinations and diagnostic procedures.

Referral to a psychiatrist usually takes place only when patients continue to complain of incapacitating symptoms in the absence of objective findings from examinations and laboratory procedures. Reasons for referral also include eccentric and quarrelsome behavior. Frequently patients confront their physicians with the embarrassing question, "If all of the tests are negative, why do I still have symptoms?" To gain the patient's compliance and adherence to treatment, after a diagnosis of a PTSD, the most important step is explanation-education.

At the onset it is imperative that prior medical records be obtained and patiently explained to the patient. Sometimes reference to an anatomy atlas or the utilization of other visual aids helps clear up misconceptions that patients may have about their bodies. Consultation with physicians, especially those doctors who continue to see the patient, mitigates contradiction, allays patients' suspicions of organic etiology for their disorder, and facilitates cooperation.

The development of a Stress Disorder can best be explained by a reiteration of the patient's history in a logical, chronological sequence. To respond with anxiety following exposure to a traumatic event is a normal reaction, the patient is told, and one need not be ashamed of nervousness, trembling and shaking sensations, nausea, or vomiting. Palpitations, tachycardia, hyperventilation, and a variety of other anxiety symptoms may occur normally following exposure to a traumatic event, the explanation continues. These symptoms result from an activation of the autonomic nervous system when the environmental trauma impacts on one or a combination of the five senses; however, the patient is emphatically told, prolongation of an anxiety response beyond several weeks represents a pathologic mental reaction called PTSD.

The patient's symptoms are enumerated and explanations are given to account for their presence and continuation. Obsessive preoccupation with the trauma, an encephalic process, generates pathologic anxiety and distinguishes Stage I from Stage II. Many prominent symptoms during Stage II as listed in Chapter three can be due to pathologic anxiety. Autonomic hyperactivity accounts for alterations in heart rate, difficulties in breathing, gastrointestinal disturbance, light-headedness, dizziness, tingling sensations in the arms or legs, hot flashes or flushing, excessive sweating, and feeling faint. Symptoms of increased motor tension include trembling or shaking of the hands or body, restlessness, fatigue, muscle aches, and headaches. Pain originally resulting from physical trauma to muscles and ligaments is aggravated by increased motor tension. The patient's anxious state is characterized by apprehensive expectation, with ruminations about the trauma and frequent speculations about a more disastrous consequence. Flashbacks are usually precipitated by an environmental stimulus and may be associated with feelings of unreality. Sleep disturbance, usually problems in falling asleep or interrupted sleep, difficulties in concentration, and irritability are caused by hyperattentiveness to the trauma. Dreams can be so disturbing that patients awaken in the middle of the night, panic stricken with nightclothes damp from perspiration. Repeated episodes of nightmares cause patients to dread sleep, further aggravating insomnia. When avoidance behavior exists, mechanisms of a phobia or phobic anxiety are explained to the patient in terms of a conditioning process directly related to the original traumatic incident. Objects of situations closely resembling the source of the trauma trigger episodes of anxiety often followed by phobic avoidance, but the patient is reassured that specific treatment reverses this process.

During Stage III, PTSD becomes chronic and the patient develops fixed opinions concerning disablement. Glib explanations of PTSD and disability must be avoided. The patient should be taken slowly through the various stages of PTSD with a detailed explanation concerning the reasons for symptoms. The idea of permanent disability must be dispelled by a reiteration of medical reports indicating that no evidence of a serious physical defect exists. Paradoxically some patients, especially if they are seriously depressed, become suspicious when the physician proffers an optimistic and hopeful outlook for the future. The seemingly unrelenting course of Chronic PTSD, unaffected by previous therapeutic attempts, provides patients with ample reason for pessimism. Chronic PTSD patients tend to take a global view of disability and an all-or-none attitude concerning illness and wellness. Patients during the educative phase of treatment must be dissuaded from these extreme and rigid negative positions concerning their disorder in favor of a posture of gradual return to normal functioning. Over the course of treatment, the patient is resolutely told, symptoms will become less intense and less frequent, and in time the disability will be minimized. Initially patients may be unmoved by pronouncements from physicians that they will overcome their disorder. An adroitness in explaining, instructing, interpreting, persuading, and even exhorting facilitates the acceptance of the idea that a positive change in behavior is not only possible, but probable (Frank 1961, 1978).

Pathologic anxiety permeates every aspect of PTSD; patients, however, often fail to grasp the significance of this observation. Other issues obfuscate the importance of pathologic anxiety, as patients ruminate about the traumatic incident and obsess about disability. Patients often insist that they want to be the way they were before the traumatic incident. This expectation can frustrate treatment since one cannot turn the clock backward. A trauma disrupts lives, the patient must be told, and wanting to turn the clock back and make things the way they were suggests an unrealistic magical wish. A more fruitful goal that can be pursued during the course of treatment consists of understanding and identifying the sources of pathologic anxiety — the Three E's. Throughout the course of therapy, whenever the patient complains of symptoms, the relationship of symptomatic behavior to the Three E's must be explained and emphasized. A reluctance to accept the idea of the Three E's and pathologic anxiety must be countered with illustrations from the patient's history and current behavior. A Self-Assessment Form (Table 6-1) helps patients to organize behavioral information in a form that contributes to the educative process. When theoretical concepts are translated into real-life experiences, the exercise becomes more meaningful and therapeutically useful.

Many patients become visibly apprehensive when relating the history and onset of the traumatic event, even after they have engaged in this narration several times before. This experience can be used to advantage by the clinician when pointing out the relationship between recalling and retelling of the trauma and the renewal of anxiety symptoms. In these instances, an explanation of retraumatization and the Spiral Effect is appropriate. The "video tape of the mind" analogy is a useful device to explain retraumatization, whereas a chart (Figure 2-1) illustrates the Spiral Effect. As has been mentioned in Chapter two, endogenous events stimulate encephalic activities, in turn stimulating pathologic anxiety or stress. Increased motor tension makes physical symptoms more apparent, sometimes painfully so, which in turn stimulates more encephalic activity and pathologic anxiety — the Spiral Effect. Unless patients become

TABLE 6-1
Self-Assessment Form

Name _____
Date _____

Time	Sources of Anxiety			Antianxiety Intervention			Comment
	Environmental	Endogenous	Encephalic	Environmental	Endogenous	Encephalic	

Selected Behavior

Global Rating 0-1-2-3-4-5-6-7-8-9-10

Source: Reprinted from *Stress Strategies: The treatment of the Anxiety Disorder* (Scrignar, 1983). Reproduced with permission.

knowledgeable about the Spiral Effect, they are likely to conjure a more exotic explanation of their symptoms, usually a vague and mysterious physical ailment. As treatment proceeds it is periodically necessary to restate the principle of retraumatization and the Spiral Effect.

The rationale for treatment is based upon the premise that pathologic anxiety is largely learned and conditioned. Relearning and deconditioning form the main therapeutic thrust. As each element of the treatment program is added, the patient must be instructed on its significance and reason for employment. Explanation-education continues throughout treatment and must be done repeatedly in order for patients to thoroughly assimilate the salient points of theory and therapy before making positive changes in behavior.

Training in Relaxation

All relaxation techniques (Schultz and Luther 1969; Wallace 1970; Jacobsen 1974; Shapiro 1977) produce the beneficial physiological result of reducing motor tension and lowering the activity of the autonomic nervous system. Just as the Three E's combine to produce pathologic symptoms and behavior in PTSD, relaxation reverses their negative effects and promotes a feeling of well-being. A quiet environment, the use of pleasant visual images, and a focus on pleasant internal sensations, such as relaxed feelings in muscles, soothing respiratory sensations, warm feelings in the abdomen, and a pervasive relaxed feeling throughout the body facilitate the effectiveness of various relaxation methods. The observation that many of these principles have been incorporated into yoga, transcendental meditation, and prayer attests to the universality and agelessness of these empirically derived procedures. Although many relaxation methods exist and may be equally efficacious, progressive muscle relaxation (PMR) (Jacobsen 1974) and hypnosis (Cheek and LaCron 1968; Kroger and Fezler 1976) are recommended for clinical use in the treatment of PTSD, because both are easy to learn and apply in context with the positive use of the Three E's.

PMR

Jacobsen's technique (1974) of PMR is probably the most widely used method of muscle relaxation and is preferred by the author.

Before the procedure an explanation is given to patients regarding the relationship between relaxation and stress. The patient is asked to sit, preferably in a comfortable reclining chair, close the eyes, listen, and follow instructions. After several deep breaths, the patient is asked to breathe normally and then to make a fist with the right hand. "Focus your mind on the sensations in your right forearm, wrist, hand, and fingers," the patient is told, "and pay attention to the tight and uncomfortable sensations of tension in that part of your body." After 10 or 15 seconds has elapsed, the patient is requested to open the hand and relax the right lower arm, wrist, and fingers, paying particular attention to the sensations of relaxation, which are usually indicated by a tingly sensation or heavy feeling. "The more you concentrate, the more that part of your body will relax," it is pointed out to the patient. The procedure of contracting and relaxing proceeds to other muscles, until all of the major muscle groups in the body have been relaxed. At the conclusion of the exercise, most patients report a subjective feeling of tranquility and deep relaxation. The time required to complete the relaxation sequence varies depending upon the degree of tension present in the patient, but usually 30 minutes will suffice. Some patients report residual tension in certain muscle groups, which requires additional time and more practice. Like the learning of any skill, "practice makes perfect," and 10 to 15 hours of training leads to proficiency.

Patients should also be familiar with the technique of partial passive relaxation, which can be done unobtrusively, in any position, with the eyes open, and without actively contracting the muscles. Passive relaxation starts with several slow, deep breaths during which the patient monitors the air passing in and out of the lungs. By first noting the presence of existing tension, the patient is asked during exhalation to passively relax the shoulders, arms, hands, and fingers, and next the neck, head, upper back, and lower back, and finally, depending upon the position of the patient's body, the hips and legs. To deepen the state of relaxation, the patient is asked to spread the feeling of relaxation from the chest to the abdomen and then to various other body parts during each exhalation. This unobtrusive method of partial passive relaxation affords the patient a means of controlling stress while walking, driving, standing, and sitting. It is a strange but exhilarating experience for patients who have long been victims of stress to counter their symptoms with a self-imposed process.

The key to the successful utilization of PMR lies in the recognition of symptoms as a manifestation of Stress Disorder and not caused by a vague and undiagnosable physical ailment. Muscle aches, pain, nausea, excessive sweating, headaches, diarrhea, dizziness, tachycardia, dyspnea, and other stress-related symptoms can serve as cues for the employment of PMR. Even insomnia can be alleviated when PMR is practiced while attempting sleep. To gain proficiency and achieve maximal advantage from PMR, patients must practice the technique at least once daily for several weeks.

A prerecorded instructional audio cassette for use at home assists patients in mastering PMR. Many relaxation tapes and records are currently on the market, but clinicians should consider recording their own. While the voice of the narrator of professionally prepared tapes may be more mellifluous, most patients prefer to hear the voice of their own therapist. The hours of practice required to master muscle relaxation are made less arduous and less costly by the use of an audio cassette. As time passes, relaxation eventually becomes an almost automatic response to stress.

Hypnosis and Self-Hypnosis

To help raise the shroud of mysticism, patients should be told that all hypnosis is self-hypnosis, since subjects place themselves in the hypnotic state and the clinician or hypnotist functions as a teacher. Self-hypnosis is a skill that can be achieved quickly by some people and with practice by others. In the state of mind called hypnosis, there is enhancement of bodily relaxation, concentration, and receptivity to suggestions.

Hypnotic relaxation begins with suggestions to recumbent patients to close their eyes and concentrate on the voice of the therapist. Further instructions go something like this: "If you should hear any sounds other than the sound of my voice, let them go in one ear and out the other. Similarly, if you should have thoughts going through your mind, thoughts not related to what I am talking about, try to push those thoughts out of your mind when and if they should occur." The patient is then asked to take three consecutive deep breaths and at the conclusion of the third to breathe normally. Next the patient is told to concentrate on any feelings or sensations that may be present in the feet. The patient is requested to note the tingling sensations in the toes and on the bottom, top, and heels of the feet. These sensations are labeled as "your own personal relaxation feelings." In a slow and repetitious fashion, the patient is directed to notice these "personal relaxation feelings" moving slowly up the body from the feet to the legs, hips, stomach, chest, back, shoulders, arms, hands, fingers, neck, head, and face. A counting sequence of ten to zero with interspersed suggestions of relaxation deepens the hypnotic state. An intensification of the relaxation results when patients are asked to visualize – clearly and vividly – pleasant scenes such as lying on the beach, walking through a flower-laden garden, or perhaps a prearranged scene that elicits pleasant and peaceful feelings. At this point the patient may be given positive suggestions or cognitive corrections, which will be discussed in more detail in the section on encephalic reconditioning.

For patients who complain of pain, hypnosis can act as a powerful anodyne. The relaxed state of hypnosis, in itself, reduces the awareness of pain, but a visual technique sometimes is superior. The patient is asked to visualize a "pain gauge" with the number zero (no pain) on the left and ten (maximal pain) on the right. The patient is then requested to evaluate his or her current perception of pain by visualizing the gauge needle on the appropriate number. Suggestions are given to the patient to move the needle of the gauge to the left as much as possible by concentration and willful effort. Time is allotted to accomplish this, and although zero may not be reached, as the needle moves to the left the patient begins to notice a subjective reduction of pain. This simple mental device affords the patient a means of changing the perception and memory of pain, thereby reducing physical discomfort.

All hypnotic sessions can be individually recorded on an audio cassette and given to the patient for use at home. Audio cassettes permit patients to experience hypnotic phenomena outside the clinician's office, thereby saving time and money. Occasionally, patients exhibit concern or even alarm about using tapes with hypnotic suggestions, fearing some adverse consequence. Such apprehension is needless and can be quickly quelled by the simple statement that the worst thing that can happen is that the positive suggestions concerning relaxation and amelioration of discomfort will not be effective. Most patients, however, derive benefits from audio cassettes and sharpen their skills of self-hypnosis.

Some clinicians argue that there is no difference between PMR and hypnosis. Undeniably, the two techniques are similar and exert influence on the same psychophysiological systems. Hypnosis, however, has the added advantage of utilizing a broader range of visual and verbal suggestions and the disadvantage of being cloaked in mysticism and myth that may frighten certain patients. PMR and hypnosis both can serve as a nonmedicinal means of controlling stress symptoms, pain, and physical discomfort. Both should become part of the patient's coping repertoire.

Encephalic Reconditioning

Encephalic events are of paramount importance in the continuance of PTSD. In fact, without the essential ingredients of retraumatization and the Spiral Effect, it is doubtful whether pathologic symptoms would be maintained. The repetitious replaying of the video tapes of the mind portraying the traumatic incident with grisly elaborations involving more serious injury or death sensitizes the patient, thus aggravating the disorder. The video tapes of the mind contain inaccuracies, distortions, and untruths, often omitting the fact that the patient survived the trauma and is still alive. Similarly, innocuous physical sensations elicit thoughts of grave physical disturbance, thus initiating the Spiral Effect. As a general rule, the more time a patient spends envisaging the trauma and misinterpreting somatic sensations, the more frequent and intense become pathologic symptoms and the degree of disability. Unquestionably, obsessive preoccupation with the trauma and its consequences is the most pernicious aspect of PTSD and to a large extent perpetuates the disorder.

In the context of this book, the term "encephalic reconditioning" refers to clinical procedures that alter negative encephalic activity by changing verbal or visual images for the purpose of lowering stress. Modifying the emotional impact of certain beliefs, perceptions, visual images, and thoughts is no new idea. Guided affective imagery (Kosbad 1974), fantasy evocation (Klinger 1970; Gottschalk 1974), imagery conditioning (Kroger and Fezler 1976), and cognitive restructuring (Beck 1976; Meichenbaum 1977) have a wide range of clinical applications in psychotherapy, clinical hypnosis, and behavior therapy (Meichenbaum and Cameron 1983). Encephalic reconditioning for PTSD patients includes the following clinical techniques: thought stopping, positive encephalic practice (thought substitution), and the four positive reinforcing statements. Hypnosis can be used in encephalic reconditioning to alter negative self-statements and to promote positive visual images.

Thought Stopping

A simple and effective way to reduce thoughts and images that evoke stress is through a stopping procedure (Bain 1928; Taylor 1963; Yamagami 1971). While in the consulting room, the patient is asked to close the eyes and to produce stressful thoughts and images related to the trauma. After about 1 minute, the clinician shouts, "Stop! Get out of there!" or "Stop the action!" The patient is momentarily shaken but will invariably report that the encephalic processes were interrupted. The procedure is repeated, but now the patient is instructed to silently but emphatically repeat the phrases "Stop! Get out of there!" or "Stop the action!" each time that the therapist signals by a light tap on the hand. The patient is then requested to employ the stopping procedure independently as often as necessary to control and reduce the anxiety generating encephalic events. A rubber band can be worn around the wrist and snapped simultaneously when the patient silently shouts, "Stop! Get out of there!" (Mahoney 1971). The combination of momentary pain and the simultaneous phrase is often more effective in stopping unwanted mental activity. Most patients are amazed and pleased with the results.

Positive Encephalic Practice

Positive encephalic practice consists of substituting new "video tapes" that have a happy and pleasant ending in place of old ones with a traumatic theme. It is salutary for patients to visualize themselves coping with their symptoms and problems, for it breeds confidence and assuages anxiety. Visualizing the completion of productive tasks also provides patients with personal pleasure and satisfaction. Other scenes of a relaxing nature can evolve from fantasy or by a retrieval of past pleasant memories of happy events. Patients are instructed to utilize positive encephalic practice twice daily for 10 to 15 minutes. When patients begin to ruminate or obsess about their trauma, it is important that relaxing scenes be substituted immediately. Positive encephalic practice sessions conducted by the clinician in the consulting room can be recorded on an audio cassette and given to the patient for practice at home. The use of recordings regularizes and structures home practice, thus minimizing procrastination. When successful, positive encephalic practice, a form of thought substitution, reduces pathologic anxiety and contributes to the reversal of PTSD.

The Four Positive Reinforcing Statements

Somatic sensations, whether physical residuals of the traumatic incident or anxiety induced, remind patients of their trauma and increase anxiety — the Spiral Effect. In spite of repeated reassurance and normal physical examinations, PTSD patients incorrectly interpret normal physiological sensations or minor muscular spasms as evidence of some serious physical defect. Erroneous self-statements concerning somatic sensations serve to heighten pathologic anxiety and increase motor tension, thus making the physical sensation more evident. The Spiral Effect can be interrupted by the utilization of the four positive reinforcing statements. Whenever patients first notice any physical sensations that might be misinterpreted, they are instructed to repeat, silently but with conviction, the following statements:

1. "I feel uncomfortable." (This confirms that the feeling is not imaginary and that they are experiencing uncomfortable physical sensations.)
2. "I have had these feelings before and nothing really bad has ever happened." (This is a true statement, for no dire or irreversible consequences have ever resulted from these feelings.)
3. "There is nothing seriously wrong with me." (This is also a true statement. The patient's physical examinations and various laboratory procedures have disclosed no serious abnormalities.)
4. "I am experiencing the effects of pathologic anxiety." (This is a correct assessment.) "I shall employ antianxiety interventions and these uncomfortable feelings will pass more quickly." (The patient then practices PMR or self-hypnosis.)

The four positive reinforcing statements are all true. Patients must be convinced of this and encouraged to recite them whenever any of the somatic manifestations of PTSD are felt.

Hypnosis and Encephalic Reconditioning

Hypnosis is a natural adjuvant to encephalic reconditioning, since both involve the modification of visual and verbal images to achieve a therapeutic goal. Following a formal hypnotic induction as described earlier, patients are more attentive and become better listeners. The clinician's statements therefore impact more profoundly, which allows for easier correction of patient misconceptions. Specific suggestions, given under hypnosis, can also reinforce the influence of the four positive reinforcing statements and serve to develop pleasant scenarios during positive encephalic practice. Posthypnotic suggestions can cue patients to visualize pleasant scenes whenever they focus on physical sensations or think about the bad effects of the trauma. In addition, hypnosis can aid in the treatment of depression by encephalic reconditioning. Age-regression allows patients to relive the trauma to permit abreaction, catharsis, and cognitive correction.

Abreaction

A reenactment of the past traumatic experience can produce dramatic results with good hypnotic subjects, especially if the trauma is of recent origin. Following a formal hypnotic induction, care must be taken to secure permission from the patient, in the form of a finger signal or verbal assent, to go back to the time of the trauma and to reexperience it. The clinician then encourages the subject to relive and relate the details of the trauma. As catharsis occurs, fearful emotions emerge and patients may begin to cry, tremble, and exhibit other signs of extreme anguish and agitation, invariably including the fear of dying. Following revivification of the trauma and abreaction, patients must be reassured that everything is all right. Encephalic corrections include specific statements such as, "You have gone through a terrible trauma, but you have survived. You were not killed or seriously injured. You are okay." Direct suggestions should also include statements encouraging the patient to disassociate the fearful emotions from the memory of the trauma and to discourage future ruminations.

In acute cases of PTSD, abreaction under hypnosis affords the patient an opportunity for a quick and dramatic cure. In chronic cases patients are less likely to derive salutary benefits from abreaction;

however, suggestions correcting misconceptions about their original trauma may be beneficial (Spiegel 1981). Abreaction utilizing the intravenous administration of sodium pentathol or sodium amytal (narcosynthesis) has been used with some success with Vietnam-era combat veterans who have developed PTSD (Kolb and Mutalipassi 1982). In chronic cases, however, abreaction alone, whether induced by hypnosis or barbiturate drugs does not resolve PTSD, but in conjunction with a comprehensive therapeutic approach it can be helpful.

Depression

Positive suggestions given to patients under hypnosis can allay the dispirited, demoralized, pessimistic, and depressed mood that is often a secondary manifestation of PTSD. Depressed patients have a tendency to overgeneralize, making a dismal mood pervasive and disproportionate to reality. Positive events and experiences get lost in a mental morass of gloom and doom. Extrication from melancholy can be assisted by the use of positive suggestions given under hypnosis. Typical suggestions include: "Your frame of mind and general attitude will become more and more optimistic and positive as time goes on. You will begin to think more and more optimistically and positively about yourself, your relationships with people who are important to you, and things that you will be doing today, tomorrow, and in the near future and . . . You will feel better . . . and . . . You will begin to act and behave in a more positive manner." To allow the patient to practice positive thinking, while still under hypnosis, the clinician states, "I am going to be quiet in a minute and during that silent period I want you to give yourself some positive suggestions about issues important to you." The session is concluded with the suggestion that, with time and practice, thinking optimistically and positively about one's life will become easier. When the sessions are recorded and the audio cassette given to patients, learning is facilitated and treatment hastened.

Cognition

The techniques of encephalic reconditioning have been previously elaborated upon by others and labeled as "cognitive therapy" or "cognitive behavior therapy" (Beck 1976; Meichenbaum 1977;

Meichenbaum and Cameron 1983). These terms imply a new and different therapeutic approach, although cognition has always been an important part of every medical therapy and, of course, is at the core of most psychotherapies (Wolpe 1978). Additionally, cognitive therapy is too narrow a term to describe brain functioning and can deflect attention from the fact that cognition represents only one of the many functions of the brain involved in the production of emotions and behavior. The term "encephalic" seems superior because it invites attention to the brain where definitive answers to the problem of stress and anxiety ultimately reside.

Medication

Many patients with PTSD have consulted numerous physicians and have taken a wide range of psychotropic agents that have not been entirely successful, since otherwise they would not be seeking further help. Their previous response to medication can assist the physician in selection, in order to avoid prescribing insufficient dosages or nontherapeutic agents. The clinician must be alerted to patterns of drug abuse or dependence, as patients with Chronic PTSD, especially those who complain vociferously of pain, overuse prescription drugs and sometimes resort to self-treatment. Abuse of alcohol, barbiturates, narcotic analgesics, and other sedative and hypnotic agents is not uncommon (Quitkin et al. 1972; Ludwig 1979; Mielke and Winstead 1981). If possible, it is desirable at the onset of treatment to discontinue or limit the use of all narcotic analgesics and psychotropic medication so that a baseline of symptomatic behavior may be obtained. In this way the patient's complaints are more accurately measured and the effects of future medications are more objectively evaluated.

During the initial stage of treatment, when patients exhibit high levels of anxiety that markedly interfere with life, one of the benzodiazepines can be prescribed. Diazepam (Valium), lorazepam (Ativan), and alprazolam (Xanax) (Dunner 1983) are safe, predictable, and effective and can complement other antianxiety interventions (Hollister et al. 1980; Shader et al. 1981). Throughout the course of treatment, if a crisis arises and anxiety severely impairs the patient, one of the benzodiazapines may be utilized as needed.

Recently, investigators have reported preliminary results utilizing the β-adrenergic blocker propanolol hydrochloride (Inderal) and the anticonvulsant clonazepam (Clonopin) in the treatment of PTSD (Burris 1983; Kolb and Mutalipassi 1982). No controlled studies have been conducted, and the number of PTSD patients treated thus far with these two medications is small. More research is obviously needed before specific recommendations can be made.

In the event that depressive symptoms are prominent, one of the cyclic antidepressants can be prescribed (Gallant and Simpson 1976). Antidepressants can also lessen agitation, somatic symptoms, and insomnia, which often accompany depression. The choice of a specific antidepressant depends upon the clinician's experience and the effect desired. When insomnia is a prominent feature, a more sedating antidepressant can be given in one evening dose. Since many PTSD patients are very sensitive to physiological sensations, it is wise to choose an antidepressant that has minimal anticholinergic side effects. The starting dose of antidepressants should be low, with a gradual increase until a therapeutic level of the antidepressant is reached. In the author's experience, trazadone hydrochloride (Desyrel) and maprotiline hydrochloride (Ludiomil) are often efficacious in treating the depression of Chronic PTSD patients. Some physicians prefer a monoamine oxidase inhibitor (Robinson et al. 1978) such as phenalzine sulfate (Nardil), which has been used in the treatment of Traumatic War Neurosis (Hogben and Cornfield 1981). It should be noted, however, that certain dietary precautions must be observed by patients taking an monoamine oxidase inhibitor (Table 6-2; McCabe and Tsuang 1982).

Even after the patient's depressive symptoms have diminished or disappeared, the antidepressant should be maintained until there is a definite change in the life of the patient. When the patient discloses positive changes in mood, better sleep, diminished somatic symptoms, involvement in sexual and social/recreational activities, and a general improvement in life circumstances, including a resumption of work, the dosage of the antidepressant can be slowly reduced over a period of 2 to 3 months and eventually discontinued.

Sleep disturbance merits the clinician's special attention. Patients who do not sleep thrash restlessly about in bed at night and awaken fatigued. During periods of insomnia, patients are likely to obsess about their trauma, increasing anxiety and further decreasing the

TABLE 6-2
Foods and Substances to Be Avoided When Taking Monoamine Oxidase Inhibitors

Foods with significant amounts of tyramine

Beer
Red wine (especially Chianti)
Other alcoholic beverages in large quantities
Beef or chicken livers
Brewer's yeast
Canned figs
Cheese (nonprocessed cheese and cream cheese are allowable)
Fava or broad beans (Italian green beans)
Game
Herring
Summer sausage

The following foods may cause problems when consumed in large quantities

Ripe avocado
Ripe fresh banana
Sour cream
Soy sauce
Yogurt

Some nonfood vasopressor agents

Amphetamines
Anorexiants
Certain cold remedies
Dopa
Epinephrine
Nasal decongestants
Norepinephrine

Source: Reprinted from *Stress Strategies*: The Treatment of the Anxiety Disorder (Scrignar 1983). Reproduced with permission.

likelihood of sleep. During sleepless nights retraumatization often takes place as the video tapes of the mind continuously replay the traumatic event and its aftermath. On the following morning, the sensitizing effect of mental activity and fatigue undermines treatment. Patients should be told to avoid taking naps during the day in order to regularize sleep. Before taking any sedatives for insomnia, patients are advised to attempt sleep by listening to a PMR or self-hypnosis tape. Suggestions regarding the treatment of insomnia (Table 6-3) can be given to promote sleep. If these methods fail, medication is prescribed to induce sleep. Flurazepam (Dalmane),

TABLE 6-3
Treatment of Insomnia or Difficulty Falling Asleep

1. Lie down intending to go sleep *only* when you are sleepy.

2. Do not use your bed for anything except sleep; that is, do not read, smoke, listen to radio, or talk to roommate once you intend to go to sleep.

3. If you find yourself unable to fall asleep, get up and go into another room or sit up. Stay as long as you wish and then return to the bedroom to sleep.

   Although you should not watch the clock, you should get out of bed if you do not fall asleep after 10 minutes. *Remember, the goal is to associate your bed with falling asleep quickly.* If you are in bed more than 10 minutes without falling asleep and have not gotten up, you are not following these instructions.

   If you still cannot fall asleep, repeat previous steps. Do this as often as necessary throughout the night.

4. Get up at the same time every morning, no matter how little sleep you got during the night. This will help your body acquire consistent sleep rhythm.

5. Do not nap during the daytime or lie in the bed for any other reason such as reading.

Our goal is to have you associate your bed with falling asleep quickly.

Source: Bloom, W. A., and Gallant, D. M., Southeast Louisiana State Hospital, Mandeville, Louisiana. Reproduced with permission.

temazepam (Restoril), and triazolam (Halcion), prescribed 30 minutes before bedtime usually combat insomnia. Patients have to be reminded periodically to listen to relaxation tapes before resorting to medication. Sedatives can be used to best advantage during the initial stages of treatment, and care must be taken to discourage long-term usage so that patients will not become psychologically dependent. Adequate sleep is essential, because a rested patient responds more readily to the total treatment regimen.

The therapeutic objective is to teach the patient to effectively cope with stress nonpharmacologically. Treatment gains can then be attributed to the patient and not wholly to the medication. Personal independence, not dependence on drugs, is the ultimate goal.

Systematic Desensitization

Any situation, conveyance, or place where a trauma has occurred and from which PTSD has developed have the capability of being a phobic stimulus. Even when patients do not avoid situational aspects of their trauma, phobic anxiety is almost always present. Persons involved in automobile or airplane accidents frequently develop phobias or phobic anxiety related to traveling in those conveyances. Although some phobias impose personal inconvenience, others affect a person's vocation and livelihood. Teamsters who have been involved in a truck accident may avoid driving, and workers who are injured in an industrial plant may develop a phobia of the premises and avoid work. Often it is not prudence but a phobia that motivates victims of a trauma to avoid the scene of the accident. When a phobia or phobic anxiety is associated with PTSD, systematic desensitization or graded exposure is the treatment of choice and has been found to be successful in 80 to 90 percent of phobias (Wolpe 1958, 1982; Paul 1968; Mavissakalian and Barlow 1981). This therapeutic technique is based on the principle that when patients are gradually exposed under specified conditions to a phobic or anxiety-evoking stimulus, they will eventually become habituated or deconditioned to the anxiety occasioned by the phobic stimuli. Systematic desensitization may be employed in the consulting room by using imaginal techniques (Keane and Kaloupek 1982) or, if practicable, by gradually exposing the patient to phobic situations in real life (in vivo desensitization). Prolonged exposure (flooding), if tolerated by patients, can be extremely useful and has been reported to be successful in the treatment of Vietnam-era veterans (Fairbank and Keane 1982; Keane et al. 1983).

Construction of Hierarchy

The first step in desensitizing phobic PTSD patients consists of developing a hierarchy of anxiety-evoking situations based on a unified theme involving the traumatic incident. Depending upon the circumstances of the trauma, patients may have become so anxious that they avoid driving automobiles, flying in airplanes, operating a truck or heavy machinery, going into high places, or being around fire or combustible materials. Scenarios based upon the appropriate theme are developed and hierarchically arranged according to the intensity of anxiety that would be evoked if the patient were in that situation (Scrignar 1974). When constructing hierarchies, precise measures such as distance, time, quantity, and a temporal sequence give the best results. For example, a patient who was involved in an accident atop the tenth level of a tower at an oil refinery developed Acrophobia and could not return to work checking gauges and valves located at each of the ten levels of the tower. Prior to desensitization a hierarchy was constructed utilizing vertical distance or height as the variable. The least anxiety-evoking item on the hierarchy was: "I am on the ground looking up at the tower." The most anxiety-evoking scene chosen by the patient was being on the tenth level where the accident occurred and he experienced an acute anxiety attack.

The most versatile variable used in constructing a hierarchy is a temporal sequence. All activities or actions have a starting and finishing point, but with patients, the time taken to complete a phobic activity is correlated with increasing anxiety. For example, a person involved in an airplane accident who now refuses to fly may be desensitized of that phobia by using the following hierarchy (Scrignar et al. 1973):

Fear of Flying Hierarchy:
Low to High Anxiety

1. You are at home thinking about flying.
2. You make a decision to fly and call the airline to order your tickets.

3. It is the day of the flight and you are at home packing and preparing for your flight.
4. You are driving to the airport.
5. You enter the airport terminal, go to the appropriate airline counter, check your luggage, and validate your ticket.
6. You walk to your concourse, pause at the security check, then go to the gate where your flight will depart.
7. You secure a boarding pass and go to the waiting area to await the call for boarding the aircraft.
8. You board the aircraft, select your seat, and fasten your seatbelt.
9. The aircraft doors close, the jet engines start, and the airplane begins taxiing down the runway.
10. The airplane takes off.
11. You are at cruising altitude. Drinks and food are being served as the airplane flies to your destination.

For patients who have been involved in an automobile accident and have subsequently developed a phobia of driving, the distance driven from home can be the hierarchical variable. Proximity to the phobic stimulus was the variable used for a patient who had been burned in an industrial accident and feared fire or potentially flammable materials. Even the sight of someone lighting a cigarette evoked high levels of anxiety, and the patient avoided all situations where fire might be encountered. Standing 10 feet from a flaming burner on a gas stove elicited the least anxiety, whereas turning on the gas jet and watching the flames was the most anxiety-evoking item on the hierarchy.

Imaginal Desensitization

Imaginal desensitization (Wolpe 1958, 1982) begins after the patient has become proficient in the technique of PMR and a hierarchy has been developed. The procedure is simple and effective.

The patient is asked to sit in a comfortable chair, preferably one that reclines, close his or her eyes, and spend several minutes getting completely relaxed.
The least anxiety-evoking item on the hierarchy is read to the patient. The patient is asked to visualize that scene as clearly and as realistically as possible.

After 15 to 20 seconds, the therapist says, "Erase that scene from your mind and relax." This is a signal for the patient to take a deep breath, hold it, count to five, slowly breathe out, and relax. The counting sequence helps erase the scene from the patient's mind and facilitates relaxation.

When the patient is reasonably relaxed, the anxiety experienced while visualizing the scene is rated on a scale from 0 to 100 (Wolpe 1982).

The procedure is repeated until the patient reports little or no anxiety while visualizing the scene. Then the next lowest item on the hierarchy is presented as above.

The anxiety reduction experienced during imaginal desensitization transfers to situations in real life.

In Vivo Desensitization

Some clinicians feel that in vivo desensitization or exposure is preferable to imaginal techniques (Marks 1981; Mavissakalian and Barlow 1981). If no logistical impediments preclude an in vivo approach, it is the method of choice. As in imaginal desensitization, exposure to the lower items of the hierarchy takes place first, followed in a graduated sequence by the more anxiety evoking ones. In vivo desensitization can be facilitated when the patient is accompanied by the clinician who serves as a nonaxious model (Rosenthal and Bandura 1978) and also gives praise and precise feedback on the amount of improvement (Agras et al. 1969). Care must be taken neither to bring patients along too quickly nor to push them into phobic situations without their agreement, because they may experience an anxiety or panic attack. When this happens, the unexpected anxiety retards treatment and the patient may refuse to cooperate in the future. During desensitization or exposure treatment, patients must experience a definite lowering of anxiety while they are in the phobic situation if treatment is to be successful (Mavissakalian and Barlow 1981). It is good practice to end each in vivo desensitization session with positive gains, because this diminishes anticipatory anxiety and encourages a positive anticipatory attitude.

The key to success in desensitization, whether done in the imagination or in the environment, is persistence. When treating PTSD patients, systematic desensitization is held in abeyance until other antianxiety interventions have been implemented, for phobic anxiety and phobias may abate when the patient's generalized anxiety level diminishes.

Family Conferences

Sound practice argues for arranging a meeting with the patient and significant others. The involvement of a father, mother, spouse, lover, or close friend adds an important dimension to treatment. The objectives of a family conference include: enlisting the family members' cooperation; gathering additional information about the patient; and determining the family members' role in the reinforcement of symptoms and teaching concepts regarding the reinforcement of positive behavior.

The family conference begins with an explanation, in nontechnical terms, of the patient's PTSD. The significance of the patient's symptoms is explained to the family member(s), and any fixed opinion concerning permanent disability should be purposely dislodged in favor of a coping one. Since family members have been closest to the problem, they should be asked about their observations of the patient's behavior. Useful information can be obtained concerning the patient's coping patterns, degree of emotional detachment from the family, involvement in recreational/social activities, and use or abuse of alcohol and other drugs. Sleep disturbance, nightmares, a "personality change," hypersensitivity to sudden environmental stimuli, preoccupation with bodily sensations, and symptoms of depression can be verified during family conferences. A spouse or lover can confirm a lack of sexual desire or other psychosexual dysfunctions.

The family member can be invited to comment and to furnish additional information and suggestions that augment the treatment program. "How has family life been affected by the patient's illness?" "What changes do you think will be necessary to improve family life?" These questions immediately involve the family members in treatment and provide important information. Relatives of patients add extra pairs of eyes and ears to treatment, provide information concerning outcome, and increase the patient's compliance with treatment recommendations. It is the clinician's responsibility to titrate and moderate the role of the family members, since arguments and acrimony may emerge if family members are perceived as spies who will snitch on all failures to comply with treatment. To counter this perception, family members must verbally reinforce positive gains made by the patient and discuss this progress during family conferences. As treatment proceeds it becomes obvious to all that the entire family benefits from success.

Marital conflicts frequently arise as a direct result of the altered relationship between spouses caused by the PTSD. Sometimes, however, marital disharmony antedates the onset of the Stress Disorder. Frequent arguments, decrease in sexual activity, diminished frequency of shared pleasures, and difficulties in communication indicate marital disharmony necessitating therapy.

Conjugal conferences can become an arena for invective and hate unless certain precautions are taken. The couple must be instructed that the first rule of successful marital therapy consists in setting aside past grievances and concentrating on the current marital relationship. This ahistoric approach, emphasizing changes in current marital interaction and deemphasizing past grievances, affords a couple the best means of improving their marriage (Stuart 1980). Any departure from this rule by either party receives quick attention from the therapist, who intervenes and emphatically states that arguments or bickering will not be tolerated. Within a very short time, problem areas can be identified and commitments obtained from the couple to change specific behaviors. Compromises can be negotiated in the areas of child management, housekeeping chores, money management, lovemaking, social and recreational pursuits, and talking together harmoniously (Stuart 1975). Reciprocated positive feedback sustains improvement, whereas a continual failure to adhere to the terms of an agreement portends protracted unhappiness or divorce.

Assertive Training

Not all patients with a PTSD have problems with assertion, but those who do must be identified. The consequences of anger, unpleasantness, lack of consideration, and sarcasm, as well as an inability to express gratitude or appreciation contribute to symptomatic behavior. A retributive attitude toward those believed to be responsible for the trauma and ensuant disability fuels a desire for monetary compensation. Litigation often springs from the anger engendered by the belief of negligence on the part of others. Patients frequently rail about the stupidity and carelessness of those people perceived to be culpable for the trauma. An absence of appreciation for the efforts of clinicians and other helping persons are assertive deficiencies that impact directly upon the quality of care the patient receives. Disagreeable and unappreciative persons frequently are rejected by clinician and friends alike and, owing to lack of insight, PTSD patients interpret such actions as proof of the uncaring nature of people.

Outbursts of temper, aggressive acts, or just thinking angrily activates the autonomic nervous system and produces uncomfortable physical sensations that contribute to the patient's distress. Although anger is appropriate at times, patients should be taught when it is not. Popular psychiatric parlance pronounces that open expression of anger should be promoted because of its therapeutic effect. This is unsound advice, because although a patient may experience momentary relief, the long-range effects of open hostility and acrimony accrue to one's detriment.

PTSD patients often confuse anger and aggression with assertion (Dawley and Wenrich 1976; Alberti and Emmons 1978). Aggression is a militant act with the willful intent of harming someone, either verbally or physically. Assertion, on the other hand, is primarily an affirmation of one's personal rights, including expressions of affection, and is an action that enhances self-esteem and mitigates pathologic anxiety. This differentiation is important and should be discussed with patients who confuse the two. For example, if a patient feels aggrieved because of a perception that the PTSD resulted from the negligence of others, the appropriate course to follow is to solicit the services of an attorney. The redress of wrongs can be arbitrated or adjudicated calmly and it is hoped, objectively in a courtroom. Patients need not distress themselves or others by the meaningless maneuver of hurling insults or invective toward their perceived antagonist. Aggression in a civilized society almost always proves to be a self-injurious action, whereas assertion more frequently leads to the attainment of desired goals.

Thinking angrily, a less obvious aggressive action, contributes to feelings of dis-ease. During periods of disability involving inactivity, patients have abundant chances to think about unpleasant things. Like the old adage, "An idle mind is the devil's workshop," inactive patients have ample opportunity to think angry thoughts and become very self-centered, impatient, and irritable. Teaching patients techniques of self-control based on behavioral principles reduces the tendency for aggressive outbursts (Feindler and Fremouw 1983).

One might assume that most patients with a PTSD always act or think angrily and interact aggressively with people, but of course this is not true. Many patients exhibit passive, nonassertive behavior and are quiet and withdrawn. Nonassertiveness or a lack of social skills directly influences treatment when there is an inhibition of self-action leading to patterns of indecisiveness and procrastination. Since a successful outcome of treatment depends upon the implementation of various therapeutic techniques, failure to act decisively when performing muscle relaxation, encephalic reconditioning, beginning exercise programs, seeking work, or initiating social/recreational activities thwarts progress. When procrastination patterns extend to other areas of life and become extreme, owing to pathologic anxiety or lack of social skills, the unfinished business can become a burden and a source of additional anxiety.

Assertive training consists of a varied combination of behavioral rehearsal, modeling, instructions, feedback (Marks 1981), and encephalic reconditioning. Encephalic reconditioning, especially thought stopping and positive encephalic practice, can reduce the flow of hostile thoughts. When the patient begins to act assertively, angry thoughts will usually diminish and disappear. Learning how to act assertively with others and initiating self-action can best be achieved by behavioral rehearsal and graded task assignments (Wolpe 1982). Before behavioral rehearsal begins, the patient identifies the nonassertive situations and the people who are involved. The situations are discussed and several assertive "scripts" are created and ranked in accordance with the degree of difficulty and the amount of anxiety each situation would elicit. The "easier," less anxiety-evoking situations are chosen first and enacted in the consulting room with the clinician playing the role of the other person. These behavioral rehearsal sessions may be recorded on a video or audio cassette and played back for analysis and critique (Server 1972). The same situation is rehearsed again, and a comparison between the first and second attempt usually facilitates learning because the patient invariably does better the second time. Homework includes assignments for patients to practice assertion in real-life settings, starting with the easier situations and then moving to the more difficult ones. Acting assertively is an interpersonal skill and, like other skills, improves with practice and time.

Procrastination patterns respond to the successful completion of graded task assignments (Curran and Gilbert 1975). Patients begin by compiling a hierarchical procrastination list that starts with the simpler tasks and progresses to the more difficult and anxiety-evoking ones (Scrignar 1983). It must be kept in mind that patients procrastinate not only on arduous tasks, such as filling out reports, writing letters, and paying bills, but also regarding involvement in such matters as deciding to take a vacation, visit a friend, or engage in some new pleasurable social activity. Failure to act on these issues can result in a future source of anxiety and eliminate a future source of enjoyment. After the hierarchical procrastination list has been compiled, each situation is discussed at length with the patient. Information concerning self-assertiveness as it applies to each item on the hierarchy assists patients in decision making and eventually in assertive action. Following instruction, assignments begin with one or two of the less difficult items on the list, which are to be completed before the patient returns for the next session. As patients reap the rewards of assertion, procrastination diminishes. Change is slow, but adherence to the principles of assertive training yields results, and behavioral rehearsal assignments become pleasurable exercises.

Problem Solving

Unresolved problems which aggravate a PTSD are a source of anxiety. During family conferences and assertive training sessions, many common problems involving family life, interpersonal issues, and decision making are addressed and resolved. Of the remaining problems, all that may be required is sound counsel from the clinician. PTSD patients often develop tunnel vision and are unable to see alternatives to their dilemmas. Through discussion the clinician presents information and opinions that widen the patient's vision and make it easier to envisage and decide upon solutions.

Often when patients file a civil law suit, it creates conflict, which tends to intensify anxiety. Some patients become obsessed with their tort action and constantly complain of court delays and real or imagined injustices, which contribute to stress. When the clinician is familiar with the legal process, information concerning depositions and courtroom procedures allays the patient's apprehension. To place litigation in perspective, sometimes it is helpful to express the opinion that the legal process is impersonal and revolves around monetary issues. Advice to solicit a trustworthy, competent attorney who can attend to all aspects of legal matters also mitigates anxiety.

A problem that causes considerable distress in unemployed patients is lack of money. A state of impecuniousness alters the living standard and imposes hardships on all members of a family. If the patient had been the breadwinner, the burden of insolvency adds more stress. No solution is perfect, but temporary remedies include: assistance from governmental agencies, instructions on money management and budgeting, dependence on relatives, and employment of the well spouse. Monetary insufficiency can also serve as an impetus to motivate a patient to work in a limited capacity or to obtain a different job.

Occasionally problems may have resisted solutions because the patient simply did not possess the requisite information upon which to base a plan of action. Governmental bureaucracies at the federal, state, and local levels often offer seemingly insurmountable obstacles to the solution of simple problems, and the clinician can serve as a cicerone, guiding the patient through the maze of bureaucratic procedures. Letters, phone calls, or advice from the clinician often remove bureaucratic barriers and break the impasse to a viable remedy. When problems that were a source of anxiety are eliminated, the patient profits.

In some circles advice giving by clinicians, especially psychiatrists, is viewed with skepticism, yet a physician or other clinician as a respected authority figure can have a profound positive influence upon a patient by giving sound advice. Successful people in all walks of life consult experts for guidance and counsel, and the clinician can provide this service or direct the patient to an appropriate resource. Advice giving under these circumstances should not be discouraged, but promoted as of value to the patient.

Exercise and Nutrition

It is axiomatic to state that persons function best when they exercise regularly and eat properly. This maxim, however, has specific significance for patients with Chronic PTSD who may avoid physical activity and neglect nutrition. The body, like a machine, requires proper maintenance and fueling. Proper exercise and good nutrition contribute to successful treatment of PTSD.

Exercise

The benefits of exercise cannot be stored; rather, physical fitness requires regular involvement in some physical activity. Fitness flags quickly when idleness ensues, especially if injury causes physical inactivity. In cases of Chronic PTSD, physical discomfort can persist long after the expected time of healing and can nurture the idea of an unsound body. There is some evidence for this idea, because prolonged physical inactivity causes muscles to become flabby, strength to ebb, and the body to become easily fatigued. Verification of physical infirmity and defect seems to occur when patients engage in minor acts of physical exertion or short spurts of arduous activity and later complain of muscular aches and pains. After a while patients honestly believe they cannot perform certain physical actions and attribute failure to some pathologic process within the body. In reality, poor physical conditioning caused by lack of exercise is responsible for most physical limitations. In spite of repeated physical examinations and various laboratory procedures that disclose no organic pathology, some patients are loath to accept this conclusion. This may lead to an impasse in treatment, since patients may obstinately refuse to comply with recommendations to return to work, to assume more responsibility at home, to engage in more social/recreational activities, and, of course, to embark upon an exercise program.

To dissuade patients from erroneous ideas concerning their physical status and to persuade them of the value of exercise, an explanation for the presence of any current physical discomfort or pain is mandatory. The sources of the patient's pain and discomfort can usually be traced to: chronic anxiety and increased motor tension; residual injury related to the original trauma; and muscular aches and pains owing to poor muscle tone. As anxiety is alleviated by self-hypnosis and relaxation exercises during treatment, the patient is told motor tension will be greatly reduced. Minor aches and pains caused by poor muscle tone can be corrected by physiotherapy and exercise. Encephalic reconditioning is used to teach the patient how to cope with residual pain.

Brief instruction in anatomy utilizing an atlas to illustrate the affected anatomical areas augments the educational process and is usually enthusiastically received by patients who formerly harbored ignorance concerning the functioning of their body. Although patients may be experiencing some pain and physical discomfort, the main message, "There is nothing seriously wrong with you," must be conveyed along with the recommendation that a sensible, well-designed exercise program would be of great value. Confirmation of this statement by an orthopedic surgeon reduces the patient's apprehension and increases compliance.

Many medical centers and hospitals have physical fitness clinics or wellness centers where an individual's physical state of health can be evaluated. Trained personnel in these centers utilizing special instruments and equipment can measure cardiopulmonary functioning, percentage of total body fat, and muscular strength prior to the preparation of individualized exercise programs. In the absence of human performance centers in the community, well-staffed and -organized health clubs, spas, and similar groups devoted to physical health are acceptable alternatives. Some patients prefer unsupervised exercise, but this must be avoided or carefully controlled, lest overexertion lead to pain and discourage future exercise. To ensure compliance and adherence with the prescription of regular exercise, part of each therapy session with the patients should include a discussion concerning physical progress. When a medical center or health club conducts the program, ongoing communication with the agency maximizes compliance and successful outcome.

The recommendation to engage in regular exercise carries with it the implicit messages that "there is nothing seriously wrong with you" and "you are capable of improving your physical health." When patients begin to derive the benefits from exercise, enhanced strength and endurance also reinforce the idea of physical soundness. Some pain may still be present, but as patients learn to cope, discomfort becomes subordinated to a more active life-style. Fatigue and listlessness caused by chronic anxiety also respond favorably to a program of gradated exercise. More energy, sounder sleep, increased interest in sex, improved appetite, and a physical and psychological feeling of well-being all accrue as a result of regular exercise.

Nutrition

An inquiry into the dietary habits of the PTSD patient should always include the quantities of alcohol, coffee, tea, other caffeine-containing products, and proprietary medications that are consumed. Caffeine and sympathomimetic substances directly affect the nervous system and abet anxiety (Goldstein et al. 1969; Greden 1979; Rapoport et al. 1981). By the use of a log, the eating habits of the patients are surveyed, and if diets are not adequate, information concerning the daily minimum requirements of essential foodstuffs (proteins, carbohydrates, fats, vitamins, and minerals) is provided. Overweight patients should be placed on an appropriate diet based on behavior modification (Scrignar 1980; Stuart and Davis 1982). If the clinician does not feel totally competent in this area, consultation with a nutritionist or dietician assists in the analysis and formulation of a good nutritional program.

Group Treatment

Treatment conducted in groups has the advantage of economy in terms of time and money (Marks 1981). Many of the therapeutic interventions mentioned — explanation-education, training in relaxation, encephalic reconditioning, assertive training, problem solving, and exercise — can be conducted in a group setting. Although more difficult, systematic desensitization and family conferences are also amenable to a group approach. The manner in which group treatment is conducted determines therapeutic outcome. PTSD patients do poorly in psychodynamically oriented groups, which are insight oriented and concentrate on uncovering repressed pretraumatic conflicts (Walker and Nash 1981). "Rap group therapy" (Brende 1981) has evolved from experience with Vietnam-era veterans with PTSD. Advocates of rap group therapy have assumed that catharsis and "therapeutic revivification" of traumas experienced in Vietnam are beneficial. Actually, catharsis by itself has limited value in Chronic PTSD because the reliving of traumatic experiences, as occurs in rap sessions, can be detrimental because retraumatization and a resurgence of symptoms can occur (Rosenheim and Elizur 1977; Walker and Nash 1981).

If the clinician has many PTSD patients, group treatment does offer the best utilization of time. Individual attention, especially at the beginning of treatment, is necessary. Once patients become stabilized, however, transfer to a group setting may facilitate progress, provided the patient has easy access to the therapist on an individual basis. The following general rules are suggested for group treatment.

The groups should be open ended.
Emphasis is placed on the here and now, and patients should be discouraged from retelling the details of their trauma.
Goal setting and problem solving in an atmosphere of mutual assistance should be encouraged.
All positive gains made by patients should be verbally reinforced by the clinician.
When patients complain of symptoms, group discussion should center around the proper selection and implementation of therapeutic options.
Symptomatic improvement and successful behavior change are indications for termination. As a group member is "graduated," an appropriate ceremony conveying best wishes from the clinician and other group members forms closure and may inspire others to challenge, not succumb, to stress.

Self-Assessment

Recording the occurrence and frequency of selected symptoms helps to control and regulate targeted behavior and is a way of assessing outcome of treatment (Fisher et al. 1982; Mahoney and Arnoff 1979). Too often, PTSD patients complain of symptoms as if they were occurring throughout the entire day. Additionally, they may negate therapeutic recommendations as if they had absolutely no effect on altering symptoms or pathologic behaviors. For example, patients will complain of insomnia or physical discomfort, suggesting that they never sleep and are in constant pain. Similarly, patients may report that PMR or self-hypnosis had absolutely no effect in inducing somnolence or ameliorating pain. Neither patients nor clinicians receive encouragement from these nihilistic reports, but fortunately these assessments are usually in error. When patients are asked to record the total number of hours spent napping or sleeping during the day and night or to record hourly, on a scale from zero to ten, the intensity of pain or physical discomfort that they experience, the symptomatic profile discloses significant variations. The all-or-nothing reports — "I have the symptoms *all* the time and *nothing* seems to work to alleviate it" — are not only untrue but hinder treatment. Unknowingly, the patient makes these inaccurate estimates of pathology and response to treatment because "that's the way it seems." Unless there is a dramatic and profound change in symptoms, patients will report no change. The small but steady positive alterations in behavior, the usual response to treatment, are either ignored or minimized, and thus distort therapeutic gains.

Patients must be persuaded that accurate self-assessment is one way to control and regulate selected behaviors. By the use of a Self-Assessment Form (Table 6-1), patients record the occurrence and source of pathologic anxiety as well as selected target behaviors. Since pathologic anxiety is a crucial element in PTSD, the Three E's, which both stimulate and alleviate anxiety, must be identified and recorded. On the left side of the Self-Assessment Form, the patient records the source of pathologic anxiety, and on the right side the interventions employed to reduce anxiety. Space is also included for comments related to outcome. An example of a typical entry for a PTSD patient who was involved in an automobile accident and has phobic anxiety while riding in a car might be:

Sources of Anxiety

Environment — Riding in a car driven by a friend

Endogenous — Heart beginning to beat rapidly, I feel tightness in my chest and have a dizzy feeling

Encephalic — I think I am going to faint or maybe lose control of myself

Antianxiety Interventions

Environment — Stayed in the car, conversed with my friend as a distraction

Endogenous — Initiated muscle relaxation, especially slow deep breathing

Encephalic — Repeated the four positive reinforcing statements and told myself everything would be all right

Comment — After several minutes, the anxiety symptoms went away, my heart slowed, and the tightness in my chest and dizziness were alleviated. Soon, I began to feel better and more in control.

The SIC (Table 4-3) can be administered periodically to assess the effect of treatment. The items on the SIC can be scored: 4 points for "practically all of the time," 3 points for "very often," 2 points for "often," 1 point for "sometimes," and 0 points for "not at all." The total can be compared with that from a previous administration of the SIC, thus giving some indication of the effects of treatment. The results can be graphed and shown to the patient to reinforce change. Other items that the patient may record are: participation in exercise (specify in detail), participation in social/recreational activities (specify in detail), time spent in a phobic situation, presence and duration of any somatic symptoms, amount of alcohol consumed, quantity and type of medication taken, and the intensity (low, moderate, severe) and place where anxiety is experienced. The record should include an assessment of positive coping behaviors and other signs of improvement. At the conclusion of each day the patient is asked to make a global rating of progress, based on a scale of zero (no progress) to ten (excellent progress).

Recording events facilitates self-analysis and self-management of pathologic behavior and associated symptoms. The information also furnishes the clinician with data concerning the patient's progress, upon which an adjustment of the therapeutic regimen depends. When patients are doing well, they should be praised. If they founder, however, appropriate adjustment in treatment must be initiated. The goal of treatment is not complete tranquility, for patients must learn to differentiate between anxiety and pathologic anxiety and, most importantly, to cope with the consequences of trauma.

Related Issues — Work and Social/Recreational Activities

Work

PTSD disrupts a person's life and often interferes with the ability to work. Work is defined as any productive activity that regularly utilizes a person's mental and physical energy and consumes a significant amount of time each day, for which an individual receives a reward, usually money. The manifestations of PTSD — pain, physical discomfort, chronic anxiety, fatigue, phobic anxiety, and depression — interfere with performance at work, frequently resulting in unemployment. The consequences of unemployment are all bad, but generally lack of money places the most stress on the patient. Insolvency is demoralizing, attracting bill collectors and limiting the purchase of food and clothing, while creating a host of other problems that impact on all members of a family. The patient's time, normally spent working, is not spent on leisure but wasted on worry, an encephalic activity that generates more anxiety, further encumbering the patient.

When a physical injury is associated with the development of PTSD, somatic symptoms sometimes persist long after the expected time of healing, and patients feel physically incapable of performing even minor tasks. They also eschew more arduous activity, fearing an aggravation of an injury. Patients who cling to the belief of an organic defect seem bereft of psychological insight and choose to concentrate, in vain, on a physical cause and surgical cure for their condition. Wisdom dictates that clinicians communicate with the patient's surgeon in order to avoid mixed messages concerning physical impairment and fitness for work. Moreover, physiotherapy and other medical treatments can complement the psychological treatment of PTSD, so that patients can return to work as soon as possible. A quick return to work is always desirable, but without the patient's approval and consent, this recommendation meets with resistance. Often, patients become truculent if they feel that their doctor is insensitive or in cahoots with the company. Recommendations to return to work are therefore met with hostility and noncompliance.

Patients must be persuaded that work will not aggravate their condition, but rather will be part of the rehabilitative process. Sometimes a recommendation to return to limited or light duty with gradual resumption of regular tasks hastens a patient's recovery. When work requires hard labor or employers are uncooperative, reemployment under these circumstances may not be possible. Although a change in occupation and vocational rehabilitation may become necessary, this means a longer road to recovery.

Reports, letters, and phone calls from the clinician can expedite an unemployed patient's return to work. Personal attention helps remove administrative red tape that may have blocked reemployment. For example, a 43-year-old oil refinery worker was involved in an explosion in which he received minor physical injuries and developed a PTSD with a phobia of the work premises. Following imaginal desensitization for his phobia, a phone call was made to the company physician. The principles underlying PTSD, particularly the worker's phobia, were explained to the company doctor who was requested to allow the patient to visit the oil refinery, including his immediate work area, for the purpose of in vivo desensitization. The patient's supervisor, who was originally not predisposed to this request, acquiesced following approval by the company physician. The patient was desensitized of his phobia, returned to work, and successfully resumed his job.

Although work has a high priority in treatment, the symptoms of PTSD must have abated to a large extent before this goal is met. To be successful the recommendation of a return to work must be titrated with symptomatic improvement. Pending personal injury litigation or weekly worker's compensation payments complicate efforts regarding employment.

Social/Recreational Activities

When patients experience chronic anxiety, physical discomfort, and/or depression, they derive little delight from social/recreational activities. Concentration on the trauma and its consequences causes a self-centeredness that draws attention from enjoyable activities. PTSD is a desocializing condition, and patients soon become withdrawn and isolated from family and friends, thus diminishing potentially pleasing interactions with others. During the later stages of treatment, patients frequently need guidelines to reestablish old pleasures and discover new ones. It is during family conferences that discussions concerning social/recreational activities are best conducted. At this time it is imperative to secure a commitment from the patient and spouse to engage in one or more mutually satisfying activities during the coming week. The involvement of the spouse increases the patient's compliance, and the pleasure derived from the activity reinforces a repeat performance. Patients are well on their way to recovery when the environment provides enjoyment, the physiological sensations of the body feel good, and the cognitive apparatus of the mind begins to presage pleasure. The patient's improvement measured by enjoyment in social/recreational activities is a good index of progress.

TERMINATION

Treatment for Chronic PTSD, like any other chronic illness, is imperfect, and criteria for termination lack precision. There is no dramatic reduction of symptoms, except in those exceptional cases responding to hypnosis and abreaction. Rather, a slow and sometimes tedious return to normal functioning occurs. Pending litigation may retard treatment, but it is questionable whether successful litigation hastens recovery. More often than not, dogged adherence to the treatment described in this book and the passage of time are the important ingredients of recovery. Successful treatment can be demonstrated when patients report a significant reduction or elimination of symptoms as determined on the SIC and an improvement in work performance, family life, social/recreational activities, and improved coping skills. As patients make progress, the frequency in sessions diminishes from weekly to twice monthly, then to monthly until termination. To ensure a stable improvement during the first year, the patient should be seen in the office every 3 months for a current status review. Thereafter, a mental status examination is conducted annually, similar to an annual physical examination. Continued contact with patients, without fostering undue dependency, prevents exacerbation of symptoms. When patients learn to cope adequately with the everyday stresses of life by utilizing appropriate therapeutic techniques, treatment is considered to be successful.

SEVEN

LEGAL ISSUES

PTSD is of interest to lawyers and mental health professionals during personal injury suits, worker's compensation disputes, and criminal cases when PTSD is used as an insanity defense. The type and severity of mental suffering or degree of incapacity imposed by the Stress Disorder become a matter for arbitration or trial. Lawyers need to know the basis upon which mental health professionals formulate conclusions and should become familiar with the elements that constitute a thorough forensic evaluation. Finally, the theoretical and practical aspects of PTSD are blended when psychiatrists or psychologists testify during depositions or trials, and lawyers should become conversant with medical language, psychiatric constructs, and the application of both to a client's case. Mental health professionals who participate in forensic proceedings should also be familiar with the legal concepts underlying tort, worker's compensation, and criminal law as they relate to the evaluation of a patient and testimony in court. In this way judges and jury who make the final decision in forensic matters may have access to clear and concise thinking and lucid testimony upon which to render judgment.

TORT AND PTSD

Tort stems from the root word "torquere," as does the word "torture"; and, in a sense, that is what is claimed by clients in personal injury cases. Everyone understands that torture consists not only of the affliction of intense physical pain but also includes anguish of the mind. In fact, the most effective forms of torture involve subtleties requiring little or no infliction of physical pain (Zunzunegui 1982). In a personal injury suit, a tort action generally claims that a trauma has caused damages resulting from the negligence or intentional action of the defendant. If the injury was physical and can be objectively evaluated, few problems arise in elaborating its extent and the resultant disability. Part of the claim may also include a desire to be compensated for pain and mental suffering, a legal principle that is firmly established and time honored. During legal proceedings, if the defendant is at fault, damages are awarded to the plaintiff and the case is closed.

In the past the courts have been reluctant to accept pain and suffering as compensable entities. Understandably, physical defect related to a trauma occupied the principle attention of judges and lawyers because physical injury was observable and could be objectively measured. The less tangible emotional accompaniment of a trauma was difficult to describe and quantify, and for many years, the judiciary was unwilling to accept mental consequences of an accident as a compensable entity. As knowledge in the behavioral sciences grew, the resistance to the concept of trauma and mental disorder lessened. During World War II physicians who were specialists in psychiatry for the first time studied the effects of combat stress upon a large number of soldiers (Kardiner and Spiegel 1947). The concept of Traumatic Neurosis emerged and became widely recognized, so that by the late 1940s, testimony related to this psychiatric syndrome was accepted by many courts. Since that time experience has shown that traumatic events may bring about a disabling mental disorder that can be either a combination of physical and mental disorders or solely a residual mental incapacity continuing after the physical injury has healed (Malone and Johnson 1980). Finally, in 1980, the APA for the first time incorporated into the *DSM* the term "Post-Traumatic Stress Disorder."

PTSD as a Clinical Entity

It is now clearly established that a clinical entity, PTSD, can result from a trauma and that such a trauma need not be accompanied by an observable physical defect. Confusion arises when lawyers or other persons unfamiliar with the onset and course of PTSD attempt to understand the post-traumatic relationship between PTSD and physical injury. Such persons should be guided by the following principles: <u>(1) PTSD can exist whether the victim of a trauma suffered demonstrable physical injury or not. (2) The presence, absence, or diminished state of organic pathology due to a trauma are not the indicators of the existence or severity of a PTSD. (3) PTSD does not accompany all traumatic incidents involving physical injury.</u> Lawyers and the laity frequently make two incorrect assumptions about trauma and a Stress Disorder. The first is that the severity of a physical injury correlates with the severity of a PTSD. The second is that a PTSD is dependent upon physical injury, so that if no physical pathology is present, either because none occurred as a result of the trauma or healing has occurred and no physical defect is demonstrable, PTSD should not be present. A tort action based solely on PTSD is quite appropriate and medically justifiable. PTSD should be considered an autonomous entity related to a trauma but not dependent upon physical injury. As has been pointed out earlier (Chapters two and three), the trauma perceived as a life-threatening event must stimulate the victim's autonomic nervous system by one or, more likely, a combination of the five sensory pathways to the brain. Any physical injury that may occur as a result of the trauma is not primary to the production of PTSD. Later, if the physical injury is not remediable and the PTSD becomes chronic, both contribute to disability; <u>they may seem inextricable, but they are still independent disorders (Sierles et al. 1983)</u>.

Official medical recognition in 1980 of a Stress Disorder following trauma together with the increased public awareness of PTSD fostered by publicity given to Vietnam-era combat veterans with a Stress Disorder, have resulted in more forensic usage of PTSD. Already common in worker's compensation cases and in personal injury suits, PTSD has also been used as a criminal defense mitigating criminal responsibility, as will be discussed later. It can be expected that in the future the legal use of PTSD will expand.

WORKER'S COMPENSATION

Worker's compensation, unlike tort litigation, which is an adversarial contest to right a wrong between contestants, is an insurance system to supply security to injured workers to meet their marginal needs during a period of disability. Worker's compensation differs from the conventional damage suit in two important respects: (1) Fault on the part of either employer or employee is eliminated. (2) Compensation is substituted for damages and payable according to a definite schedule based on the type of injury sustained by the worker (Malone 1951). Worker's compensation is a mechanism for providing cash wage benefits and medical care to employees involved in work-related accidents that produce injury. The cost is ultimately placed on the consumer through the medium of insurance premiums, which are passed on in the cost of the product when possible (Larson 1972). Larson (1972) wrote: "Workman's compensation is fundamentally different from tort liability: (1) in its basic test of liability — work connection rather than fault; (2) in its underlying philosophy — social protection rather than righting a wrong; in the nature of the injuries compensated; (3) in the elements of damage; (4) in the defenses available; (5) in the amount of compensation; (6) in the ownership of the award; (7) in the significance of insurance."

History

During the period of the Industrial Revolution, there was a sharp increase in the number of factories along with an abrupt rise of injuries to workers employed in the factory system. Regrettably, there was a simultaneous decrease in the employee's common law remedies for injuries. During the nineteenth century, employees were at a disadvantage because defenses were exclusively products of that period's individualistic common law designed for the protection of an infant industry. The defenses, irreligiously labeled "the unholy trinity," were: contributory negligence; assumption of risks; and the fellow-servant rule in which employers were not responsible for the negligence of an employee that resulted in an injury to another employee. All shared the common characteristic that employees who accepted dangerous employment did so as free agents and were thereafter obliged to watch out for themselves (Malone 1951). Reform to protect an injured employee was obviously in order.

In the nineteenth century, Prussia enacted a law making railroads liable to their employees (as well as passengers) for accidents, excepting acts of God and negligence of the plaintiff. Later, in 1884, the German Reichstag adopted the first modern compensation system, 13 years before England and 25 years before the first U.S. statute (Larson 1972). The original accident insurance law was restricted to a limited number of occupations, such as mining, manufacturing, and transportation; however, coverage was extended several times by amendment, and finally in 1911 it embraced all employment (Bradbury 1917). In Great Britain, Parliament adopted the Workman's Compensation Act in 1897. It differed from the German act by placing the responsibility for compensation exclusively on the shoulders of the employer who was permitted to carry this insurance with private companies. Initially only highly dangerous employment was included in the act; however, various amendments followed, broadening the act to include additional occupations, until in 1980 it was almost universal in scope (Employer's Liability Report 1912). In the United States the state of New York in 1910 passed an act with compulsory coverage of certain hazardous occupations, but this was held unconstitutional by the Court of Appeals in 1911. In 1913, however, New York adopted a constitutional amendment permitting a compulsory law, and it was passed in the same year. By 1920 all but eight states had passed compensation acts, and by 1930 all but four states had adopted worker's compensation statutes. Mississippi, the last state to pass a compensation statute, did so in 1949.

Compensation acts contain a compromise called the Compensation Principle: "The employer gives up the immunity he otherwise would enjoy in cases where he is not at fault, and the employee surrenders his former right to full damages and accepts instead, a more modest claim for bare essentials, represented by compensation" (McCalb 1942). Workers who are suffering from PTSD should be entitled to such benefits.

Five major objectives of a modern worker's compensation program as identified by the National Committee on State Workman's Compensation Laws are: provision of sufficient medical care; accessibility to rehabilitation services; encouragement of safety; prompt and effective system for delivery of benefits; and prompt and effective system for delivery of services (Supplemental Studies 1973). Physicians, including psychiatrists, are involved in four of the five objectives when they provide medical care and educational programs during primary, secondary, and tertiary prevention (Chapter eight).

CRIMINAL RESPONSIBILITY

The M'Naughten Rule

In 1843, amidst the political turmoil of mid-nineteenth century England, a deluded Scotsman named Danny M'Naughten believed that he was being persecuted by the Tories. Acting on this belief, M'Naughten attempted to assassinate the prime minister, Sir Robert Peel, but by mistake killed Peel's personal secretary, Henry Drummond. M'Naughten's trial and subsequent acquittal by reason of insanity aroused Queen Victoria's attention. A few years earlier in 1840, the queen and Prince Albert were almost victims of an assassination by Edward Oxford, who also was acquitted on the grounds of insanity. The two attempted assassinations of important personages of the realm impelled the House of Lords to submit certain questions to the judges of England for a clarification and authoritative statement of the existing law (Glueck 1962). After deliberation, Chief Justice Tindal, speaking for 14 of the 15 judges, enunciated the now-famous M'Naughten Rule (Bromberg 1979):

> "To establish a defense on the ground of insanity, it must be clearly proven that at the time of committing of the act, the party accused was laboring under such a defect of reason, from disease of the mind, as not to know the nature and quality of the act he was doing, or, if he did know it . . . he did not know he was doing what was wrong" (Guttmacher and Weihofen 1952; Davidson 1965).

The insanity defense saved Danny M'Naughten from the gallows and resulted in the rule that bears his name, also called the Right and Wrong Test, but M'Naughten was never again to see the light of day and freedom. In 1843 he was committed to the Bethlehem Hospital and was later transferred to the Broadmoor Asylum where he died in 1865, spending the last 22 years of his life in confinement (Diamond 1956).

The Irresistible Impulse Test

The doctrine of irresistible impulse had some status in English law before it was swept away by M'Naughten. Criticism of the

M'Naughten Rule, especially from the United States, around the narrowness of the concept regarding legal insanity. Cognition, "knowing the difference between right and wrong at the time of committing the act," was the essential element determining criminal responsibility in the M'Naughten Rule (Glueck 1962; Silving 1967). Opponents clamored for a broader definition of insanity to include other facets of mental functioning. Isaac Ray, the leading U.S. forensic psychiatrist, in his famous book *A Treatise on the Medical Jurisprudence of Insanity* (1962) was an outspoken proponent of including the "irresistible impulse" and the concept of moral insanity into rules determining criminal responsibility. In 1886 the state of Alabama first adopted an Irresistible Impulse Rule. And, for the first time in the United States, volitional impairment joined the cognitive defect of M'Naughten as a defense mitigating criminal responsibility. "When the will was dominated by uncontrollable impulses and emotions resulting in a criminal act, the defendant was not responsible for his actions" (Robitscher 1966). An irresistible impulse is not to be confused with "unresisted impulses," where reason is temporarily blinded by anger, jealousy, or other overwhelming passions not the result of a mental condition (Robitscher 1966). The Irresistible Impulse Test expands the M'Naughten Rule, for "the defendant may have known what he was doing and known that it was wrong, but nevertheless may have been unable to resist an overwhelming impulse to commit the crime" (Glueck 1962). The test is included in the American Law Institute (ALI) Standard, as will be discussed later.

The Durham Rule

The seeds for Durham were sown by the New Hampshire Court (State versus Pike 1869) and reaffirmed in State versus Jones (1871). The court, in a decision that stands today, ruled that "if the killing (of Jones' wife) was the offspring or product of mental disease, the defendant should be acquitted." In 1954 Judge David Bazelon of the U.S. Court of Appeals for the District of Columbia Circuit reviewed Durham's conviction for housebreaking (1954). The appeal was based on the claim that the Right and Wrong Rule and the Irresistible Impulse Test should be superseded as obsolete.

Monte Durham was a ne'er-do-well and a psychiatric veteran who, after he was discharged from the U.S. Navy for "profound personality disorder," was arrested and convicted for passing bad checks, theft, and housebreaking. Following the decision that bears his name, Durham was convicted of housebreaking and petty larceny. During hospitalizations he received the following psychiatric diagnoses: "psychosis with psychopathoic personality," "without mental disorder," "psychopathic personality," "schizophrenic reaction, paranoid type, chronic" (Guttmacher and Weihofen 1952).

Judge Bazelon noted that the psychiatric testimony was unequivocal in that Durham was of unsound mind at the time of the crime. The judge concluded that the prevailing tests were not satisfactory criteria for determining criminal responsibility and should therefore be superseded. The Durham Rule that emerged is essentially the same as the New Hampshire Doctrine: "An accused is not criminally responsible if his unlawful act was the product of mental disease or mental defect" (Slovenko 1973). The Durham or Product Rule was never widely adopted by either federal or state courts. In a subsequent decision Judge Bazelon, apparently disenchanted with inadequate psychiatric testimony, in Washington versus the United States (1967) admonished psychiatrists and furnished guidelines and explanatory instructions advising psychiatrists of the kind of information they are expected to provide as expert witnesses.

Rejection of the Durham Rule by most jurisdictions acknowledged the reality that a broad definition of legal insanity would include almost all criminal defendants; and society, psychiatry, and the law were not ready for such an experiment. By 1972 the Court of Appeals, all nine members sitting *en banc*, including Judge Bazelon, voted to reject the Durham Rule in favor of the ALI Standard.

The ALI Test

The ALI Test for criminal responsibility is a combination of the Right-Wrong Rule and an update of the Irresistible Impulse Test. The elements of cognition, volition, and capacity to control behavior are included (Slovenko 1963):

> "A person is not responsible for criminal conduct if at the time of such conduct, as a result of mental disease or defect, he lacks substantial

capacity either to appreciate the criminality of his conduct or to conform his conduct to the requirements of law."

It is noted that the term "mental disease" or "defect" does not include abnormalities of behavior manifested only by repeated criminal or otherwise antisocial conduct. The ALI's model penal code, which was prepared during the years 1952 to 1962, allows improved opportunity for the inclusion of psychiatric testimony while rejecting the Durham concept by excluding abnormalities of behavior manifested only by repeated criminal behavior or antisocial conduct (Silving 1967).

In 1961 Judge Biggs of the U.S. Court of Appeals for the Third Circuit formulated the Currens Test (United States versus Currens 1961), which modified the ALI Rule by eliminating the phrase "either to appreciate the criminality of his conduct or," and adding to the phrase "requirements of law" the words "which he is alleged to have violated." By eliminating the word "appreciate," which emphasizes cognition in the M'Naughten sense, Judge Biggs felt this allowed for all symptoms to be put before the jury. Indeed, Currens, a 22-year-old man convicted of purchasing a car under false pretenses and driving it to a distant state (a violation of the Dyer Act) had been diagnosed as "sociopath with development under stress of schizophrenic signs of the undifferentiated type" (Glueck 1962). In articulating the Currens Test the court was allowing the inclusion of a broader range of psychiatric testimony. Like the Durham Rule, however, it has never gained widespread acceptance.

The ALI Test has become the accepted standard in the federal system and has also been adopted by about one-half of the states. It is considered generally satisfactory as a test for criminal responsibility. In the post-Hinckley era, however, the insanity defense has come under fire, and there are cries for its abolishment or restricted use.

APA Statement on the Insanity Defense

"The first comprehensive position statement on the insanity defense to be developed and adopted by the APA" was published in 1983 (APA 1983). Following the Hinckley verdict, in which the accused attempted assassin of President Reagan was found not guilty by reason of insanity, attention was focused on the wording of the insanity defense, post-trial mechanisms for containing the "insane acquittees," and the effect of abolishing the insanity defense. The APA's position as approved by the Board of Trustees is that "the insanity defense should be retained in some form" and "retention of the insanity defense is essential to the moral integrity of the criminal law."

The APA's insanity defense workgroup then asked and answered certain questions: "Should a guilty but mentally ill verdict be adopted in the law, to either supplement or take the place of the traditional insanity defense?" Correctly, the APA is skeptical about this commonsense solution and states that this is "the easy way out." The net result of such a verdict would be that mentally ill defendants adjudicated guilty would be sent to a prison where no or limited psychiatric treatment exists. The insanity acquittees would no doubt be segregated in maximum security areas of prison, receiving neither psychiatric treatment nor the rights and privileges accorded most other prisoners. Moreover, it is unlikely that the woefully inadequate psychiatric facilities in prisons will get any better. The guilty but mentally ill verdict is an atavism that rejects the idea of humane psychiatric treatment for insanity acquittees. Pointing out that in the state of Michigan where the guilty but mentally ill verdict was first used in the United States, convicted felons with mental disorders received no more treatment than they would have prior to the enactment of the law, the APA workgroup concluded that "such a plea may cause important moral, legal, psychiatric, and pragmatic problems."

In answer to the question "Should the legal standards now in use concerning the insanity defense be modified?" the APA workgroup suggested that the more important question is whether or not judges will allow psychiatrists to testify concerning the broad range of mental functioning that would be relevant for the jury's deliberation. The workgroup added that only serious mental disorders such as psychosis should lead to the exculpation of a defendant, and any revision of the insanity defense should include psychosis as an essential ingredient. Approval, if not endorsement, of Bonnie's (1982, 1983) model statute on the insanity defense coincides with the APA stand that only severe mental disorders be considered in future statutes concerning criminal responsibility.

A person charged with a criminal offense should be found not guilty by reason of insanity if it is shown that as a result of mental disease or mental retardation he was unable to appreciate the wrongfulness of his conduct at the time of the offense.

As used in this standard, the terms mental disease or mental retardation includes only those severely abnormal mental conditions that grossly and demonstrably impair a person's perception or understanding of reality and that are not attributable primarily to the voluntary ingestion of alcohol or other psychoactive substance.

On the question "Should the burden of proof always rest on the prosecution?" the APA is reluctant to take a position. Relating that one-half of the states in all federal courts require that the state bear the burden to prove the defendant sane and the other half of the states and the District of Columbia assign the burden to the defendant to prove insanity, the APA states, "This matter clearly requires further empirical study." As a lawyer once told the author, "The state has all the guns," referring to the power and financial resources of the government and the sometimes pitiful resources of the defendant. There is no question that if the defendant has to prove insanity, the number of successful acquittals on the grounds of insanity will diminish.

The fourth question that the APA workgroup asks and attempts to answer is, "Should psychiatric testimony be limited to statements of mental condition?" Sensitivity to the criticism concerning the "battle of the experts" seems to underlie the cautious answer to this question. The APA is not opposed to legislatures restricting psychiatric testimony about the "ultimate issues," such as whether or not the defendant was, in their judgment, "sane" or "insane," "responsible" or not, etc. The APA agrees that psychiatrists must be permitted to testify about the defendant's psychiatric diagnosis, mental state, and motivation at the time of the alleged criminal act so as to permit the jury or judge to reach the ultimate conclusion about which "they and only they are expert." One would have difficulty in agreeing that the jury members are experts at reaching the ultimate conclusion, but, of course, judge or jury do make the final determination of guilty or not guilty by reason of insanity. The answer to this question seems more a public relations statement designed to eliminate or smooth over widely publicized differences in opinions of expert witnesses. Psychiatrists can and should give their expert opinion (for it is only that) regarding any connection between mental disease or defect and criminal responsibility as defined by the law. Whether this opinion is accepted or rejected is a matter for the fact finder.

The critical question, which has little to do with tests for criminal responsibility or the battle of the experts, is asked last: "What should be done with defendants following not guilty by reason of insanity verdicts?" Everyone knowledgeable about forensic psychiatry would agree that "this is an area for reform. . . ." The APA (1983) suggests the following guidelines for legislation with the disposition of violent insanity acquittees:

> "Special legislation should be designed for those persons charged with violent offenses who have been found 'not guilty by reason of insanity'.
> Confinement and release decisions should be made by a Board constituted to include psychiatrists and other professionals representing the criminal justice system — akin to a parole board.
> Release should be conditional upon having a treatment supervision plan in place with the necessary resources available to implement it.
> The Board having jurisdiction over released insanity acquittees should have clear authority to reconfine.
> When psychiatric treatment within a hospital setting has obtained the maximal treatment benefit possible but the Board believes that for other reasons confinement is still necessary, the insanity acquittee should be transferred to the most appropriate non-hospital facility."

Whether federal and state governments will expend the necessary funds to implement these post-trial recommendations remains to be seen. As pointed out in the APA report, insanity acquittees represent a small portion, less than 1 percent, of all felony cases (Pasewark 1981). In austere financial times, it is doubtful that the needs of such a small group of insanity acquittees will be met. Those who commit crimes and are acquitted on the grounds of insanity draw little sympathy from the public and less attention from politicians who are unlikely to appropriate funds for reform. The argument about the insanity defense goes on, but the means to redress any wrongs or injustices in the system at the post-trial phase will probably go unanswered, unless there is a concerted campaign for reform.

CRIMINAL BEHAVIOR AND PTSD

Ordinarily, persons with a PTSD are in contact with reality and do not display any symptoms of psychosis such as hallucinations or delusions. Pathologic anxiety lies at the core of PTSD; however, some patients, especially those who are subjected to additional stress, develop a transient dissociative reaction with episodes of depersonalization and/or derealization. Most of the time, these feelings of unreality only frighten patients, but in some instances they may result in erratic behavior that may be criminal. The question of criminal responsibility, therefore, is pertinent, as it relates to any criminal acts occurring during a dissociative reaction. Since a person may not be responsible for criminal conduct during a dissociative reaction, an elaboration and description of the reaction is in order.

Dissociative Reaction — Depersonalization/Derealization

According to the *DSM-III* (1980), "the symptoms of depersonalization involve an alteration in the perception or experience of the self so that the usual sense of one's own reality is temporarily lost or changed." During periods of depersonalization, patients often report that they feel like spectators and look at various parts of their body as if they belong to someone else. The sensation of self-estrangement makes patients feel "mechanical" and not in complete control of their actions. During periods of derealization, which may occur independently of or be associated with depersonalization, patients relate that their external environment looks strange, different, unusual, and unreal. Sensory awareness can be heightened or dimmed, and there may be a perceived change in the size or shapes of objects in the surroundings. People in the immediate environment look different and may be perceived as dead or mechanical. During these periods of unreality, the onset of which is rapid and the subsidence more gradual, persons can become extremely fearful and agitated. In addition, patients often report a disturbance of the subjective sense of time and difficulties or slowness in recall.

Whenever pathologic anxiety reaches Levels 4 or 5, and especially if the heightened anxiety is maintained, persons may have a dissociative reaction and experience feelings of unreality —

depersonalization/derealization. Persons with PTSD may experience such a response during Stage I, the time of the traumatic incident, or more commonly, following impact, Stages II and III. Victims may feel they are going insane or out of control and begin to act strangely or bizarrely. The onset occurs quickly, frightening the patient; however, gradually the feelings of unreality diminish in intensity and eventually disappear altogether. The entire experience may linger in the mind of the PTSD patient, who wonders about its significance and the possibility of a recurrence. Generally, patients report that they were "stunned" or "in shock" and may or may not attribute the altered feeling state to the original trauma.

The level of anxiety that a person experiences in Stages II and III of PTSD depends upon life circumstances, coping skills, and therapeutic interventions. When pathologic anxiety is high (Levels 3 or 4), patients are extremely vulnerable to environmental stressors, related or unrelated to the original trauma. It is at these times that anxiety can escalate and patients may experience a dissociative episode.

A search for the sources of anxiety — the Three E's — will reveal the stimuli responsible for the dissociative state. At times, obsessive concern about the trauma and preoccupation with somatic symptoms are sufficient explanations for heightened anxiety. More often, however, environmental events play a significant role in raising anxiety to the point that the patient experiences a dissociative reaction. Family disputes, interpersonal conflicts, unemployment, financial worries, and a host of other problems mentioned in Chapters three and four can fuel pathologic anxiety, predisposing a person to the development of a dissociative reaction.

In the chronic stage of PTSD, patients are vulnerable to episodes of depersonalization/derealization because they are continuously anxious, depressed, and fatigued. In the *DSM-III* (1980) are listed the predisposing factors for depersonalization, a form of Dissociative Disorder: "fatigue, recovery from substance intoxication, hypnosis, meditation, physical pain, anxiety, depression, and severe stress such as military combat or an automobile accident." It is evident that many of the predisposing factors listed are to be found in Chronic PTSD patients.

A dissociative reaction with feelings of unreality may also be present in Schizophrenia, Affective Disorders, Organic Mental Disorders (especially intoxication or withdrawal), epilepsy, and Depersonalization Disorder, a form of Dissociative Disorder not associated with PTSD. It is possible for PTSD to coexist with another mental (Sierles et al. 1983) or neurologic disorder such as those mentioned previously, and in these cases, the more severe psychiatric disorder or epilepsy is more likely to be the primary cause of the dissociative reaction.

THE CRIMINAL PROCESS AND PTSD

From the time of arrest, a mentally disordered defendant charged with a criminal offense passes through various stages of the criminal process. Beginning with the pretrial stage, hearings are conducted to ascertain the defendant's mental competency to stand trial. A determination of criminal responsibility takes place during the trial, the most dramatic stage during which the "battle between the experts" receives much attention and widespread publicity. Disposition of the accused following acquittal on the grounds of insanity, the post-trial phase, is anticlimatic and relatively invisible, although it is the most important step of the legal process. When insanity is raised as a criminal defense, the law provides different procedures for the pretrial, trial, and post-trial stages of criminal procedure, and different issues confront lawyers, mental health professionals, and the court.

The Pretrial Stage

When the plea of not guilty because of insanity is raised by the defendant's attorney, a sanity commission, consisting of two or more physicians (usually psychiatrists), is convened to determine the accused's present mental capacity to proceed. The mental examination focuses on two questions: Does the defendant understand the proceedings against him? Can the defendant cooperate and communicate with the attorney during the preparation of the case (Scrignar 1967a)? The determination of a defendant's mental competency to stand trial thus depends upon his or her cognitive intactness and communicative ability. This is as it should be, because defendants certainly cannot properly defend themselves if they do not understand the proceedings against them or cannot communicate and cooperate with legal counsel in the preparation of their case.

When it is pleaded that a defendant was suffering from a PTSD and was experiencing a loss of reality at the time the criminal act was committed, a sanity commission is generally convened to determine the accused's current mental status. Unless the defendant is experiencing a dissociative reaction — episode of depersonalization or derealization — at the time of the mental status examination the accused is likely to be found mentally competent to stand trial. No cognitive impairment or loss of ability to cooperate and communicate with an attorney will be discovered. Defendants will look "near-normal"; however, a thorough mental status examination will reveal symptoms of pathologic anxiety and probably depression together with other signs and symptoms mentioned in Chapter four. After a judicial hearing, it can be expected that most defendants diagnosed with PTSD will be remanded for trial.

The Trial Stage — The ALI Test and PTSD

For the purpose of this discussion, the ALI Test will serve as the standard for criminal responsibility because it includes components of the Right and Wrong and Irresistible Impulse Tests. The federal courts and about one-half of the states embrace the ALI Test, one-third of state jurisdictions endorse the M'Naughten Rule, and six states include a variation of the Irresistible Impulse Test. The question to be addressed during the trial stage is: At the time of the alleged criminal conduct, as a result of mental disease or defect, did the defendant lack substantial capacity either to appreciate the criminality of his conduct or to conform his conduct to the requirements of law? PTSD is certainly a mental disease or defect. During a dissociative reaction, persons do lack "substantial capacity either to appreciate the criminality of their conduct or to conform their conduct to the requirements of law." Furthermore, PTSD is a clinical entity that ordinarily does not include abnormalities of behavior manifested by repeated criminal or otherwise antisocial conduct. Cognition and volition are impaired during the dissociative episode involving a temporary loss of reality, and defendants at this time lack substantial capacity to appreciate (know, understand) the criminality of their conduct and to conform their conduct (control impulses) to the requirements of law. It would therefore seem evident that PTSD would be an acceptable defense in a criminal trial, utilizing the ALI Standard.

During the trial, the defense attorney must first establish that prior to a trauma, the defendant manifested no signs or symptoms characteristic of a PTSD and, ideally, demonstrated no evidence of treatment for a mental disorder. The trauma and its effects should be elaborated in detail, so that the jury understands and identifies with the defendant's state of mind at that time. The expert witness explains the defendant's PTSD, emphasizing how a dissociative reaction interferes with the perception of reality. Next, a connection must be established between the patient's PTSD and mental state at the time of the "alleged" criminal act. Any similarity between the traumatic scene and the scene of the crime helps to explain a flashback and a dissociative episode during which an irrational criminal act may have been committed. Finally, the expert witness concludes testimony by offering an opinion of the defendant's mental state at the time of the alleged criminal conduct in accordance with the court's rules relating to criminal responsibility.

Historically, questions arise regarding the appropriateness of utilizing PTSD as an insanity defense. The insanity defense originally evolved to deal humanely with homicidal psychotic defendants, so deranged that, "like children," they should be protected from the usual penalties imposed by law. A successful plea of not guilty by reason of insanity meant for these defendants charged with murder that the death penalty would not be imposed, and the "acquitted" defendant would be remanded to a state hospital for treatment rather than to a prison for punishment. Release from a medical setting could be obtained only when it was determined that, following treatment, the insanity acquittee was a danger neither to self nor to society.

The popularity of PTSD as an insanity defense will probably grow. Two cases involving Vietnam-era veterans accused of committing violent acts (State versus Heads 1981; People versus Wood 1982) utilized PTSD as an insanity defense and have been adjudicated successfully. Generally during a criminal trial, two stories are told to the jury regarding the defendant's past life, circumstances of the crime, the defendant's motivation, and, in insanity defenses, the state of mind of the defendant at the time of the alleged criminal conduct. The ultimate issues of guilt or innocence, responsibility or irresponsibility, are determined by the fact finders, the judge or jury. Too often the public assumes that the mental health professional, who is only a participant in the criminal process, makes the ultimate decision of not guilty by reason of insanity. The post-Hinckley antipsychiatric clamor for the abolishment of the insanity defense will die down with time. Thoughtful people will realize that the insanity defense is utilized by only a small number of criminal defendants and represents a token to rational humanity in the criminal justice system.

The Post-Trial Stage

The undercurrent that covertly permeates all aspects of the trial is the disposition of defendants who are adjudicated not guilty by reason of insanity. Upon acquittal on the grounds of insanity, the public has visions of a maniacal ogre being released from prison to feed on hapless citizens. In most cases following an adjudication of not guilty by reason of insanity, the acquitted person is committed to a mental hospital for further evaluation and treatment (Scrignar 1971). Incarceration may last for a lifetime, as in the case of Daniel M'Naughten, or until hospital physicians and the court are convinced that the mentally disordered insanity acquittee has recovered and is not a danger to self or society. The determination of dangerousness is difficult, and insanity acquittees involved in acts of violence pose a special problem for the predictive powers of mental health professionals. Predicting future dangerousness becomes more complicated when insanity acquittees require ongoing psychopharmacologic treatment (Scrignar 1967b). The question of who is going to take responsibility for the future behavior of an individual adjudicated not guilty by reason of insanity arises. Certainly not the prosecutor, defense attorney, or even the "expert witnesses," all of whom usually bow out after the trial has been concluded. Judges have legal authority to commit the insanity acquittee to a maximum security hospital or a similar facility, but once this is done, they retire to their chambers. During the post-trial stage, the burden falls on the physicians and staff of hospitals designated to accept such acquittees. Clearly, in the past, this has not been an entirely satisfactory procedure.

The APA in its statement on the insanity defense (1983) recognizes the importance of the post-trial stage, especially in reference to violent insanity acquittees. The APA has recommended that special legislation should constitute a board to include psychiatrists and other professionals representing the criminal justice system with the authority to confine, release, and reconfine insanity acquittees. Not mentioned in the APA report, but implied, is that the legislature should also appropriate funds for the administration and implementation of such a system. The best interests of the individual and society are served when the law and the behavioral sciences work together during the post-trial stage of the legal process.

A challenge confronts the court and mental health professionals who have the responsibility for supervising and treating PTSD insanity acquittees. These acquittees are not as seriously ill as persons suffering from psychosis. Pathologic anxiety and dissociative episodes can usually be treated in a relatively short period of time. Hospital treatment may not be required; however, in lieu of alternative treatment systems, it can be expected that most PTSD acquittees will be committed to a maximum security hospital for further observation. Even though PTSD is not a severe psychiatric disorder, certain precautions regarding confinement, release, supervision, and treatment should be taken, especially in the case of violent acquittees. As patients move from the inpatient to the outpatient phase, the coordination of supervision and treatment is absolutely essential. Periodic reports to the court regarding the PTSD acquittee's progress and compliance with treatment should be mandatory. The involvement of a multidisciplinary board to review all cases at designated intervals ensures that the best interests of the individual and society are served. Such a system can provide better supervision than most probation and parole agencies and better ongoing treatment than most mental health clinics. Ironically, PTSD may serve as the impetus for reform within the criminal justice system for a long-neglected group, the insanity acquittees.

PSYCHIATRIC EVALUATION

Whether used during civil or criminal proceedings or solely for treatment purposes, a psychiatric evaluation must take into consideration the patient's pretraumatic history, response to trauma, and adaptation following trauma. When the three periods — pretraumatic, traumatic, and post-traumatic — are compared and contrasted, the effects of trauma are more readily apparent. The information upon which a psychiatric evaluation is based and from which conclusions are drawn should include, whenever possible, data from sources other than the identified patient. Too often, clinicians fail to verify information by interviewing persons other than the patient and reviewing pertinent records. During legal proceedings, lawyers properly pounce on those clinicians with unsubstantiated opinions. Even when litigation is not pending, a well-documented history of the present illness and past history lead to a better organized and more effective treatment program.

Spouses and other family members should always be interviewed, because persons closest to the patient before and after the trauma shed light on symptoms and pathologic behavior. If the circumstances require it, interviews with friends, fellow workers, and employers may clarify and verify certain aspects of the patient's history. The patient's past medical history, particularly previous psychiatric treatment, gives clues to past physical and psychological health (Volle 1975). The patient's account is usually accurate, but it is desirable to obtain previous medical records, especially if litigation is pending. Other records that can be obtained and that will give some indication of a patient's pretraumatic personality include: report cards from school, diplomas, employment records, military service files, police and arrest records, and documentation regarding previous litigation.

A complete psychiatric evaluation includes pretraumatic, traumatic, and post-traumatic history.

Pretraumatic History

Educational history: The highest level of education attained and all trade schools, vocational schools, night schools, or technical courses attended are listed. If the patient is a student, report cards should be obtained and grades prior to and after the traumatic incident compared.

History of employment: A chronologic list of all jobs held by the patient with length of employment and reasons for change of employment is recorded.

Military service: When the patient had been in the military, the branch of service, length of service, highest rank achieved, rank at discharge, and type of discharge (e.g., honorable, medical discharge under honorable circumstances, general discharge, or dishonorable discharge) are stated. If the patient's total time spent in the military service is not commensurate with usual terms of 2, 3, or 4 years, specific questions should be asked regarding reasons for an early discharge. In the case of Vietnam-era veterans being evaluated for disability or who are involved in civil or criminal actions, a more extensive evaluation of service in the military is necessary (Lipkin et al. 1983).

History of antisocial behavior: Any history of delinquent or criminal behavior is listed here. Questions concerning arrests by the police for any offense, minor or major, as a juvenile or adult, with reference to adjudication and final disposition are documented when possible by police records. Traffic offenses except for driving while intoxicated can be excluded. The patient's police record prior to and following the traumatic incident should be compared.

History of previous litigation: A history of a worker's compensation claim or personal injury litigation should be listed and verified if possible. The results of the litigation, the amount of award, and whether the suit was settled in or out of court should be described. The patient's physical and mental state prior to and following the litigation can be included.

Medical history: The patient's medical history prior to the trauma is chronicled. Previous hospitalizations, surgery, and medical treatment for all illnesses are briefly listed. Specific questions concerning involvement in accidents are asked. Patients are requested to make a general statement of their state of health prior to the trauma (e.g., health was excellent, good, fair, or poor).

Previous psychiatric treatment: History of treatment either in a hospital or as an outpatient by a psychiatrist, psychologist, social worker, or counselor with dates and results is included. Specific questions about treatment received from the family doctor for "nervous trouble" or illnesses associated with stress help clarify the patient's pretraumatic mental status.

Substance use: A list of all prescribed medications, the dosage, frequency, and therapeutic response, both pre- and post-trauma, is included here. Questions concerning illicit drug use and alcohol consumption should also be asked. Evidence of Substance Use

Disorder before and after the trauma is documented whenever possible.

Family history: A brief survey of the physical and mental health of the patient's parents is taken. Specific questions concerning anxiety-related illnesses are asked. Some statement regarding the atmosphere of the home should also be included. If the parents are deceased, the reason for death is noted. The general state of health with an emphasis on anxiety-related illnesses of all siblings is listed.

Marital history: The duration of marriage, number of children, and a brief statement from the patient regarding marital satisfaction, including sexual functioning before and after the trauma are examined. An interview with the spouse should be conducted to corroborate the patient's impressions. The number of children, previous marriages, and reasons for separation or divorce are enumerated.

History of the Trauma

Impact: Details concerning the patient's perception of and reaction to the trauma must be obtained. Patients are usually extremely conscious and hyperaware of impending danger and will often report that they remember the trauma as if "it were in slow motion." Because it is anxiety evoking, patients at times are reluctant to talk about their trauma in detail; therefore, when taking a history, sensitivity is required on the part of the clinician.

Impact: The patient's self-talk just before impact is especially important. Often patients will remember thoughts that they were going to die or be seriously injured. Thoughts occurring at the time of the trauma often become intrusive following the trauma and are a source of pathologic anxiety.

Visual images related to the trauma: Various elements of the traumatic scene become firmly etched on the mind of the patient. When these scenes are replayed in the mind, like a video tape, retraumatization occurs. How the traumatic scene is imprinted upon the mind may be of importance regarding subsequent behavior.

Autonomic nervous system reaction: Symptoms of tachycardia, palpitations, tightness of the chest, and difficulties in breathing manifest themselves at the time of the trauma. Immediately afterward, patients frequently report trembling of their entire body, nausea, at times vomiting, unsteadiness of gait, profuse sweating, and a "feeling of shock." Unless asked specifically, patients will often gloss over these symptoms, sometimes feeling ashamed of the gross manifestations of fear.

Physical symptoms: The absence or presence of pain or physical discomfort should be recorded. The patient's perception of the seriousness of the injury at the time of the trauma and afterward can be compared with the results of subsequent physical examinations.

Post-Traumatic History

Immediately after the trauma: Patients' access to assistance determines the amount of time they are in acute distress. During war trauma, natural disasters, incarceration as a prisoner, or systematic torture help may not be forthcoming and stress is prolonged. More common, following an accident patients are often taken to the emergency room of a hospital or go home. If the patient receives an examination for treatment in a hospital, the history should be corroborated by hospital records. It is important to secure from patients an account of what they thought was wrong with them and what the physicians at the hospital told them. If, after examination, the patient was sent home, questions should be asked regarding the prescription of medications and recommendations they received from the emergency room physician.

The immediate post-traumatic period: The patient's response to trauma during the first several weeks should be determined. Questions concerning sleep disturbance, nightmares, intrusive memories and ruminations about the trauma, anxiety symptoms, and physical discomfort or pain should be asked. Analgesics, sedatives, and antianxiety agents can chemically diminish pain, induce sleep, and ameliorate anxiety; these effects must be taken into consideration during the evaluation.

Treatment immediately following the trauma: If the patient was hospitalized, medical records will indicate the results of examinations and nature of treatment rendered. The dates and reasons for outpatient treatment will also be reflected in medical records, but should be part of the patient's history. The patient's response to treatment should be briefly but comprehensively stated.

All medical treatment prior to the psychiatric/psychological consultation: Chronologic documentation of all treatment received from the time of the trauma to the present places into perspective the course of the patient's illness. The patient should always be asked to assess the results of all treatment and to answer the question, "What do you think is wrong with you?" At times it may be necessary to consult with the patient's physicians, especially if there is some doubt relating to organicity.

Mental Status Examination

The patient's general appearance, stream of speech, content of thought, and sensorium are evaluated in the context of pretraumatic, traumatic, and post-traumatic events. Symptoms and behavior changes occurring post-traumatically are assessed in terms of a Stress Disorder. The ASP and SIC assist in determining the effect of the trauma upon the current functioning of the patient. Interviews with other persons and all available records are considered before a final diagnosis is made and a conclusive opinion rendered.

Personal injury: The temporal relationship between the trauma and psychiatric disorder, as it relates to cause, is determined. The degree of disability and prognosis are compensable and therefore are of great importance in issues of tort. The clinician must estimate the length and the cost of future treatment and specify the impairment believed to have resulted from the Stress Disorder.

Worker's compensation: The relatedness of the trauma to the psychiatric disorder and current ability to work are important issues. If the person involved in a work-related accident is disabled, an opinion regarding prognosis with recommendations related to treatment and rehabilitation is given.

Criminal responsibility: When the insanity defense is used in criminal trials, the issue of criminal responsibility revolves around the defendant's state of mind at the time of the alleged criminal act. First, it must be demonstrated that a trauma precipitated a PTSD. Second, an additional link must be established to show that the PTSD negated criminal responsibility (Raifman 1983).

FORENSIC ISSUES DURING THE TRIAL

In the author's experience, a concise, well-written psychiatric report clearly concluding that the trauma did or did not result in a PTSD and that if present, the PTSD resulted in impairment of the individual is sufficient in most cases for plaintiff and defense attorney to arbitrate personal injury suits or worker's compensation claims. In civil cases, sometimes depositions are requested when either the defense or the plaintiff attorney requires additional information or clarification of the psychiatric report. If, after the deposition, arbitration does not lead to settlement of the case of claim, the psychiatrist or psychologist is subpoenaed to testify as an expert witness in court or at a hearing.

In criminal cases a well-reasoned psychiatric or psychological report can assist the district attorney, defense attorney, and judge during pretrial discussions when post-trial issues are arbitrated. Mental health professionals can participate in informal hearings in the judge's chambers where the defendant's mental disorder can be discussed. The issues of PTSD, criminal conduct, treatment, prognosis, and what is best for the defendant and for society can be addressed. If the case goes to trial, the psychiatrist or psychologist testifies as an expert witness to explain PTSD or its absence to the court and to render an opinion regarding criminal responsibility.

Civil Law

During a trial plaintiff and defense attorneys in the adversarial atmosphere of the courtroom attempt to prove opposite points of view. The attorneys will marshal psychiatric testimony to support their different positions. It is important for clinicians to understand the opposing viewpoints of the plaintiff and defense attorneys in order to participate in a meaningful manner. Pallid and ambiguous conclusions do little to assist in the legal process. Based upon the available evidence, past medical records, psychiatric evaluation, current mental status examination, and information from other sources, the clinician should be able to state an opinion regarding diagnosis and, if indicated, prognosis and treatment.

Plaintiff's Position

The attorney for the plaintiff will attempt to prove that a trauma took place and was responsible for the production of an officially recognized psychiatric disorder — PTSD. The plaintiff's attorney will utilize the testimony of mental health professionals first to educate the judge and jury about PTSD and second to establish the relationship between the trauma and the PTSD. The degree of disability imposed by the PTSD and requirements for future treatment are issues of vital importance. The following are a list of questions likely to be asked by a plaintiff's attorney of an expert witness:

Qualification as an expert witness: "Please state your name, educational background, professional experience, specialty, board certification, academic appointments, publications, and memberships in organizations, and indicate whether you have ever been qualified as an expert witness in a court of law."

Have you ever had occasion to examine the plaintiff?: "Please state the dates of all examinations and/or treatment. Please indicate all sources of information upon which you have based your expert opinion, including interviews of all persons other than the plaintiff and all records and reports that you have reviewed."

Please state the results of your findings: The history is related in a chronologic sequence. As has been suggested by Erlinder (1983b), a framework for explaining the diagnosis of PTSD requires close examination of three well-defined time periods: the time period preceding the traumatic event; the traumatic event itself; and the time period following the traumatic event in which behavioral changes can be observed. When the history of the traumatic event is described, special emphasis is placed on the patient's psychophysiological reactions moments before, during, and immediately after impact. All symptoms occurring at these times are enumerated and their significance described. The results of all examinations, tests, and laboratory findings are summarized.

An analysis of interviews and a summary of reports and records that have been reviewed are presented. A simple declarative sentence concluding whether the trauma did or did not precipitate a psychiatric disorder — PTSD — ends this part of the testimony.

What is a PTSD?: During the explanation of PTSD, the plaintiff's history is utilized to illustrate the onset and persistence of symptoms. In this manner the judge and jury can be cogently educated about PTSD as it relates directly to the plaintiff. Concepts of the Three E's, retraumatization, and Spiral Effect can best be explained by utilizing visual aids or a blackboard. The question of how symptoms of a PTSD can be maintained long after the trauma has occurred can be easily illustrated and answered by using a chart similar to that in Figure 2-1. An environmental event initiates the Stress Disorder, the judge and jury are told, but encephalic events that result in future retraumatization sustain pathologic anxiety and the disorder. The accident is recorded in the mind like an image on a video tape, which can be replayed time and time again, eliciting similar or sometimes more intense emotional reactions than those that occurred at the time of the trauma. A judge and jury easily understand this analogy, which can be further compared to those thoughts of a malingerer who has no mental video tape of a trauma, but instead dreams of acquiring wealth, property, or personal advantage. When physical symptoms are present, the same chart can be used to illustrate the Spiral Effect. It is explained that somatic symptoms activate mental images of the trauma, thus stimulating more pathologic anxiety, which in turn intensifies physical symptoms, producing a self-perpetuating cycle and the Spiral Effect. The Spiral Effect chart (Figure 2-1) can be used to explain how environmental events similar or identical to those present at the time of the trauma can also stimulate encephalic activity, causing retraumatization and increased anxiety.

What is the relationship of the plaintiff's PTSD to the trauma?: Using visual aids whenever possible, the expert should go through a step-by-step reenactment of the effect of the trauma upon the plaintiff. Ideally, a graphic description of the trauma and its aftermath attempts to put the jury into the shoes of the plaintiff, thus allowing identification to take place.

How is a PTSD treated?: A brief summary of the treatment principles and concepts mentioned in Chapter six is usually more than judge and jury would like to hear.

How long will the plaintiff require treatment?: This is a difficult question to answer. After making an evaluation of the plaintiff's mental status and evaluating strengths and weaknesses, an informed guess is all that can be expected. If the plaintiff is still symptomatic at the time of the trial or hearing, it is important to state that cure does not follow adjudication, and treatment following judicial disposition will be needed. The question concerning length of treatment has monetary significance, since this fact will be taken into consideration if damages are awarded to the plaintiff. Thus, the expert witness must state a definite length of time and translate this into a sum of money. In the experience of the author, it is best to state a minimum and maximum time required for treatment and a range of medical costs.

Does the plaintiff's PTSD prevent him or her from working?: The plaintiff's job and the skills required to perform his or her employment together with the severity of the PTSD determine the answer to this question. If the accident was work related, the plaintiff may have developed a phobia of the work premises and cannot return to work until proper treatment, involving systematic desensitization, has been rendered. The issue of work is especially important in worker's compensation cases.

How has the trauma and subsequent PTSD affected the plaintiff's life?: To what extent is the plaintiff currently impaired? This can be answered by pointing out any difficulties the plaintiff is having in family relationships, marital life including sexual functioning, interpersonal relationships, social/recreational activities, financial matters, employment and any deficit of behavior attributable to the trauma. This question addresses any impairment the plaintiff may have experienced as a result of the trauma and hence has importance in the awarding of damages.

Do you feel that the plaintiff is malingering?: The question of Malingering is always an issue whenever a diagnosis of PTSD is made, especially in the absence of any objective physical findings. Most plaintiffs' attorneys feel that the question of Malingering is best brought up during direct examination, anticipating similar questions during cross-examination.

Again, will you please tell the jury what the relationship was between the trauma and the plaintiff's psychiatric disorder — the PTSD?: At the end of direct examination, most plaintiffs' attorneys ask the expert witness to reiterate his or her conclusions regarding the relationship between the trauma and the PTSD.

The Defense Position

The objective of the defense attorney is to portray the plaintiff as a malingerer or to demonstrate that if any psychiatric disorder exists, it was present before the traumatic incident. From the standpoint of the defense, the veracity of the plaintiff and the competence of the expert witness are at issue. When attempts to arbitrate fail and a tort action comes to trial, there are usually legitimate differences between the opposing sides. The defense usually has expert witnesses to counter the plaintiff's psychiatrists or psychologists, and the scene is set for the "battle of the experts." During cross-examination of the plaintiff's expert witness, the following are likely to be asked:

Assault of credentials: The defense attorney probes into the professional background of the plaintiff's expert witness, attempting to find weaknesses that may undermine the credibility and confidence of the mental health professional. Expert witnesses who have limited experience in the courtroom may be vulnerable to such an attack. Those professionals, unaccustomed to being challenged, may become angry and defensive, thereby weakening the effect of their testimony. The establishment of a witness as an expert takes place before any testimony prior to direct examination.

Upon what do you base your diagnosis?: This is a good question, especially if the expert witness has based his or her opinion only on information provided by the plaintiff. A prepared expert witness will answer this by stating the number of hours spent interviewing and evaluating the plaintiff, the spouse, and other relatives or friends, and review all reports and records that have been used to formulate an opinion. When the expert witness is not sufficiently prepared and has not based his or her testimony on a broad base of data, the second question is already formulated for the defense attorney.

Isn't it true, doctor, that all or most of your testimony merely restates what the plaintiff has told you?: On one occasion, while testifying in federal court, the author answered this question in mock indignation with another question: "What do you think I am, a Xerox machine?" The question can be better answered by restating all of the elements that went into the conclusion and opinion. To a psychiatrist or psychologist, a mental status examination is equivalent to the physical examination of an internist. Experience and judgment, as in a good physical examination, are required to evaluate a patient's history and mental processes. No objective tests are available at present to conclusively support a diagnosis of PTSD; however, behavior can be observed and evaluated by the mental health professional and others. PTSD, unlike many mental disorders that are explained by invisible intrapsychic conflicts, is precipitated by an observable environmental event, and many of the signs and symptoms can be observed and validated (Erlinder 1983b). Sometimes defense attorneys attempting to demonstrate that psychiatric testimony is nonscientific and a lot of "guess work" will ask several questions about subjectivity. The best policy is to answer all of these questions politely and calmly, emphasizing whenever possible that PTSD is a mental disorder recognized by the APA in its *DSM* (1980) and that the plaintiff fulfills the essential criteria for the disorder.

What is malingering?: Familiarity with the characteristics of Malingering, Antisocial Personality Disorder, and Factitious Disorder is required when answering this question (Chapter five).

How do you know that the plaintiff is not a malingerer?: In all honesty one can never be 100 percent sure that a patient is or is not malingering. However, based upon the expert's clinical experience, a definite opinion can be rendered regarding the plaintiff's credibility. Most plaintiffs will have a tendency to exaggerate symptoms, but such hyperbole is not tantamount to Malingering. When the patient has a past history of antisocial behavior though not necessarily an Antisocial Personality Disorder, this unquestionably weakens the plaintiff's case. Depending upon the proclivities of the defense attorney, a series of questions may be asked about Malingering, all designed to cast doubt upon the credibility of the plaintiff as well as the testimony of the expert witness.

Are some persons predisposed to a PTSD?: Although most behavioral scientists who are involved in personal injury cases feel that this is so, no carefully controlled scientific study has ever been conducted to establish this (Chapter three). It is a moot point as far as the law is concerned, for the defense "takes the victim as he finds him." The defense attorney, however, may attempt to demonstrate that the plaintiff's psychiatric disorder was a preexisting condition and has little or nothing to do with the alleged trauma.

Previous history of mental disorder: When the plaintiff has a past history of treatment for a mental disorder, the following questions are likely to be asked: "What is the relationship between the patient's previous mental disorder and current mental status?" "Is the plaintiff's current mental status an extension of a previously diagnosed mental disorder?" "If the plaintiff did not have a previous mental disorder, would a PTSD have developed?" When issues of predisposition or prior mental disorder are raised, and the plaintiff has developed a PTSD after a trauma, the appearance of the characteristic signs and symptoms of a PTSD post-traumatically with no evidence of these symptoms pretraumatically clearly defines the relationship between trauma and subsequent symptoms. The absence of nightmares, intrusive memories, flashbacks, etc. pretraumatically and their appearance only after exposure to a well-defined trauma makes mute the argument that the disorder predated the trauma.

What is a "normal" person's response to trauma?: Referral to Stage I — response to trauma — as described in Chapters three and four answers this question.

Tangential information: The defense attorney may ask a series of short precise questions relating to tangential findings in the mental status examination: "Is the plaintiff in good contact with reality?" "Is the plaintiff psychotic?" "Is the plaintiff delusional?" "Has the patient ever hallucinated?" "Is the plaintiff well oriented?" "Is the plaintiff's intelligence within normal limits?" "Does the plaintiff have any objective evidence of brain damage?" These questions are answered briefly, usually with a "yes" or "no."

Bias of the expert: The defense may ask questions aimed at uncovering the bias of the expert witness: "When testifying as an expert witness in the past, what percentage of the time did you testify in favor of the plaintiff; what percentage in favor of the defense?" "During the last several years, how many clients have you examined for the plaintiff's attorney?" "What is your fee for testifying as an expert witness and who is paying your fee?" These questions should be answered dispassionately and briefly.

Detracting tactics: The defense may ask a series of questions related to psychiatry, psychology, mental disorders, and PTSD, which are intended to demonstrate to judge and jury that psychiatry is unscientific, imprecise, and just short of "witchcraft." This tactic can backfire if the defense attorney is not well versed in concepts, nomenclature, and terminology of psychiatry, psychology, and mental disorders.

Criminal Law

PTSD is relatively new as an insanity defense and the "case law" is limited. Defenses based on PTSD have been advanced in cases ranging from murder, attempted murder, assault including rape, and weapon offenses to nonviolent crimes such as burglary, robbery, drug conspiracies, and tax fraud (Erlinder 1983a).

Murder, Attempted Murder, and PTSD

A Louisiana case involving a defendant charged with murder (State versus Heads 1981) was the first in which PTSD and the insanity defense were used successfully during a jury trial.

> Mr. Heads, estranged from his wife, broke into his sister-in-law's house, brandishing and firing a pistol. After running out of ammunition, Mr. Heads got a rifle from his car and resumed firing. One shot struck and killed his sister-in-law's husband. Mr. Heads was arrested, tried, and found guilty of murder in 1978 and was sentenced to life imprisonment. Through a series of appeals not related to PTSD, Heads was retried in October 1981. By this time, the APA officially recognized PTSD as a diagnostic category. Head's attorney explained his client's behavior on the basis of a PTSD related to his combat experiences in Vietnam. The Vietnam veteran was found not guilty because of insanity.

A 1982 case, People versus Wood (1982), also utilized PTSD and the insanity defense.

Mr. Wood, a Vietnam-era veteran, attempted to murder his foreman following a dispute at work. In an ingenious and meticulously prepared presentation, Wood's attorney demonstrated to a jury that his client's conduct was related to combat experiences in Vietnam and was the result of PTSD. After an adjudication of not guilty by reason of insanity, it was determined at a post-trial commitment hearing that Mr. Wood was not dangerous at the time of the hearing and would not be dangerous in the future. He was released to receive outpatient treatment supervised by the court.

The two cases shared the following characteristics: (1) Both Heads and Wood were Vietnam-era veterans; (2) Except for the conduct that led to the criminal charges, both had little or no involvement with the law; (3) PTSD and the insanity defense were argued before a jury; (4) Both men were found not guilty by reason of insanity. Unlike Heads, Wood did not testify at the trial, and he was released following trial with the proviso of court-supervised outpatient treatment.

Rape and PTSD

The presence of PTSD in a victim claiming sexual assault has been used by prosecuting attorneys to bolster their cases. In a Kansas case (State versus Marks 1982), the defense asserted that sexual relations were consensual, whereas the woman contended that she was raped. There were no eye witnesses, and evidence rested on the credibility of the complainant and defendant. During the trial a mental health professional testified that the woman suffered from a Rape Trauma Syndrome (PTSD) that indicated that a forcible assault had indeed taken place. The judge allowed the testimony, stating that it was relevant when the defendant argued that the victim consented to sexual intercourse, and as such the expert witness' opinion did not invade the providence of the jury. On appeal the State Supreme Court upheld the lower court's ruling that allowed the expert to testify. In a case with the opposite outcome (Minnesota versus Saldana 1982), the State Supreme Court overturned the conviction of a defendant accused of rape because an expert witness testified that the complainant suffered from a Rape Trauma Syndrome (PTSD). The expert testimony was rejected because it "does not assist a jury in its fact finding function," and "may not be introduced until further evidence of the scientific accuracy and reliability of the syndrome can be established." A new trial in which the expert would not be allowed to testify was ordered. There is no doubt that in the future, expert testimony concerning rape and PTSD will become more common and acceptable to the court (Burgess 1983). It will not be surprising if some women who have been raped in the past and have subsequently been charged with committing a criminal act will plead insanity related to a Rape Trauma Syndrome (PTSD).

Assault, Self-Defense, and PTSD

Battered women who kill abusing spouses may attempt to plead insanity, diminished responsibility, or self-defense based on PTSD to explain their actions (Raifman 1983). It is possible for any person who has been exposed to a trauma and developed a PTSD to claim a connection between altered mental functioning and criminal conduct. Paradoxically, many view PTSD sufferers such as Vietnam-era veterans as dangerous and hence claim that homicide in self-defense against the PTSD sufferer would be justifiable. The vicissitudes of PTSD and the law seem bound only by the imagination of attorneys, but common sense and the restraint of a judge and jury usually prevail and will determine the limits of PTSD and the criminal law.

The Defendant's Position

When PTSD is used in the insanity defense, the defendant's attorney proceeds much in the same fashion as in a personal injury suit. The emphasis and objective are, of course, different — awarding of damages in a personal injury suit and acquittal of the client in a criminal proceeding. The dilemma facing the defendant's attorney is that of an obviously guilty client and a crime usually discordant with the life history of the defendant prior to a trauma.

The attorney for the defendant will attempt to prove that a trauma took place and was responsible for the production in the client of an officially recognized psychiatric disorder — PTSD. Furthermore, the attorney desires to establish that the PTSD rendered the client not criminally responsible at the time the crime was allegedly committed. The tactics and strategy for the utilization of PTSD in the insanity defense vary, but extensive preparation on the part of the defendant's attorney and mental health professional is absolutely necessary. The following outline may be useful in organizing information:

Explanation of a PTSD: The emotional response of an individual to a trauma during Stages I to III is explained and illustrated, whenever possible, with appropriate tables, charts, and other visual aids. After presenting the clinical course and usual signs and symptoms associated with PTSD, it is always wise to state that PTSD is officially recognized by the APA.

A detailed and documented history of the defendant's life before, during, and after the trauma: The traumatic incident should be described in great detail, with an emphasis on the impact on the defendant. Signs, symptoms, and behavior occurring post-traumatically should, whenever possible, be verified by sources other than the defendant. Dissociative episodes occurring before the alleged criminal conduct should be fully documented and described.

The alleged criminal act: The circumstances surrounding the criminal conduct alleged by the prosecution must be detailed and documented whenever possible. Any similarities between the traumatic incident experienced by the defendant (accident, rape, combat experiences) and the circumstances of the crime should be highlighted. The concept of a flashback or automatism must be explained to the fact finders.

Dissociative reaction: A dissociative state with feelings of unreality and derealization/depersonalization must be defined and explained to the judge and jury in language that can be easily comprehended. The defendant's state of mind, a dissociative state, at the time of the alleged criminal act must be connected to the circumstances and events that were present when the act was committed. In turn, this must be linked to the defendant's PTSD and the trauma that precipitated it.

Criminal responsibility: At the conclusion of testimony during the trial, the mental health professional must make a statement concerning the state of mind of the defendant as it pertains to the test for criminal responsibility used in that jurisdiction. For example, if the ALI Test were applicable, the expert would be asked the following question: "Did the defendant, as a result of mental disease or defect, lack substantial capacity either to appreciate the criminality of his (her) conduct or to conform his (her) conduct to the requirements of law?" If the defendant experienced a trauma, developed a PTSD, and experienced a dissociative reaction at the time of any alleged criminal conduct, the answer to the above question would be in the affirmative.

The Prosecutor's Position

The prosecutor will attempt to denigrate the testimony of the defense's expert as "intellectual balderdash" designed to excuse an obviously guilty defendant from the penalty usually imposed on all law breakers and will present "experts" to support this position. Whenever possible, the prosecutor will introduce and emphasize information detrimental to the defendant, for example, prior antisocial history, abuse of alcohol or other substances, and other evidence indicating that the defendant is a reprobate deserving punishment, not acquittal on the grounds of insanity. If the expert witness is verbose, tending toward polysyllabic explanation, the prosecutor's job is made easier, for all that is required is to let the expert babble on. The fact finders may "tune out" the expert who speaks with sophisticated semantics from a rarefied atmosphere. A tactic of the prosecutor that can nullify the impact of the expert's testimony is to facetiously challenge certain conclusions in the hope that this will anger the mental health professional. Clever prosecutors will make the most out of unflattering characteristics of the expert witness, such as pomposity, grandiosity, dogmatism, and an unwillingness to concede even small or inconsequential points of view.

The ultimate issue during the trial is the defendant's state of mind at the time of the commission of the alleged criminal act. Since it is unlikely that the mental health professional was present at that time, the prosecutor will ask how the expert can be so certain about the defendant's state of mind at a specific point in time. The best answer is to reiterate all of the data upon which a conclusion was reached and end with the statement that the opinion is based on "reasonable professional certainty."

Prosecutors are on the alert for any inconsistencies or inaccuracies, however small or unimportant, in the testimony of the mental health professional. Seemingly inconsequential statements or lapses of memory although not directly related to the major issue at hand may be seized by the prosecutor to undermine other aspects of the expert's testimony. If a mistake has been made, it is better for the mental health professional to admit it, apologize, and calmly correct it. Thorough preparation on the part of the expert witness minimizes embarrassing confrontations in the courtroom.

The prosecutor's strategy during the trial is to describe the crime in the most heinous manner possible and to picture the perpetrator, the defendant, as an evil person totally in control of all mental faculties and deserving punishment. The tactic is to portray the expert witness as an instrument of the defendant to prevent the dispensing of deserved justice — a guilty verdict.

Conclusion

Even experienced witnesses encounter surprise in the courtroom when they are confronted with information that was either unavailable or not forthcoming during the evaluation process. A philosophical attitude, willingness to admit error, and humbleness are the best defenses when challenged with unforeseen events during the trial. As a gleeful attorney once said before asking an embarrassing question, "There is nothing personal in this. We just want to get to the truth of matters." It may not be personal, but when one is under scrutiny in the public glare of the courtroom, embarrassment is personally uncomfortable. Proper preparation is the best protection against unpleasant experiences in court.

Some writers denounce psychiatric testimony (Ziskin 1981) and recommend that mental health professionals not participate in the adversarial process of a trial. Whether these commentators are timid and wish not to take part in adversarial proceedings or are pompous professionals not accustomed to having their views challenged is not for the author to say, but the use of mental health professionals in the courtroom is well established and, like it or not, is here to stay.

For those who enjoy the repartee of verbal confrontation and an opportunity to match wits with an adversary, the courtroom offers an arena for such an engagement. Somehow, when all is done, the truth usually emerges and justice is served as the judge and jury sort through fact and conflicting testimony and arrive at a decision.

THE FUTURE

Psychiatry and the behavioral sciences have made considerable progress over the last 50 years. It can be expected in the future that as technology continues to advance, the biochemical and physiological processes of the brain will be correlated with specific behavior and treatment will become more refined. This utopian view is not as far-fetched as it may seem, when one considers the direction of basic research in the behavioral sciences. Advances in psychopharmacology since the 1950s illustrate but one facet of progress. Effective medication now exists to treat psychosis, Affective Disorders, and pathologic anxiety. Biochemical tests that correlate chemical substances with clinical syndromes have been developed (Brown et al. 1979), and it can be expected that more and better-refined blood tests will evolve to confirm the presence of various psychiatric disorders. Sophisticated instrumentation like computerized axial tomography and positron emission tomography scans (Heath et al. 1979, 1982) and more recently nuclear magnetic resonance can visualize brain structures and functions. It can be expected that more progress will be made in this area. Although it is premature to introduce these procedures as evidence in court (an attempt was made to do so in the Hinckley trial, and was rejected by the presiding judge), admissability in the not-too-distant future is almost a certainty.

In the case of PTSD, there can be no question that objective tests will be developed to quantify pathologic anxiety and identify brain structures associated with dissociative reactions. As evolving psychiatric concepts become based on objective criteria, treatment will become more predictable and effective. Advances in psychiatry must be taken seriously by the court in criminal matters. The days when experts render opinions based solely on subjective data are rapidly passing. In the future, when discussing the psychological reactions to trauma, experts in both civil and criminal cases are more likely to be scientists trained in biochemistry, physiology, and computer technology. Disagreements will still occur, but they will be based on the interpretation and analysis of more objective data. At the present time, PTSD, unlike many psychiatric disorders, offers lawyers and mental health professionals the opportunity to gather evidence external to the person who experiences symptoms (Erlinder 1983b) and integrate this data during the presentation of the case in court. The emergence of PTSD in the courtroom ushers in a new frontier for the law and the behavioral sciences.

EIGHT
PREVENTION

Under a public health classification, there are three types of prevention: primary, secondary, and tertiary (Weston 1975). Primary prevention refers to the elimination of those factors that cause or contribute to the development of disease. Early detection of disease and the implementation of treatment at the earliest possible time is called secondary prevention. Tertiary prevention has been defined as the elimination or reduction of residual disability after illness.

In the field of psychiatry, prevention has been described (Caplan 1961, 1964) as that body of professional knowledge both theoretical and practical that may be utilized to plan and carry out programs for reducing: the incidence of mental health disorders of all types in the population (primary prevention); the duration of a significant number of those mental disorders that do occur (secondary prevention); and the impairment that may result from these mental disorders (tertiary prevention).

PREVENTION AND PTSD

Programs and interventions designed to reduce the risk and hence the incidence of PTSD constitute primary prevention. After a PTSD has developed, the identification and prompt treatment of the disorder reduce risks to health and shorten the duration of the mental disorder — secondary prevention. Programs of tertiary prevention decrease the prevalence of Chronic PTSD and reduce morbidity and impairment.

Primary Prevention of PTSD

Although stress following trauma has been observed and noted over the years, its codification as a mental disorder by the APA occurred only recently with the publication of the third edition of the *DSM* (1980). Undoubtedly, official recognition of PTSD has been assisted by the wide publicity given to Stress Disorders in Vietnam-era veterans. Television programs have alerted the citizenry to the deleterious effects of war stress upon soldiers and fostered public awareness of the concept of PTSD. However, outside professional circles, there is a lack of awareness of the relationship between a mental disorder and civilian trauma. News programs and documentaries occasionally record human emotional suffering caused by natural catastrophes or human-caused disasters, and these reports often mention that emotional reactions following a trauma may exist long after all physical wounds have healed. Therefore, the idea that accidents or industrial trauma may precipitate a psychiatric disorder is slowly being disseminated by the video and print media, which is a form of primary prevention.

Places where industrial organization exists offer the best opportunity for implementing programs of primary prevention (Mclean 1975). Most large companies employ safety experts who conduct meetings on a regular basis to reduce or eliminate the occurrence of accidents that cause physical injury. However, information related to mental health and mental disorders is usually excluded, when its addition would require little extra effort. The theme that all accidents, regardless of the extent of physical injury, are stressful should be highlighted. There is no mind-body dichotomy, rather the brain and body together respond to a trauma. An understanding of this fact by workers could maximize acceptance of psychiatric treatment if an accident were to occur in the future. Too often, workers equate mental disorders with "craziness" or feel that an emotional response to trauma indicates weakness or a "lack of manliness." These myths can be erased from the minds of workers during safety meetings. There are a wide range of emotional reactions to trauma, the employees can be told, and most mental symptoms dissipate and eventually disappear with time. Industrial psychiatrists or psychologists can elaborate on treatment interventions that are available when mental symptoms persist beyond 4 to 6 weeks. During primary prevention educational programs are aimed at explaining, in easily understood terms, the concepts of the Three E's, pathologic anxiety, retraumatization, and the Spiral Effect.

Case histories or video-taped interviews with persons who have developed a PTSD can augment primary prevention by demonstrating the psychiatric signs and symptoms following an accident as well as treatment approaches. It is important to emphasize that if a PTSD develops, effective treatment is available. Once workers are acquainted with the concept of PTSD, no surprises await them if they are involved in an accident and experience symptoms of a Stress Disorder. Cries of faker or malingerer by fellow workers and supervisors can be quelled when the relationship between trauma and stress is understood.

Programs of primary prevention in an industrial setting are easy to implement if management supports the concept. However, in small or poorly administered companies, primary prevention becomes a more difficult goal to attain. Outside an industrial setting, primary prevention becomes a public health responsibility. Here, persons must depend upon information available through governmental health and safety agencies and the public media. Television and radio programs on public broadcasting systems and articles in popular periodicals can be of great assistance in the dissemination of information concerning trauma and stress. Unfortunately, as has been discovered in the "wellness movement," persons seem unmotivated to act in their own behalf until circumstances necessitate action. Nonmandatory programs emphasizing principles of primary prevention as it relates to trauma and stress might be difficult to put in place, but their implementation is not an impossible task.

Secondary Prevention

Persons who develop a PTSD know that something is wrong with them but tend to attribute symptoms to some physical process. Likewise, relatives and friends notice changes in the patient's demeanor following a trauma, but unless previously instructed feel helpless to intervene. Quick identification and detection of persons suspected of having a PTSD depend upon the observer's familiarity with key signs and symptoms exhibited by an individual following exposure to a trauma. When physical injury is present, ministration to fractures, lacerations, or bruises understandably supersedes attention to the emotional consequences of the trauma, but mental reactions must not be ignored. Any trauma, however slight or seemingly inconsequential, is capable of precipitating a PTSD. When persons display or complain of the cardinal characteristics of PTSD (Table 8-1), prompt action is warranted.

One need not have the clinical skills of a psychiatrist or psychologist to make a determination that a traumatized person has changed in the manner described in Table 8-1. In fact, those who have been closest to the patient before the accident may be in a better position to note the reaction to trauma and subsequent changes in behavior. In work-related trauma, supervisors and fellow employees will certainly notice differences in overt behavior. Such observations can be the impetus for referral of the traumatized person to an appropriate mental health professional.

In industrial settings, a nurse, paramedic, or industrial physician usually has first contact with a traumatized worker. After the injury has been assessed, it is wise to engage patients in a discussion concerning their emotional response to the trauma. Relating the details of the accident to the company nurse or doctor allows for catharsis and attests to management's interest in the worker's welfare. Both can be extremely therapeutic and are a part of secondary prevention. Injured individuals who are near retirement age are particularly sensitive to the psychological effects of trauma because injury seems to magnify the perception of waning power due to aging. Therefore, older workers should receive more emotional support from supervisors and professionals. Persons who have been involved in previous accidents or have a past history of mental illness should also be sorted out for more intensive psychiatric evaluation. To ensure compliance, sensitivity and good judgment must be mixed when injured persons are referred to psychiatrists for evaluation and treatment following trauma.

For many persons involved in a traumatic incident, professional assistance may first be encountered in the emergency room of a hospital. Commonly, if the injury is not severe as confirmed by examinations and X-rays, emergency room physicians send the patient home with instructions to contact the family doctor if symptoms persist. Quick dismissal by the emergency room physician without adequate explanation plants in the mind of the patient the idea of an incomplete examination with the possibility of an undetected physical defect. Persons may awaken the next day racked with

TABLE 8-1
Cardinal Characteristics of Post-Traumatic Stress Disorder

Nervousness
   The person is apprehensive, on edge, tense, jumpy, easily startled, and fearful.

Preoccupation with the trauma
   The person talks a great deal about the accident, speculating that more serious injury or even death could have occurred.

Pain or physical discomfort
   The person complains of pain or physical discomfort that appears disproportionate to the actual injury incurred.

Sleeplessness
   The patient complains of insomnia with resultant tiredness and fatigue.

Flashbacks and nightmares
   The person relives the trauma during flashbacks or nightmares with similar emotional reactions as if the accident were happening again. Intrusive thoughts related to the trauma are common.

Deterioration of performance
   The person experiences inability or difficulty in carrying out usual life activities such as work, family responsibilities, social/recreation, or any activity engaged in before the trauma.

Phobia
   The person experiences fearfulness and avoidance of the place where the accident occurred or extreme apprehension associated with some activity related to the trauma.

Personality change
   The person becomes withdrawn, moody, irritable, distracted, forgetful, and unlike his or her usual self.

Dudgeon
   The person gives expression to frequent unprovoked outbursts of anger with complaints about the carelessness of others and a retributive attitude. Quarrelsome behavior may be evident.

Table 8-1, continued

Depression
At some point following the trauma the person feels "blue" or "down in the dumps." A loss of self-confidence, a pessimistic attitude, brooding about past events, or feeling sorry for self may be noted. Social withdrawal and a look of sadness on the face of a person formerly cheerful and outgoing may be extant.

Source: Compiled by author.

pain caused by sprained muscles and a belief that they are seriously injured. Family doctors or specialists are consulted and examinations including X-rays repeated. If no serious physical abnormalities are diagnosed, patients are usually sent home with prescriptions for muscle relaxants, pain medication, and physiotherapy. Failure to respond to this regimen often leads physicians to the sardonic conclusion that the patients have a high serum porcelain level and are crocks. Unenthusiastic treatment or referral and dismissal of the patient can result when the clinician misses the diagnosis of PTSD. The opportunity for secondary prevention is lost, and the patient proceeds to the chronic stage of the Stress Disorder. In the experience of the author, the preceding sequence of events is too common. Even when the trauma has resulted in observable physical injury, including fractures or lacerations, physicians are frequently perplexed when symptoms persist long after the expected time of healing. In many instances the psychological response to trauma is ignored or minimized and a diagnosis of PTSD never considered.

Whether they be experts in traumatology (orthopedic surgeons, neurosurgeons, forensic psychiatrists) or family doctors, physicians must be alerted to the signs and symptoms of PTSD in those patients who report for examination and treatment following a trauma. In addition to the history of the traumatic incident and the presence of the signs or symptoms mentioned in Table 8-1 and elaborated in Chapter four, other factors should alert the clinician to the patient's psychological vulnerability to trauma. A past history of an Anxiety Disorder or an anxiety-related illness should suggest a predisposition to PTSD. A family history indicating that one or both parents of the patient have suffered from an Anxiety Disorder or anxiety-related illness should also raise the suspicion of a possible psychopathologic response to trauma. In addition, physicians and other clinicians should be on guard to the likelihood of PTSD when patients remain symptomatic in spite of vigorous medical treatment with minimal objective evidence of organic disease or defect. The normal psychological response to trauma involves a gradual diminution of symptoms, so when symptoms remain or intensify, a Stress Disorder should be suspected and a psychiatric consultation ordered. Clinicians should always secure information from relatives or friends to expand the patient's history and substantiate symptomatic behavior. Early detection and intervention mean prophylaxis and secondary prevention, for when PTSD becomes chronic, treatment and resolution of the disorder are more difficult.

Tertiary Prevention

When PTSD goes unrecognized and undiagnosed, treatment is not forthcoming and the disorder becomes chronic. Patients suffer and complain of the symptoms related to Stage III (Chapter four). Disability, which may lead to lifelong invalidism, leaves persons demoralized and despondent. Untreated Chronic PTSD can lead to unemployment, insolvency, disruption of family life, Substance Use Disorder, depression, alienation from others, suicide, and a possible lifetime of nonproductivity. Tertiary prevention attempts to reduce or eliminate these chronic aftereffects of PTSD.

Frequently, Chronic PTSD patients are grouped and labeled as suffering from Disproportionate Disability Syndrome, Catastrophic Disability Syndrome, or some other "catch-all" classification. Such appellations focus attention on chronic, unrelenting, end-stage disablement and fail to place in perspective the onset and course leading to disability. As in secondary prevention, tertiary prevention depends upon the correct identification of persons suffering from a PTSD. However, chronicity often obscures the basic Stress Disorder, making diagnosis difficult. If the characteristics (Table 8-1) persist in a patient following a well-documented trauma, this should alert the clinician to the possibility of Chronic PTSD. In addition, the continuance of symptoms in lieu of objective physical findings and lack of response to usual medical treatment should be reason enough for psychiatric consultation.

Practical considerations involving tertiary prevention arise when certain questions are asked: Who will identify and refer Chronic PTSD patients? To whom should such patients be referred? Any of the persons listed in Table 8-2 could recognize or refer Stage III PTSD patients, and treatment would be available from those qualified professionals. In many instances, however, the mental health profession participates in neither the identification nor the treatment of such patients. Psychiatrists, psychologists, and social workers are seldom consulted unless litigation is pending or directors of rehabilitation or pain units request consultation. Unfortunately, unless psychiatrists, other mental health professionals, and personnel in conventional mental health clinics or traditional psychiatric hospitals have expertise in the identification and treatment of Chronic PTSD, they are likely to be ill suited to treat the Chronic PTSD patient. It is not that mental health professionals and the staff of psychiatric institutions are incapable of managing and treating Chronic PTSD patients, but rather their personnel and programs are not geared to deal with this difficult patient population. Patients who complain constantly, show slow or no progress in treatment, miss appointments, display little gratitude, lack insight, and seem not to profit from traditional psychiatric approaches not surprisingly have little appeal for many clinicians. It is hoped that this will change in the future.

How, then, can the Chronic PTSD patient be helped? A multidisciplinary approach would best meet the needs of the patient. A psychiatrist temperamentally suited and educationally equipped to manage the chronic patient should head the treatment team. Although a wide range of problems and issues is prominent, PTSD is primarily a psychiatric disorder. Therefore, psychiatric direction is paramount. Ideally, a treatment program should include inpatient and outpatient facilities. The patient need not be hospitalized, which is very expensive, but should have access to hospital services whenever needed. A residential center, day hospital, or clinic could serve as a place where evaluations are conducted, outreach programs developed, and all services coordinated. Intensive involvement with the patient and family maximizes compliance with treatment recommendations. A comprehensive, multidisciplinary approach should continue during all phases of treatment and include individual sessions, group treatment, family conferences, as well as consultation with occupational/rehabilitation therapists and other specialists.

TABLE 8-2
Persons in Contact with Patient following Trauma

Relatives or friends

Employer (supervisor)

Industrial nurse, paramedic, physician (if available and trauma occurred at workplace)

Emergency room physician

Family doctor

Medical specialist
    Orthopedic surgeon
    Neurosurgeon
    Other

Physiotherapist

Vocational rehabilitation specialist, occupational therapist

Laywer

Pain unit/rehabilitation center personnel
    Surgeon (neuro or orthopedic)
    Psychiatrist
    Psychologist
    Nurse
    Social worker
    Support personnel (aides, rehabilitation experts, etc.)

Psychiatrist, psychologist, social worker

Mental health clinic, psychiatric hospital personnel

Forensic psychiatrist

Source: Compiled by author.

The establishment of a trauma center to meet the psychological needs of the victims of trauma could be modeled upon the pain units or rehabilitation centers that exist in many communities. As mentioned, an inpatient phase is optional. However, initially, patients and their families must be intensively involved in a broad-based treatment program to counter the debilitating effects of Chronic PTSD. In this manner the goal of tertiary prevention can be met.

CONCLUSION

The treatment concepts and strategies mentioned in Chapter six are applicable to the primary, secondary, and tertiary prevention of PTSD. Whether these interventions are used to educate persons to prevent or lessen the emotional impact of a trauma (primary prevention), to intervene promptly following a trauma (secondary prevention), or to eliminate or reduce chronicity (tertiary prevention), morbidity is lowered. Prevention, often ignored in the behavioral sciences, is important and particularly applicable in modifying a person's psychological response to trauma.

NINE
CASE HISTORIES

CASE ONE: AIRPLANE CRASH

Mr. A, a married businessman in his early thirties, was in a commercial jet liner crash, following which he developed insomnia, nightmares of airplanes crashing, severe headaches, generalized anxiety, problems in concentration, and marital conflicts with a diminished interest in sex. He also felt anxious when he heard or saw a jet aircraft. A phobia of flying in airplanes restricted his travel and interfered with his business enterprises.

History of Present Illness

Three months after the crash Mr. A sought treatment. He recalled that his airplane had landed at an intermediate city and, following transfer of passenger and baggage, was beginning its takeoff. It was nighttime and he was in his seat dozing having concluded a long day of business. Suddenly, the undercarriage of the airplane collapsed, and the airplane skidded down the runway on its belly. The sound of metal scraping, rending, and tearing filled his ears, and when he looked out of the windows, both wings appeared to be on fire. The lights inside the airplane went out, and as the plane came to a stop, the interior of the aircraft was dimly illuminated by flames issuing from both wings. Confusion grew into pandemonium as passengers began to scream in fear and scramble for the exits. The almost complete darkness was pierced by dim emergency lights, and he hurried behind a flight attendant to one of the emergency exits. The flight attendant struggled with the latch, but it would not budge and the exit could not be opened. Other passengers pressed behind him, shoving and shouting before they were led away to another emergency exit. Mr. A felt trapped and feared for his life believing that the airplane would explode burning him to death. His heart began to pound wildly and he was gasping for breath when a flight attendant grabbed his arm and led him to another exit. He slid down an escape chute, landing heavily on his right ankle, spraining it severely. As he limped away from the burning aircraft to a safe area, he paused and watched the conflagration. He marveled at his escape from death or serious injury and began to feel nauseated as his body trembled and shook uncontrollably. Mr. A and the rest of the passengers were bussed to the airport terminal, a fitting term he later mused, where they were taken to a VIP lounge and given free spirits. He accepted the free liquor but refused tickets for the next flight home and instead took a train.

Upon returning home Mr. A had difficulty sleeping and experienced vivid nightmares about airplane crashes. Anxiety was evoked when he heard the sound of jet engines or saw an airplane. He refused to fly, although this resulted in great inconvenience and seriously affected his business. He began to obsess about accidents, injury, and death, frequently complaining of headaches and a feeling of nausea. Irritability replaced a calm and friendly demeanor, and marital problems emerged. Lovemaking became less frequent, and he experienced problems getting and maintaining an erection during sexual intercourse. He was cross with his children and caustic with his business customers. Finally, with the encouragement and insistence of his wife, he decided to seek treatment.

Past History

Mr. A's memories about his early life were scant, but he distinctly remembered being poor. As a child he felt different because he always seemed to be dressed in ill-fitting, hand-me-down clothing and had less money and possessions than other children. Academic problems and poor grades led to psychological testing and placement in a special education class where he felt further alienated.

Nevertheless, he struggled with his schoolwork and his academic performance improved. He was industrious even as a young boy, working at various odd jobs to help support his family. Following graduation from high school, he entered a trade school where he learned automechanics. His sedulousness led to success, and several years later he opened up his own automotive business, which grew and prospered. He married his childhood sweetheart and they had four children. Prior to the airplane accident, his life was in reasonable order and he was having no major difficulties.

Family History

Mr. A came from a large family. His father, a chronic alcoholic, was disabled and could not work regularly. His mother, whom he described as a hard-working and loving person, was the breadwinner in her employment as a maid. The patient was the oldest of eight siblings and, as the eldest, assumed much responsibility for household affairs early in his life. Although his family was poor, he stated they were never hungry and felt loyal to each other. He did not like or respect his father, a dissolute man who existed around the fringes of the family.

Treatment

During the *explanation-education* stage of treatment, an elaboration of the onset and course of PTSD was presented. As the plane was speeding down the runway, Mr. A became aware of the increased noise of the jet engines, followed by a feeling of sudden descent, and then a tremendous jolt. He was jarred to full consciousness by the screeching sound of metal rending and fragmenting as the bottom of the airplane scraped along the concrete runway. These stimuli, along with the sight of the plane's wings on fire and the shouts of confusion and alarm of other passengers, combined to activate the patient's autonomic nervous system. Anxiety reached a zenith when the patient was at the emergency exit that would not open and he was momentarily pinned to that door by frantically pressing passengers. Mr. A felt trapped and was certain that he could not escape and would die. Palpitations and dyspnea seemed to confirm this notion, but the patient was quickly hustled out of the airplane by the nimble flight attendants who propelled him toward the escape chute at another door. As he hit the ground, spraining his ankle, the patient's autonomic nervous system was working wildly; he felt extreme nausea and a severe shaking of his body as he staggered off to safety, away from the burning jet liner.

During this frightening sequence of events, the patient experienced the effects of intense autonomic activity, thus conditioning him adversely to various situational aspects of flying. Subsequently, whenever he saw airplanes or considered flying, he encephalically overexaggerated the dangers of air travel by visualizing airplane crashes and his certain demise. Anxiety was generated by this encephalic activity, but was reduced when the patient decided not to fly. Mechanisms of phobic behavior were explained, and it was emphasized that approach behavior (any activity that leads to a flight) increased anxiety, whereas avoidance behavior (any activity that led to a decision or action not to fly) reduced anxiety. Unfortunately, the anxiety decrement reinforced the phobic avoidance behavior.

A PTSD, the explanation continued, is sustained encephalically when a patient thinks, visualizes, or talks excessively about the traumatic incident, because this serves to maintain high levels of pathologic anxiety. Dreams reflect to a large extent the concerns of the waking state, so nightmares accompany an agitated mind overly concerned with the traumatic incident. When patients frequently dream about trauma, they often quit the struggle for sleep because somnolence is associated with upsetting nightmares, not rest. Patients yearn for sleep, yet dread it at the same time. Headaches and gastrointestinal upsets are somatic manifestations of pathologic anxiety, and these and other symptoms not present before the airplane crash would diminish as treatment proceeded, the patient was reassured.

Control and diminishment of pathologic anxiety and the induction of sleep can be achieved by learning *relaxation techniques* the patient was told. He proved to be especially adept at self-hypnosis but also learned the technique of PMR. Both methods were recorded on an audio cassette for home use. It was important he was informed to master relaxation procedures since they would be part of the desensitization process for addressing his flying phobia.

Preoccupation with thoughts of mortality may be intellectually beneficial for theologians and philosophers but it is not beneficial for patients with a PTSD. Morbid ruminations about death or injury serve only to heighten anxiety and maintain the disorder. Reliving the trauma in imagination retraumatizes patients, thus sensitizing them to various aspects of the trauma. Obsessive preoccupation with trauma, the patient is warned, is the most important reason for enduring anxiety and the sustentation of the disorder. He was taught methods of *encephalic reconditioning*. Whenever envisaging unpleasant ideas related to his trauma, he was instructed to use a stopping technique. To dispel the distressing thoughts, he was to repeat to himself as often as was necessary, "Stop! Get out of there!" When the thought or scene was expurgated from his mind, he was urged to employ positive encephalic practice or to utilize a distraction technique involving conversation with another person or the pursuit of an engaging activity.

Rather than dwell on the uncomfortable sensations of headache or nausea and speculate about the possible presence of some pernicious process within his body, Mr. A was advised to state emphatically to himself the four positive reinforcing statments: (1) I feel uncomfortable. (2) I have had these feelings before and they *always* pass. (3) There is nothing seriously wrong with me. (4) My discomfort is caused or aggravated by pathologic anxiety, and if I utilize antianxiety interventions, these uncomfortable feelings will pass more quickly. The patient was then asked to practice self-hypnosis or PMR. Listening to audio tapes with instruction related to self-hypnosis and PMR can facilitate encephalic reconditioning, Mr. A was informed. Adherence to a policy of limiting, reducing, and ultimately stopping ruminations about the trauma would pay dividends of symptomatic improvement, he was told, and was an important factor in the resolution of his PTSD.

The patient's phobia of flying was treated by *systematic desensitization*. A hierarchy was constructed similar to that found in Chapter six, and imaginal desensitization proceeded in the office. Initially, desensitization proceeded with difficulty because the patient visualized scenes that included an airplane crashing. For example, when he was asked to visualize that he was at home packing and preparing prior to driving to the airport, he simultaneously recollected his awful experience inside the disabled jet liner. The patient had to be repeatedly warned not to include as part of the desensitization scenes depicting any portion of his traumatic experience. He was also advised not to anticipate, but merely to visualize the stated scene. When this was sorted out, desensitization proceeded normally. Following imaginal desensitization the patient was encouraged to go to the airport and observe airplanes taking off and landing. This in vivo desensitization experience exposed him to the hustle and bustle of airport activity as well as to the sights and sounds of airplanes landing and taking off. Finally, Mr. A scheduled a short flight. Prior to his flight, however, he saw a news report of an airplane crash on television. He postponed his trip, and his fears about flying and thoughts about airplane crashing were rekindled. After a short delay, desensitization was reinstituted as before. The patient's confidence was somewhat shaken by the resurgence of symptoms, but soon another flight was scheduled. It was decided that prior to his initial flight, *medication* would be prescribed. The patient was instructed to take diazepam 5 milligrams the morning of his flight and to take another 5 milligrams while he was at the airport waiting to board his plane. Additional diazepam could be taken as needed during the flight. The patient, as are most flight phobic patients, was impervious to declarations that flying was the safest form of travel, but to demonstrate that desensitization had indeed lowered his anxiety, he agreed to take a short flight from New Orleans to Houston. He was accompanied on the flight by the author, and he was delighted with the outcome. Anticipatory anxiety made him feel a bit uncomfortable prior to the flight, but during the flight he was at ease most of the time. He experienced a surge of anxiety on takeoff when he heard the roar of accelerating jet engines and during landing when he felt a noticeable "bump" on descent, but his discomfort quickly subsided. Following this initial successful flight, longer flights in which he was unaccompanied were scheduled. In vivo exposure to flying led to further decreases in anxiety, and eventually Mr. A discontinued the use of diazepam. Five years following termination of treatment, he reported that he now flies with ease and no vestige of a phobia of flying remains.

A *family conference* was convened because the patient complained of marital problems, especially difficulties in getting and maintaining an erection. Mrs. A, a woman who was obviously in love with her husband, was very concerned about his welfare. She stated that since the airplane accident, her husband did not sleep well and frequently woke up in the middle of the night screaming and sweating profusely. Upon questioning, he related nightmares that involved burning airplanes and imminent death. During the conjoint conference, Mrs. A reported that her husband was irritable, on edge, tense, and would "fly off the handle" easily, which was contrary to his usual easy-going, pleasant personality. She also exclaimed that her husband seemed preoccupied with death and lamented that his inability to fly impeded his growing business and affected his profits. Mrs. A was told that her husband was suffering from a PTSD and that most of his symptoms and behavior could be attributed to this disorder. It was important for the couple to restore harmonious interaction, and this would be made easier by conjoint therapy sessions, Mrs. A was reassured. Initially, sexual disinterest and dysfunction, a common component of PTSD since anxiety and pleasurable sexual relationships are incompatible, were addressed during the family conference. The couple was placed on a modified Masters and Johnson (1970) program designed to reduce performance anxiety and overcome the problem of impotence. Both cooperated with this regimen, and within five sessions their sexual relationship was mutually satisfying.

Mr. A had just expanded his business, an automotive parts agency, and it was necessary for him to meet regularly with other dealers in various parts of the country. His phobia of flying prevented him from attending these meetings during the initial phase of treatment. *Problem-solving sessions* were conducted around this issue, and the patient made alternative arrangements to minimize any disruption to his business. At times he sent one of his employees or, if possible, drove or took the train to these meetings. Financial problems ensuant to expanding his business were not serious, but his symptoms of anxiety interfered with decisive action. Discussions helped clarify his options, rendering decision making easier. The patient had good business sense and needed only peace of mind to reflect calmly on a problem in order to arrive at a sound decision. As the patient's preoccupation with his trauma diminished, so did his anxiety and difficulties in problem solving.

The patient's *exercise and nutritional status* was discussed. Mr. A was obese and exercised little. Toward the end of treatment he was placed on a diet based on behavior modification principles (Scrignar 1980; Stuart and Davis 1982). Since he was a good hypnotic subject, a special hypnosis audio cassette tape was prepared that contained positive suggestions designed to help him adhere to his diet. In addition, Mr. A was encouraged to join an exercise club and to work out regularly. He complied with both of these requests, lost weight, and began to feel the beneficial effects of self-control related to eating and physical activity. Periodic follow-ups after termination revealed that the patient was still struggling with his weight, but had managed to maintain a weight loss of 40 pounds. He exercises erratically but remains committed to the principle "sound mind — sound body."

At the end of 29 sessions extending over a 7-month period, treatment was terminated. Quarterly follow-ups for the first year following termination disclosed that he had maintained his improvement. After termination a personal injury suit that he had filed was arbitrated out of court. A telephone follow-up 5 years later revealed that he was doing quite well. All of the patient's pathologic anxiety symptoms had subsided and he was flying freely. His sleep was sound and nightmares were very infrequent. His relationship with his wife was excellent, and he was prospering financially. The airplane accident that he was involved in is now a dim memory in his mind.

CASE TWO: ACCIDENT ON AN OIL RIG

Mr. B, a married oilfield worker in his early forties, stated that following an accident on an oil rig in the Gulf of Mexico, "my whole life has changed." He explained that he was in constant pain, which was relieved to some extent when he wore a back brace or took various analgesics. Nervousness, a fear of possible paralysis, headaches, difficulty in concentrating, insomnia, disturbing dreams, irritability, marital conflicts, diminished sexual desire, and gastrointestinal upsets interfered with his ability to enjoy life. He admitted that he thought a great deal about the accident and its consequences and wondered whether he would ever get well. Displaying despondency, the patient cried as he related that friends had noticed a personality change and told him that he was moody, withdrawn, and distant. With regret, he stated that he had instituted a lawsuit against his former employers who he believed were unsympathetic and uncaring about his injuries. Litigation, he felt, had placed additional pressures upon him.

History of Present Illness

Mr. B was working on the drilling platform of an oil rig in the Gulf of Mexico, assisting in the removal of drilling pipe "out of the hole." A "wet string" (large amount of drilling mud) poured out onto the drilling platform, making it very slippery. In the performance of his duties, he slipped and fell backward, landing very hard on his buttocks. Although he was in pain, he got up and continued working. Shortly thereafter, he slipped again falling on his lower back and buttocks. At the time, although in great pain, he thought he was not injured seriously. He continued working but when his foreman asked him to get some test equipment, he could not lift it, although ordinarily he could have done so without difficulty. The thought that he might have injured his back passed quickly through his mind, but he asked another man to get the equipment and returned to work. At the end of his shift he went to the bunkhouse and slept. Several hours later he awakened and tried to get out of bed but severe pain prevented this. Instantly, he thought that he was paralyzed. Reasoning that the two falls he had endured must have seriously injured his spine making it impossible for him to pick up the test equipment, and now to get out of his bunk, he became panic stricken. He was alone in the bunkhouse, and the noise of the drilling rig drowned out his shouts for help. His chest tightened, he thought he would suffocate; and his heart was beating so fast he feared it would burst. These acute symptoms subsided somewhat, and with great effort he crawled out of his bunk and desperately called for help. The driller (foreman), alarmed at Mr. B's condition, called for a helicopter to evacuate him to a hospital. During the 30-minute wait for the helicopter, Mr. B was in severe pain and believed that he was seriously injured and might never walk again. "My back felt like a nerve or muscle was pulled out and I was very scared."

In the hospital after receiving a complete physical examination including X-rays, Mr. B was treated with pain medication and bed rest. After 7 days of hospitalization, he was surprised when doctors discharged him with recommendations to go home and rest. Two days later, Mr. B, greatly agitated and in severe pain, returned to the emergency room of the hospital, was readmitted, and was placed in traction for 3 days. Traction relieved his pain and he was again discharged with the recommendation to take analgesic medication and get some rest. He reacted to this prescription with disbelief, and when symptoms persisted was again admitted to the hospital. Examinations, laboratory procedures, and various tests were repeated and followed with the same recommendation — discharge, medication for pain, and bed rest. Still symptomatic, Mr. B became convinced that his condition was serious, undiagnosable, and untreatable. Over the course of the next several months, thoughts that he might become paralyzed led to many visits with various doctors. In an attempt to treat his symptoms, doctors prescribed muscle relaxants, analgesics, antipsychotic agents, antianxiety agents, antidepressants, β-blockers, antacids, antispasmodics, vitamins, and a variety of drug-combination medications. In spite of this pharmacologic assault on the patient's body, his symptoms persisted.

Surgical consultation led to rehospitalization and a laminectomy and diskectomy were performed. Postoperatively the patient did well, but eventually complained of back pain radiating down his right leg. Pain was relived by bed rest, and during ambulation a lumbar corset eased his discomfort. Four months later Mr. B was admitted to a university hospital where a diganosis of degenerative disk disease with segmental instability was made. Another operative procedure, a lumbosacral fusion, was performed and his condition on discharge was good. Upon returning home, however, the patient became symptomatic. Psychiatric consultation was advised.

A mental status examination revealed a man who was extremely anxious and quite depressed. Pain was a prominent symptom, but he also suffered from generalized anxiety, sleep disturbance, frightening dreams, headaches, trembling, irritability, difficulties in concentration, fatigue, and marital problems. He was obsessed with his accident and had thoughts that he would become panic stricken and lose control. He had a long history of gastrointestinal disturbance, and 2 weeks prior to the psychiatric consultation had vomited blood, which led to a short hospitalization. His preaccident medical history included treatment for gastric ulcers and surgery to remove a gall bladder. The patient had never been evaluated nor treated for a nervous or mental disorder. There was no evidence of psychosis, and he was in good contact with reality. The patient's personal habits were good; he did not drink alcoholic beverages or smoke. There was no evidence of an antisocial personality. Previously, he had never been involved in personal injury litigation.

Past History

The patient was reared by a stepmother and father in a rural southern town. As a child he was sickly and frequently absent from school. Following the ninth grade, he quit school and worked on a farm for his father. Mr. B stated that his childhood and adolescence were not remarkable, but admitted that he was shy and preferred his own company. When he was 18 he joined the U.S. Army, served 2 years including 1 year in Europe, reached the rank of corporal and received an honorable discharge. His first marriage, which lasted 4 years, was a disaster and ended when his wife ran off with another man. Two children have resulted from his current marriage of 8 years, and he felt that he and his wife were getting along quite well until his accident. Ten years ago he was involved in another accident while working as a roustabout on an oil rig. Drill pipe was being pulled out of the hole, he related, when suddenly one of the pipes broke loose, hitting him on the head. Unconscious, he was taken to the hospital where he remained for about 3 weeks after regaining consciousness. He was unable to work for 1 year and marginally subsisted on worker's compensation. No lawsuit evolved from this accident, and he returned to work for the same company that had employed him at the time of the accident. Although he stated that he had been in good health most of his life, medical history prior to his recent trauma indicated treatment for gastric ulcers and a cholecystectomy.

Family History

The patient's mother died in childbirth, and within a year his father remarried a widow with four children. He remembered that his stepmother was very critical of him and did not like him. He felt that his two stepbrothers and two stepsisters were favored by his stepmother. He described his father as a quiet, somber man who always acceded to his wife's wishes. His reasons for joining the U.S. Army were to escape from the tedium of farm work and his stepmother's temper.

Treatment

Injury to his back, pain, and subsequent operative procedures obscured the signs and symptoms of PTSD, the patient was told during the *explanation-education* step of treatment. As physicians searched for a structural cause for his symptoms, the emotional aspects of his trauma were overlooked. Unlike in most patients who develop PTSD, the onset of Mr. B's disorder occurred several hours after the initial impact. Lying on a bed alone in a bunkhouse on an oil rig several miles offshore in the Gulf of Mexico, he awakened and discovered that he could not move. Vivid recollections of his two falls on the oil rig coupled with intense pain lent credence to the conclusion that he was paralyzed. Two E's — encephalic and endogenous — combined to produce a sudden stimulation of his autonomic nervous system. Palpitations, dyspnea, and other acute anxiety symptoms surged as his shouts for help were drowned out by the roar of machinery. Feeling helpless, panic stricken, and in great pain, Mr. B struggled to get on his feet and, finding that he could still move, thoughts of paralysis were supplanted by equally frightening ideas of impending paralysis. Laboriously, half-crawling and half-walking, he got out of bed, left the bunkhouse, and attracted the attention of his foreman, who immediately radioed for a helicopter to take him ashore to a hospital. While awaiting transportation, Mr. B suffered from severe anxiety and pain. Nausea and fear also racked his body and he began to shake violently. For almost an hour, high levels of autonomic nervous system activity, an essential element in producing a PTSD, were experienced by the patient before he arrived at the hospital.

Examinations and an assortment of laboratory procedures were inconclusive and revealed no gross abnormalities. To his surprise and confusion, Mr. B was discharged from the hospital and advised to rest and take pain medication when needed. At home he experienced intense back pain and envisaged impending paralysis, which set in motion the Spiral Effect, intensifying both anxiety and pain. Panic stricken and suffering from intense back pain, he went to the emergency room and was readmitted to the hospital. Conservative, nonsurgical treatment failed, so finally a laminectomy and diskectomy were performed, which only temporarily ameliorated pain. Symptoms of stress were present but largely overlooked or deemphasized by surgeons who concentrated instead on finding physical reasons for Mr. B's continuing discomfort. Four months later a diagnosis of mechanical back pain was made, and another surgical procedure, a lumbosacral fusion, was performed. Although the operation was judged to be successful, Mr. B remained symptomatic.

Finally, attention focused on the patient's psychological status and a psychiatric consultation was requested.

With certitude, the patient was told during explanation-education that further surgery was neither indicated nor necessary. Existing pain and anxiety could be explained by postoperative soft tissue damage and anxiety. A further search for a physical cause obfuscated the real source of his discomfort. Mechanisms underlying a PTSD were explained, emphasizing that obsessions about the trauma and the possibility of paralysis served only to perpetuate the disorder. Lowering of pathologic anxiety and control of pain could be achieved by *training in relaxation* and *encephalic reconditioning*. Dubiety greeted these suggestions, and Mr. B's anger rose as he queried, "If this is all in my imagination, why have I had two operations?" The patient's query was momentarily quieted by the explanation that his symptoms were not imaginary, but physiologically induced. He was wearing a lumbar corset, and it was difficult for him to believe that his spine had not been irreparably damaged by the original trauma. His dissatisfaction led to a discontinuance of treatment.

A month later the patient's wife, highly upset, telephoned and stated that her husband was not doing well. Mr. B had been hospitalized for several days because of bleeding gastric ulcer, and following his discharge was very depressed and talked about suicide. A *family conference* was immediately convened, during which Mrs. B said that she was at her wit's end and felt emotionally and physically spent, incapable of helping her husband. In a gloomy mood, Mr. B complained of low back pain, stomach cramps, insomnia, disturbing dreams, nervousness, irritability, restlessness, difficulties in concentration, and fatigue. He spent much of his time each day in bed, thinking about himself and the future. He obsessed about the dangerousness of working on oil rigs, reliving in imagination both of his accidents. "Even if I get over my back pain," he speculated, "I doubt whether I shall ever be able to work on an oil rig again." Untrained for any other work and in a depressed state of mind, he contemplated suicide as the best solution for his dilemma. Hospitalization in a psychiatric unit was a more responsible solution.

Upon entering the psychiatric unit, the patient was frightened but relieved as he confided that he believed he was going crazy. Bizarre nightmares, in which he was slipping and sliding on the muddied platform of an oil rig with drilling pipes and dangerous machinery imperiling him from all sides, roused him from sleep. Afterward, sweat drenched and agitated, he found further sleep impossible. Instead he lay awake, wide eyed, pondering the significance of his dreams and fantasizing dangers associated with oil rigs. During the day back pain reminded him of his accidents and reinforced the idea that oil rigs were dangerous places in which to work. Disability lasting over a year and pessimism regarding the future fueled feelings of hopelessness and depression. In the hospital during the explanation-education phase of treatment, the mechanisms underlying PTSD were reexplained, emphasizing the importance of the Three E's in the production and maintenance of his disorder. Retraumatization occurred encephalically whenever the patient visualized or thought about the accidents, thereby exposing him to the trauma in imagination many times each day. The patient's attention to back pain initiated the Spiral Effect, which intensified his pain and increased anxiety. Depression, a secondary manifestation of PTSD, was due in large part to chronic disablement and was abetted by pessimistic self-statements portending permanent invalidism.

Control of pain and lowering of anxiety can be achieved by engaging in *training in relaxation*, which must be practiced, the patient was told. This time, he mastered the techniques of self-hypnosis and PMR, which were used to advantage when he experienced pain or anxiety. Control and reduction of thoughts and mental images related to the trauma are absolutely essential and can be achieved by *encephalic reconditioning*, he was advised. Thought stopping, positive encephalic practice, and the four positive reinforcing statements were discussed and taught to the patient. He was asked to fill out a daily *self-assessment form* to help him identify the stimuli inducing pathologic anxiety and pain in order to counter them with therapeutic interventions. Pessimistic and negative self-statements, which correlate with depression (Beck 1976), were also to be recorded on the form, and he was urged to correct these. For example, the patient tended to overgeneralize and say to himself, "My life is ruined. I am no good to anyone." He was urged to substitute for these erroneous self-statements: "My life has changed but I will cope with my new circumstance. I have many positive attributes. My wife and children need me. Each day in my own way I shall get better and better." The self-assessment form provided data upon which revisions in the treatment program were based.

Because the patient was frightened and fatigued, on admission to the hospital, temazepam (Restoril) 30 milligrams was prescribed for sleep during the first week. The patient had taken many psychotropic agents and other drugs in the past with no marked clinical improvement. For this reason it was decided that no additional *medication* would be prescribed and, as it happened, no other medication was required during the course of treatment. The patient's *nutritional needs* were assessed by a dietician, and he was placed on a diet commensurate with his gastrointestinal status. An *exercise* program was developed and adapted to his physical condition. Mr. B was kept busy, and he was told that it was important for him to engage in all of the activities available on the unit. Ward personnel were assigned to monitor and encourage his participation. Weekly family conferences were convened and marital roles were redefined as he took more responsibility for housekeeping chores and the care of the children.

After 2 weeks Mr. B was given a weekend pass to go home with his wife. The couple was asked to engage in *social/recreational activities* that included the children. All progress was to be recorded in a log, which would form the basis of future discussions during family conferences. The first weekend was a huge success for the entire family. Mr. B was able to control symptoms of pathologic anxiety and pain while participating in many pleasurable activities. As he emerged from his cocoon of depression, his family was overjoyed. During subsequent weeks he continued his improvement, and on discharge, in an ebullient state, was making plans to seek work outside the oil fields in a less strenuous occupation.

As an outpatient Mr. B continued to use relaxation techniques to lower anxiety and diminish pain. In addition, anxiety-evoking and pessimistic thoughts were reduced by techniques of encephalic reconditioning. His wife felt rejuvenated and her delight became infectious when, for the first time in a year, the couple went to movie theatres, to restaurants, and to the homes of friends. Mr. B began light repairs on his car and kept busy working in his yard. He bought bicycles for his daughter and himself, and together they cycled on progressively longer outings each day. To the surprise of everyone, he took his family on a week's vacation to Disneyworld, the first real vacation they had had in a long time.

Mr. B consulted his orthopedic surgeon who was satisfied with his progress and suggested that it was no longer necessary to wear a lumbar corset. Ambulation without the brace was now possible with only minimal discomfort. The patient's sleep patterns returned to normal and he no longer had nightmares. Anxiety, irritability, ruminations about the trauma, inability to concentrate, epigastric discomfort, and fatigue all diminished, and a pleasant, almost jubilant mood replaced dysphoria. His marital relationship improved, and pleasurable sexual interaction was restored. Mr. B's easy-going ways returned, his physical status improved, and reinvolvement with his family led to a happier, more optimistic outlook on life. Other people noticed his improvement and their comments reinforced positive changes in his behavior.

After 6 weeks of hospitalization and 4 months of once-weekly outpatient treatment, Mr. B was discharged. Follow-ups over a period of 2 years disclosed that the patient maintained his improvement. His lawsuit was settled out of court, and he used part of the financial settlement to establish a small business that he has operated successfully to this day.

CASE THREE: AUTOMOBILE ACCIDENT

Mrs. C, a widow in her late forties, tearfully related that 6 months previously she was involved in an automobile accident that resulted in the death of her husband. Since that time she had had crying spells, lost 15 pounds, felt fatigued, and had difficulties sleeping. In addition to symptoms of depression, the patient complained of anxiety and agitation, frequent nightmares in which she relived the accident, headaches, hot flashes associated with sweating, heavy feelings in her chest with periodic palpitations, nausea ("I have a tight knot in my stomach all of the time"), dizzy spells, difficulties in concentration, irritability, and fears of going crazy and of being alone, especially at night. She also had a phobia of driving on expressways or bridges and experienced phobic anxiety whenever she was in an automobile. She also stated that her adolescent son was becoming a behavioral problem.

History of the Present Illness

One Saturday afternoon about 6 months ago, the patient's husband was driving her to a suburban shopping center. They were traveling on an expressway, and the traffic had backed up, forcing her husband to slow, then stop, the car. While waiting for the traffic to clear, her husband suddenly hollered, "Watch out." His warning was cut short by a terrible collision with a fully loaded dump truck traveling at high speed. The truck hit the rear of the car very hard and propelled it forward into the air. The door of the car burst open, and Mrs. C and her husband were hurled out of the vehicle onto the pavement. She got to her feet shakily and went to her husband's assistance. She looked down at him and saw that he was bleeding profusely from the head and was unconscious. Taking his head in her hands to comfort him, she noticed that his skull was cracked and brains seemed to be oozing out. Screaming hysterically, she begged onlookers to come to her aid. No help was forthcoming for almost an hour until the police cleared the traffic jam, allowing the passage of an ambulance. Inside the ambulance she was aghast at the pale gray coloring of her husband's face and collapsed when ambulance attendants told her he had multiple fractures, was critically injured, and "probably would not make it." At the hospital Mrs. C was revived and treated for minor bruises of her legs and one hand. Her husband had been pronounced dead on arrival, and afterward she felt guilty because she had survived and her husband had not.

At home Mrs. C felt terrible. Sleep was interrupted by nightmares of the accident that depicted the bloodied and crushed head of her husband. Fatigue followed insomnia, and her mood fluctuated from irritability to despair. She was plagued with thoughts about the accident, which she relived again and again in her imagination. At times she experienced intense anxiety, severe headaches, and dizzy spells, and believed she was going crazy. Heavy feelings in her chest were punctuated by palpitations. Nausea and stomach pains led to anorexia and weight loss. Her phobia of driving on elevated expressways, bridges, and in unfamiliar places limited her mobility. Elsewhere when driving alone she was tense and nervous, especially in heavy traffic. She became obsessed about the accident and the death of her husband. In a ritualistic manner she visited the cemetery two or three times a week to place flowers and to pray.

Additional stress emerged when the patient's adolescent son became unruly. After her physical symptoms intensified, mystifying her physicians, she was hospitalized for a "thorough physical examination." A myriad of examinations and tests revealed no organic basis for her symptoms. She was discharged from the hospital and told that although she had not yet gotten over the death of her husband, in time she would. Time did not heal and she was referred for psychiatric treatment.

Past History

The patient's memories of her childhood were basically happy ones. As the youngest of four children, she admitted that she was the center of attention and probably "a bit spoiled." Her preschool years passed pleasantly as did grade school. She had many friends, and was an excellent student and the "teacher's pet." Academic excellence continued in high school, where she was involved in many extracurricular activities. She also had an active social life and a "steady" boyfriend whom she married upon graduation. College was interrupted by pregnancy, and her husband got a job to support the developing family. The years passed comfortably, centered around family life. She had three children and spent the major part of the next 10 years tending to the responsibilities of wife and mother. She and her husband were well-matched. Although they had many friends, the family was close-knit and did not require much outside social interaction. At the time of the accident, her daughter and older son were married, while the younger son, in his late teens, was still living at home. In a year, when their younger son had completed high school, she and her husband planned to retire and had purchased a camper in order to leisurely tour the United States. These plans were tragically ended by the accident.

Family History

Both of the patient's parents were deceased. She remembers her father as a stern but kindly man who doted upon her when she was young. Her mother, the disciplinarian of the family, was recalled less fondly but respectfully. "Mother was a hard worker who made many demands upon herself and her family," the patient reminisced. Her family was very religious and she was inculcated with a puritan work ethic. She maintained good relationships with her parents until their death, even though they were geographically separated by over 500 miles. Her father died of heart disease and her mother of cancer.

Her two older sisters and a brother live in different states, and she maintains regular contact with them.

Treatment

The patient's trauma — the shouts of warning from her husband, collision with the speeding dump truck, being hurled into the air and onto the pavement, the sight of her seriously injured husband, the announcement of his death — was severe, and it was clear that her life would never be the same. The sequence of events leading to her husband's death impacted upon her nervous system and produced high levels of autonomic activity that culminated with her fainting in the ambulance. Subsequently, scenes of the accident and its aftermath dominated her mind and prolonged anxiety, which deepened her depression. In an agitated state, prior to psychiatric treatment, she could not piece her life together and lamented her deceased husband while pitying herself and excoriating the careless truck driver. Litigation eventually ensued.

During the *explanation-education* stage of treatment, the mental mechanisms underlying PTSD and depression were discussed. Concepts of retraumatization and cognitive causes of depression were related to the patient, emphasizing that rumination ruins recovery. Techniques of *encephalic reconditioning* can counter these obsessional proclivities, the patient was told. Time spent thinking about the accident and its consequences, particularly the death of her husband, was reduced when the patient learned the techniques of thought stopping and positive encephalic practice. She was also urged to engage in attention-capturing activities whenever she thought about the accident and to avoid protracted periods of solitude. The patient received *training in relaxation*, including both PMR and self-hypnosis. She was an adept pupil and was able to utilize these techniques to reduce anxiety and later to initiate sleep. Self-hypnosis was used as an adjuvant in encephalic reconditioning to change anxiety-evoking or pessimistic and gloomy thoughts. Audio tapes containing instructions regarding PMR and self-hypnosis were prepared for her, and it was recommended that she listen to these tapes daily. At the onset of treatment, *medication* was prescribed for depression and sleep disturbance. The tricyclic antidepressant trazodone HCl (Desyrel) was prescribed, and the patient responded well to a dose of 100 milligrams before bedtime. Insomnia was treated by flurazepam 30 milligrams before bedtime. The patient remained on trazodone for several months, but regular use of a sedative was required for only a few weeks.

Although possessing excellent secretarial skills, Mrs. C was not working and spent most of the day at home alone. Under these conditions she was vulnerable to anxiety and depression, because she had ample time and opportunity to think and morbidly obsess about the accident and its consequences. Frequent trips to the cemetery each week to pray and to place flowers at her husband's grave were exercises in self-torment and extended beyond the bounds of propriety and normal grief. During *problem-solving sessions*, she was encouraged to cease her funereal pilgrimage and to visit the grave site only at appropriate occasions, such as a birthday, anniversary, or All Saints' Day. Discussions during problem solving centered on reinvolving her in the outside world. She expressed an interest in returning to work as a secretary and taking some college courses. It was decided initially to concentrate on work, since that activity would regularize her life. From eight to five each day, her time would be occupied and she would have an opportunity to meet and talk with other people. Although her husband's life insurance left her comfortably situated, money earned as a result of work added to her security. She quickly procured a secretarial position and also enrolled for a night course at a community college.

The patient quickly improved — her anxiety lessened and her mood elevated. However, during the evening and especially on weekends, she experienced intense headaches and gastrointestinal upsets. Her *self-assessment form* revealed that symptomatic behavior was associated with thoughts about the accident, the death of her husband, loneliness, and the future. She was encouraged to continue the use of thought stopping and positive encephalic practice and to consider involvement in *social/recreational activities*. It was recommended that she join a community social organization devoted to the needs of persons who have been separated from their spouses by divorce or death. She began attending lectures, parties, dances, and other events at the community organization, and her interest in people picked up. Even though she was a pleasant woman and a good conversationalist, Mrs. C was ill at ease and awkward with men. She had been married for over 25 years and had never dated a man other than her late husband. She felt guilty and acted cautiously when talking casually to men, thinking that she was being disloyal to her deceased husband. She had to be disabused of that idea and persuaded that guilt was inappropriate. Gradually her discomfort subsided and she began enjoying herself socially. Work, school, and social engagements filled her time in a pleasing and pleasurable way. However, she reported that her younger son was becoming hostile. A *family conference* was convened to discuss the son's negativistic attitude and belligerent behavior. The boy disclosed that he was angry because his mother was involved in too many activities. He also felt that his deceased father would not approve of his mother dating other men. It soon became apparent that the son was depressed, and his complaints reflected the need for support and reassurance from his mother. These issues were discussed and resolved during family conferences in combination with several individual sessions with the boy.

After 6 months of treatment, Mrs. C was still phobic about driving across elevated expressways and bridges and in unfamiliar places. Even when driving elsewhere, she became wary and anxious when the weather was bad or the traffic heavy, fearing a rear end collision. She still could not drive or be driven near the area where the original accident took place. A program of in vivo *systematic desensitization* was developed. Desensitization began with the least anxiety-evoking driving situation in the hierarchy. The first assignment was driving on an elevated expressway in good weather with little or no traffic, until the first exit was reached. When the patient drove her car in that situation without experiencing appreciable anxiety, she was instructed to move up to a more difficult and anxiety-evoking one. The patient then began to drive longer distances in heavier traffic, which eventually included inclement weather. Bridges were added next, and the patient was advised to bring a friend during initial in vivo driving sessions. As the patient became desensitized of her fear of driving across small bridges, longer bridges were added. Finally she was able to drive across all bridges by herself. She was advised to keep a log of her driving experiences, which was discussed at each therapy session. Eventually, she was able to drive on the section of the expressway where her husband was killed.

The patient was terminated following 58 sessions of treatment extending over a 14-month period. Anxiety symptoms abated as did headaches and gastrointestinal upsets. Her phobia of driving on expressways and bridges and in unfamiliar places was successfully treated, but occasionally she was apprehensive in heavy traffic. She no longer obsessed about the accident but at times gets tearful when she thinks about the loss of her husband. Her nightmares have ceased, and her sleeping patterns have returned to normal. Her depression was alleviated and the antidepressants discontinued. Her appetite returned, and she gained the weight she had lost. The patient's youngest son settled down and now attends college. Mrs. C's social life is good. She has a steady male friend and is contemplating marriage. Three years following termination, the patient reported that her lawsuit was settled favorably and she maintained her improvement.

CASE FOUR: RAPE*

Miss D, a young elementary school teacher, had been raped and complained of an extreme fear of being alone at night. She ruminated about the possibility of someone breaking into her house, and this interfered with sleep. She was hypersensitive to night noises and exhibited a startle response whenever she heard a quick, sharp noise. The schoolteacher's anxiety symptoms were so intense and unbearable that she moved from her apartment into her parent's house where she felt more comfortable. Her phobia of being alone at night conflicted with her desire to be independent.

History of Present Illness

One and a half years prior to treatment, the patient was raped late one night in her apartment. The odious incident began when she was awakened by noises in her apartment. She opened her eyes and saw an indistinct human form in her bedroom. Her scream was cut short by a powerful hand held over her mouth. At the same instant, she felt the prick of a knife point on her neck and heard a deep voice admonishing her to be quiet or she would be dead. A few minutes later, the hand left her mouth and began tearing off her

---

*Reprinted with permission from C. B. Scrignar (1983), *Stress Strategies: The Treatment of the Anxiety Disorders*, Basel, S. Karger.

nightclothes. The sharp point of the knife was still at her throat as the man raped her. The patient felt physically numb, but her mind was racing wildly. Death or mutilation was inevitable, she thought, and her body responded with severe palpitations, dyspnea, and trembling. After he had finished, the rapist said he would not kill her. Momentary relief turned to terror when the rapist said he would murder her if she told anyone about the incident. The masked miscreant bound and gagged the young schoolteacher and left. For 1 hour she remained still, her body racked with fear, thinking that the rapist might return. Finally, with great difficulty, she freed herself and telephoned her parents. Her father rushed to the apartment and took his sobbing daughter home. Miss D refused to call the police, suspecting that the rapist was the janitor of the building and fearing further abuse and possible retaliation. Her parents reluctantly agreed, but insisted that she move out of the apartment into their house.

The young woman was still shaken after the incident and experienced nightmares, insomnia, extreme anxiety, and a hypersensitivity to night noises. She ruminated about the trauma and had vivid recollections of the rape, openly expressing the sentiment that she was lucky to be alive. While symptoms gradually subsided as time passed, she remained fearful of the dark, especially when she was alone. One year passed and Miss D, desirous of autonomous living, told her parents she would like to move into her own place. Her father purchased a small house for her located in a good neighborhood. Before the patient moved into the house, the father hired a home security specialist to make the home intruder-proof. Dead-bolt locks, burglar bars, an alarm system, and outdoor lights were installed to safeguard the patient from interlopers. At the patient's request, her mother stayed with her during the first week, but on the first night alone she was restless and could not sleep. The young woman presaged a repetition of the rape and was startled and alerted by normal nocturnal noises. On the second night, the patient, now fatigued and frantic, phoned her father and asked to be taken home. Shortly thereafter the patient sought treatment.

Past History

The patient described her childhood as happy. Until college she attended an all-girl parochial school. Miss D was an excellent student and, although shy and reserved, had many friends. She did not date until her university years and even then did so sporadically, never having a steady boyfriend. During this time she attended a university in the community and lived with her parents. Following graduation she began teaching elementary school, and 2 years later, against her parents wishes, began living by herself. She lived in her apartment successfully and happily for almost 2 years before the rape incident.

Family History

Miss D was the oldest of five children. Her parents, staunch Catholics, were hard-working people who were overly involved in the lives of their children. They tended to be overprotective, the mother especially, making unsolicited decisions for the patient. As a reaction to this control by her parents, she desired independence and got her own apartment.

Treatment

Although the violence of the rape had occurred a year and a half earlier, the patient kept the sexual assault alive by imagining a recurrence. The concept of encephalic retraumatization was related to the young schoolteacher during the *explanation-education* phase of treatment in the context of a PTSD. For over an hour during and after the rape, she suffered from the effects of high levels of autonomic nervous system activity. While in this state of autonomic arousal, she became conditioned to various elements associated with her trauma. Being alone, darkness, and night noises continued to serve as conditioned stimuli for anxiety. Over the course of a year and a half, the acute symptoms of PTSD had subsided. Anxiety, nightmares, insomnia, and ruminations were reduced in intensity and frequency. A recrudescence of symptoms occurred when she moved into her own house and was alone at night. Being alone, darkness, and night noises vivified memories of the rape, and this encephalic activity increased anxiety. The resurgence of symptoms was frightening and caused the patient to move back into her parents' home. A reduction in anxiety and a feeling of relief reinforced this pattern of phobic avoidance. Her confidence was shaken when she unsuccessfully coped with her anxiety. Nightmares and ruminations about being raped together with anxiety and insomnia fostered dependency upon her parents and interfered with the schoolteacher's desire to be independent. Coercion, the forceful subjugation and violation of individual will, is terrible, the patient was told during explanation-education, but once a vile act is over, it must be put aside and forgotten. Concepts of conditioning, phobic avoidance, and phobic anxiety were explained in the context of a PTSD (Burgess 1983). Furthermore, the patient was reassured, anxiety-reducing interventions and systematic desensitization were methods that would be utilized to successfully treat her disorder.

The patient's anxiety had become chronic. Therefore, she received *training in relaxation* consisting of PMR and self-hypnosis. The patient was to practice these techniques daily and to utilize relaxation methods whenever she felt anxious. In addition, PMR or self-hypnosis could curtail insomnia and serve as a substitute for a sedative.

Understandably, the patient was preoccupied with the circumstances of the rape, but ruminations and faulty interpretations served only to perpetuate her PTSD. Miss D had to believe that she was in a safe environment at night, and that proper precautions (dead-bolt locks, burglar bars, alarm system, outside lights) would prevent a repetition of the rape. Although this is not 100 percent true, these precautions are the best defense against assault, along with prudent judgment and common sense. Although security may be imperfect, rapists do not lurk behind every bush, and one cannot live in a state of constant fear. Miss D, while lying in bed at night, misinterpreted normal night noises as signs of a forced entry by a sadistic rapist, and these encephalic activities prophesying constant danger of an assault generated and maintained high anxiety. The conditions of darkness and being alone also stimulated thoughts and images about a sexual assault, death, and mutilation, which in turn stimulated anxiety. To counter encephalically produced anxiety, she was taught techniques of *encephalic reconditioning*. It was suggested that thought- and image-stopping procedures as well as positive encephalic practice would reduce the flow of encephalic stimuli and diminish anxiety. The patient was encouraged to practice these procedures as often as necessary and to insert appropriate self-statements correcting fallacious thinking, such as "I have taken the necessary precautions and my home is safe. Those noises I hear are the normal sounds of a slumbering city. I have experienced a terrible assault but I have survived." Encephalic reconditioning was facilitated when she filled out a *self-assessment form* daily and discussed it during sessions.

Since Miss D was extremely apprehensive and her symptoms were beginning to interfere with her work, *medication* (diazepam 5 milligrams) was prescribed three times daily for 2 weeks. Insomnia prevented proper rest and fatigue interfered with her functioning as a schoolteacher, so flurazepam hydrochloride 30 milligrams was temporarily prescribed before bedtime until she mastered techniques of muscle relaxation and self-hypnosis.

The patient's phobia was now addressed, and imaginal *systematic desensitization* proceeded with the hierarchical theme of being alone at home. The variables associated with this theme were time and illumination. Desensitization began with scenes of being alone for periods of short duration and high levels of illumination. For example, the first scene was: You are in your house alone for 10 minutes and it is broad daylight. Time spent in the house was increased and the level of illumination decreased as the hierarchy progressed. Subsequent scenes were: (1) You are in your house alone for 1 hour and it is twilight. (2) You are in your house alone for 2 hours. It is dark outside, but your house is fully lighted. (3) You are in your bedroom alone and resting with the nightlight on. (4) You are in your own bedroom alone, attempting sleep, and the room is dark.

During in vivo desensitization, the presence of the mother for a predetermined time each night and the luminosity of the bedroom were variables. As desensitization progressed, the mother's time each night was limited, and the light in the bedroom was lessened by the use of a rheostat. Undue anxiety during in vivo desensitization was to be managed by muscle relaxation, self-hypnosis, and encephalic reconditioning. Diazepam was to be used only if necessary.

With the patient's permission, a *family conference* was held and the mother was included as a member of the treatment team. Techniques of in vivo desensitization were explained to the mother as they related to the phobic portion of her daughter's PTSD. The mother was a worrier and had to be persuaded that her daughter was a grown woman who could take care of herself. The mother also had to be convinced that the security precautions to safeguard the house were adequate. With some hesitancy the mother and daughter agreed to follow the proposed treatment plan. At times, this proved to be difficult because the mother was reluctant to leave at night if her daughter displayed any anxiety. This issue was mediated and desensitization progressed satisfactorily.

Treatment terminated after 11 sessions extending over a 4-month period. Miss D was able to sleep in her own house with minimal discomfort and eventually with ease. Her nightmares and insomnia ceased. Her anxiety diminished significantly, and her ruminations about the trauma gradually subsided over time. Two years following termination, the patient was experiencing no difficulty sleeping and was able to stay in her house alone whenever she desired. Occasionally, thoughts about the rape intruded upon her mind, but she was able to use thought stopping and relaxation techniques successfully to eliminate them. She was enjoying her work as a schoolteacher and had a steady boyfriend.

CASE FIVE: THE VIETNAM-ERA VETERAN AND CRIMINAL CONDUCT

The following is a case history of a Vietnam-era combat veteran (Mr. E) who was charged with the kidnapping of persons and assault with a dangerous weapon at a VA Hospital and tried in a federal court. This case involves medical, legal, and moral issues. The information upon which this case report is based was obtained from interviews with the veteran and his mother, wife, and attorney. The following records were also reviewed: military service records from the U.S. Marine Corps, medical records from the VA Hospital, reports from the Vet Center, psychiatric reports from a court-appointed psychiatrist, and a report from the U.S. Department of Justice Bureau of Prison's Medical Center for Federal Prisoners at Springfield, Missouri. In addition, an audio cassette recording of negotiations between the veteran and authorities, which took place at a VA Hospital, was available for study. An analysis was also made of the veteran's journal (diary), which he had maintained following his discharge from the U.S. Marine Corps until the time of his arrest.

Developmental History

The veteran's family was poor, living in a government project in a section of the city that could best be characterized as a ghetto.

His father, a dissolute man, was absent from the home a great deal, so his mother bore the brunt of responsibility for the maintenance of the family. The veteran was undersized for his age, and his small stature caused others to call him "runt," "peewee," "gnat," and "small stuff." He was sickly as a youth. When he was 8 years old, his mother gave him a severe beating for what she considered to be his incorrigible behavior. Following this punishment a purplish discoloration remained in his skin. His mother became alarmed and took him to see a doctor who made a diagnosis of idiopathic thrombocytopenic purpura. Many visits to Charity Hospital clinics ensued over the next 2 years, requiring his absence from school. The boy's grades dropped and he flunked the second grade. Already sensitive about his size, he felt awkward and embarrassed because the demotion placed him in a class with younger boys, many of whom were of superior size. Embarrassment in school led to truancy, which added to absences for medical reasons and resulted in poor academic performance and further flunking. At age 10 his idiopathic thrombocytopenic purpura "spontaneously cleared." He did not regularly attend school, and when he did, he was inattentive. School counselors labeled him as "learning disabled," and he was placed in a special education class. Teachers failed to awaken his intellectual curiosity, and he stagnated, sleeping or mischievously disrupting the class. His formal education came to an end at age 15 (he was still in the fourth grade) when he adamantly refused to continue in school. His mother acquiesced with this decision. Over the next 2 years, he ran the streets and occasionally got odd jobs. Idleness allowed opportunity for delinquency, and he began to associate with older boys who acquainted him with the practice of drinking wine, popping pills, and smoking marijuana. He and his peers were arrested on three occasions for assault and battery, disturbing the peace, and theft. The charges were eventually dropped, but on one occasion he had to appear in juvenile court with his mother. At age 17 he decided to join the armed services.

The Vietnam Experience

Mr. E attempted to join the U.S. Army, but was rejected and told he was illiterate. Later, at the height of the Vietnam conflict, he applied for the U.S. Marine Corps, and the Marines, apparently less discriminating than the Army, accepted him. He successfully completed the Marine's rigorous basic training and was immediately sent to Vietnam. After arriving in Vietnam, he was given a 1-week orientation course and then sent into combat. Mr. E admitted that he was scared and for the first time in his life came into close contact with dead people. Following a combat action, it was part of his duties to find, count, and stack "like cord wood" dead bodies of North Vietnamese soldiers. He vividly remembers a woman with a baby in her arms who was burned by a white phosphorus shell and looked like a "black blob." He was given the nickname of "mini-man" and was assigned the duties of a tunnel rat. It was his responsibility to crawl into tunnels with a hand grenade and a 45-caliber pistol to ferret out Vietcong and locate caches of weapons and food. He traded his M-16 rifle for a more versatile sawed-off 12-gauge shotgun. While on patrol one day, he saw a head bob up from behind a wall and he reflexively fired at the profile. After crawling over the wall, he peered down at the first human being he had ever killed — an old, withered Vietnamese peasant whose face was "blown away." He became nauseated and vomited. Over the course of the next few months, he witnessed extensive death and carnage and was in an almost constant state of fear. Anxiety was attenuated by alcohol, and sleeplessness was soothed with soporific drugs. Although Mr. E insisted that alcohol, hashish, and heroin did not interfere with his duties, he became increasingly agitated, anxious, and fearful. Danger was everywhere, as evidenced by the sound of mortars and gunshots from snipers and the explosion of booby traps. Even though he was frightened, the veteran continued to perform his duties as a soldier. One morning he woke up with a fever, and a medical corpsman suspected Mr. E was suffering from heat stroke or malaria. He was sent to the rear for medical attention. He was not seriously ill, and after several days insisted that he be transferred back to his unit. Upon returning to his squad, he discovered that only four men were still alive. Eight of his buddies were killed by the Vietcong in an ambush. Mr. E was certain that his time was up and that he would never leave Vietnam alive. His premonition almost proved to be correct. While on night patrol a few days later, he saw a hand grenade, heard an explosion, and was knocked on his back, lapsing into unconsciousness. Later, when he awoke in the hospital, he was swathed in bandages. Thinking that he was mutilated, he became panic stricken and shouted for the nurse, who arrived shortly and calmly assured him that he was intact. He had shrapnel wounds involving his left and right upper legs, left testicle, and left forearm and hand. He was told that if he had not covered his face with his left arm, he might have been blinded. He was sent back to the United States where he spent several months in a military hospital. He signed a waiver and was given an honorable discharge, received a purple heart commendation, and was placed on 50 percent disability.

After Vietnam

Immediately after his discharge from the Marine Corps, Mr. E lived with his mother. She reported that her son was not the same person and seemed to have undergone a personality change. Before Vietnam her son had laughed and joked, but now he was sober, "held things in," and liked to stay by himself. Nervousness accompanied his withdrawn state, and nightmares about Vietnam frequently interrupted his sleep. He began to drink because alcohol "soothed his nerves," induced sleep, and stopped his mind from thinking about Vietnam. He received training in auto mechanics, but found it difficult to keep a steady job. Mr. E was likable, but his employers could not tolerate his absenteeism. Fortunately, his disability check from the U.S. Government met his minimal needs. Two years after he was discharged from the Marine Corps, Mr. E married. His wife did not know him before the war, but she related that he was quite nervous, had frequent headaches, and talked a great deal about Vietnam. She added that he had difficulties sleeping and frequently woke up terror stricken and sweating profusely. Upon becoming calm he would mutter, "It's Vietnam again." During the 10 years of their marriage, the wife said he was a good father to their three children and was a nonviolent person. "He would not hurt a fly," his wife emphatically stated. "In fact, he doesn't hunt like his friends because he dislikes killing animals." His wife insisted that even though they had tough times, their marriage had basically been a good one. She admitted that her husband drank, smoked marijuana, and used other drugs, especially when he associated with old friends who were veterans of Vietnam. During the time she has known him, the wife stated, her husband had never been arrested nor put in jail for any reason. His wife worked and together with the veteran's disability check, they had been able to meet the family's financial needs.

Three years after his discharge from the Marines, Mr. E. was admitted to the VA Hospital drug abuse program. Dissatisfied with treatment, he abruptly quit. A year later he was hospitalized and treated at the VA Hospital for acute hepatitis. Shortly afterward, he had a minor surgical operation at the VA and several admissions for alcoholism and gastritis. On one occasion he was hospitalized after experiencing severe stomach cramps and vomiting coffee-grounds material. Six years after discharge from the Marines, he was put on a methadone maintenance program, but after a few months was discharged from the program. Over the course of 10 years, Mr. E was hospitalized at the VA Hospital on 14 occasions. Although he complained of stress symptoms, sleep disturbance, and nightmares and became visibly upset when talking about Vietnam or viewing scenes of the conflict on television, a diagnosis of PTSD was never made. Substance Use Disorder was the only diagnosis rendered.

Discontentment with the VA Hospital led Mr. E to seek assistance at the Vet Center, an organization devoted to meeting the needs of veterans, primarily of the Vietnam era. Whenever he was agitated and obsessed with memories of Vietnam, he sought solace and received relief from counselors at the Vet Center. For the first time he heard the term "Post-Traumatic Stress Disorder" as applied to Vietnam-era veterans. During rap sessions Mr. E queried, "Why hasn't the VA diagnosed and treated me for this disorder?" His tirades during these sessions included a denunciation of the U.S. Government, and his angry cries were applauded by other veterans. He believed that an ungrateful government was trying to sweep the memory of Vietnam under the rug along with the men who answered the call to duty. During rap sessions, self-righteous proclamations resulted only in a temporary catharsis, for the ranting ultimately led to an intensification of dysphoric feelings. Ten days before the hostage incident, Mr. E, very upset and angry, went to the Vet Center and told his counselor that he was denied admission to the VA Hospital. The counselor attempted vainly to intercede for him.

The Diary

Since his discharge from the Marine Corps, he had the habit of secluding himself and writing in a diary whenever he got upset. His writing began in earnest in 1977, 7 years after his discharge and 5 years before the hostage incident. The following are some selected quotes:

> "I came back from Vietnam filled with hate and nightmares that keep me on drugs to sleep at night. I would like to know if I am sick but I can't make myself go see the doctor. I have a feeling of sadness and death. I am a man filled with fears, like a boy. I don't sleep at night. This makes me into what my father is, an alcoholic. I tried to get help from the VA, but they never seemed to have the time. I think what makes a man go mad is if he can't sit and say what he feels about things. My fear, at first, when I came home was the want to kill still inside of me and the hate in me is still strong. Knowing the unhappiness inside of me has made me think of doing many things, even to take my own life but my will to live and find what I want in life is keeping me going."

The diary reflected his fears while he was in Vietnam and contained questions about the war after he was discharged. Depressing words of sadness and unhappiness permeated its pages. In January 1980 he wrote:

> "How do we tell our mothers and fathers we feel proud when we know what it was really like there in Vietnam. . . . I remember one time I went to the VA Hospital because I was using too many drugs and was flipping out and went to ask for help with my life, just to have the nurse call a big red neck guard to tell me what I was doing was a no-no. If we Nam vets can't go to the hospital for help, where in the hell do they want us to go? . . . God, I would just like people to know the hell and nightmares of sleeping, but yet never being able to stop thinking. Knowing if you don't drink or use drugs you will not sleep. How many walking time bombs like me are walking around and so damn lost? They do not know if they are coming or going."

Two months prior to the hostage incident, he wrote:

> "God, why does the pain hurt me so bad? To keep living is to fear every day of my life. I only know one way and that is death. . . . My madness keeps going on and on. The hate and pain of death still walks

within me. . . . The nightmares of Vietnam still stay inside of me. . . . Every day I ask myself, 'Why don't the people in government reach out and help us in our fight to overcome the things they had us do for them?' . . . I do not know myself how long I can keep fighting this madness I have inside of me. . . . I just hope that what I feel never gets out of me. . . . At times these things get so bad I feel like I could take my life but I just keep fighting back. I guess what this is coming to one day is I still have to win or lose. . . . I feel, even in death, I can put the hate and pain to rest. I would then close my eyes with happiness in my heart. . . . When I die, Vietnam will have a lot to do with it."

Mr. E continued to agonize over and lament about Vietnam.

"I am 30 years old and I have been home 11 years now, but yet I can still hear the screams of death. The faces of the innocent men, women, and kids that we killed. We killed many we did not have to. . . . I find myself asking God to forgive me. . . . God, how it hurts. . . . Just thinking of sleep brings on fears that you are going to see all of those faces again. . . . As I write this, the smell of death is well within me. . . . How can I be sure that I am or have just gone mad? To keep going on is a fight in itself. . . . My mind and me still don't get along with each other. . . . Most people fear death or being killed but yet my biggest fear is life itself."

One month prior to the hostage incident, he addressed his youngest daughter in his diary:

"You are the purest, honesty of my life — putting the fire back in my heart. You have showed me how to love again and how to smile when I felt I didn't know how. You have made me want to wake up every day, just so I will see your happy face. My child, you have shown me how it feels just to think of someone and to feel all good inside. How can someone be so little and yet bring so much joy to everyone? You have been life for me. Without you, I would be so empty inside. You are a gift from God. With you, he sent love, life, and happiness and for this I will always love you within my heart."

The Hostage Incident

One Saturday morning Mr. E arose at 6:30, fixed himself a cup of coffee and began to read the newspaper. A story entitled "Vietnam Suicide: I Was Never Given Any Help" caught his attention.

The news story, datelined Miami, opened with a description of a Vietnam-era veteran who threw himself off an expressway bridge. "When he hit the pavement," the news story went on, "the body count from the Vietnam war went up by one." As he read and reread the account of the veteran's death by suicide, he became anxious, agitated, and angry. Very upset, he left his house to buy some Percodan, which he "shot up." The drug pacified him and he went home and slept all day. Upon awakening, he cut out the newspaper article about the suicide and pasted it into a scrapbook along with similar stories about Vietnam-era veterans. As he began scrutinizing other stories in his scrapbook, anxiety and anger mounted, and Mr. E began drinking wine to sooth his jitters. His wife, having viewed similar scenes on many occasions, quietly slipped off to bed with the expectation that he would be okay by the next day. Wine did not mollify him, so he left home at about 10:30 p.m. and went to a neighborhood bar. At the tavern he met another Vietnam-era veteran and they talked about the suicide, swapped stories about their Vietnam experiences, and commiserated about their mutual misfortune. The veterans celebrated their relationship by smoking hashish, and as time passed, Mr. E became dazed by the drug. "The hash hit me good," he remembered before he went into a state of not remembering.

At dawn of the following day, the veteran dimly recalled going to a friend's house where he borrowed a 12-gauge shotgun. Whenever he got upset, he liked to borrow his friend's gun and head out into the marshes to get away from it all. No shot was ever fired because he did not believe in hunting and killing living things. The peace and solitude of the swamp and the feeling of the shotgun cradled in his arms made him curiously calm and reposeful; these feelings were similar to those that he had first noticed in Vietnam following a battle. Later, on Sunday morning, he recalled driving his car into the emergency entrance of the VA Hospital. "Everything appeared to be extra bright, like a lot of lights were on," he stated. Mr. E walked up the stairs to the hospital entrance and then he went back to the car to get the shotgun. He related that he did not feel drunk or drugged, but that he felt different, a new experience. Everything seemed to be extra bright, in slow motion, and unreal. He walked into the hospital and down the corridor and turned into a room full of people. A patient was lying on a litter and Mr. E told an attendant to wheel him out of the room. A male nurse said, "Let everyone go and I'll stay." All of the people in the room left, except the nurse. The enormity of his action suddenly dawned upon Mr. E and he became distraught and began to cry. He put the shotgun barrel in his mouth but could not reach the trigger to fire it. Over the next several hours there were telephone conversations with police negotiators, a counselor at the Vet Center, and friends and relatives. Finally, the nurse asked if he could leave, and Mr. E assented. In response to requests from the police, Mr. E pushed the shotgun out of the room and walked out. He was quickly apprehended by two Federal Bureau of Investigation (FBI) agents and taken to a room with a priest, his wife, and some friends. After a tearful reunion, he was formally arrested and taken to prison.

Discussion

An unstable family background, chronic childhood illness, and poverty during Mr. E's developmental years certainly contributed to feelings of insecurity and nervousness. His diminutive size and continued failure in school contributed to feelings of inadequacy. Although he was involved in delinquent activities as a juvenile, he was not truly antisocial. Occasional fights, petty thievery, and drug experimentation could be considered "normal" for his socioeconomic group. It is curious that at the height of the Vietnam conflict, the U.S. Army rejected him whereas the Marine Corps accepted him. Many years later Mr. E would focus on this "happenstance" and recall the slogan of antiwar hecklers that he was "cannon fodder." As a recruit he did well during boot camp, a considerable achievement considering the spartan quality of Marine Corps basic training. While in Vietnam he was exposed to many traumatic events including the death and maiming of women, children, and buddies. Frequently, he envisioned with abhorrence the faceless form of the old Vietnamese peasant whom he had killed. Alcohol and drugs assuaged his guilt and anxiety and allowed him to continue to function as a soldier. His final trauma in Vietnam was twofold. The first occurred with the grenade explosion that wounded him. The second trauma occurred upon awakening in the hospital when he looked at his arms and legs swathed in bandages and thought that he might be armless, legless, or devoid of his genitals. His physical wounds healed and he was discharged from the Marines with a purple heart and a monthly 50 percent disability check.

Mr. E floundered in his attempt to cope with civilian life. Symptoms of stress interfered with his adjustment. Intrusive memories and vivid visual impressions of war in Vietnam generated pathologic anxiety, impaired sleep, and erupted violently in the form of flashbacks and nightmares. Clearly, he was suffering from a PTSD. Unfortunately, neither he nor his physicians at the VA Hospital recognized this. He discovered that respite from his tortuous thoughts could be achieved by drinking alcohol and using drugs. This form of self-treatment for his PTSD was not satisfactory since substance abuse created additional problems. The clinicians at the VA Hospital focused on the important but peripheral problem of drug abuse, neglecting the central issue of PTSD. Notations in his diary clearly indicated that he was struggling with the symptoms of PTSD but did not know where to turn for help. The diary also reflected an introspective and sensitive man who had strong feelings for other people. Although the veteran had used drugs intermittently over 10 years, his substance abuse was not accompanied by criminal behavior. In fact, he was never arrested, convicted, or incarcerated for a felony during the 12 years following his discharge from the U.S. Marines. Mr. E was no paragon of virtue, but he did not have an Antisocial Personality Disorder.

The Trial

During the trial in federal court, Mr. E's attorney utilized the insanity defense, asserting that the veteran, as a result of his combat experiences in Vietnam, had developed a PTSD and at the time of the alleged criminal act was not criminally responsible because he was experiencing a dissociative reaction. The federal court operates under the ALI Test, which states that "a defendant is not responsible for criminal conduct, if at the time of such conduct, as a result of mental disease or defect, he lacks substantial capacity, either to appreciate the wrongfulness of his conduct or to conform his conduct to the requirements of law." The U.S. attorney placed two physicians on the stand, one of whom was a psychiatrist, and both testified that the defendant, Mr. E, was not insane and did not meet the criteria for insanity as spelled out in the ALI Test. They also testified that the veteran had an Antisocial Personality Disorder and a Substance Use Disorder and disavowed any possibility that he was suffering from a PTSD. The defense placed two psychiatrists on the stand. Both testified that Mr. E was suffering from a PTSD and at the time of the alleged criminal conduct appeared to be suffering from a dissociative reaction. Although not psychotic in the usual sense, the defense psychiatrists agreed that the veteran seemed to fit the ALI Standard and was not criminally responsible. Furthermore, Substance Use Disorder was a secondary manifestation and was an unsuccessful attempt to self-treat his PTSD. Although he had exhibited antisocial traits as a juvenile, Mr. E had not been involved in any criminal activity since his discharge from the Marines. In addition, he displayed a strong attachment to his family, which further made questionable the diagnosis of Antisocial Personality Disorder.

The jury, the final arbitors in such matters, were perhaps more persuaded by the villainousness of Mr. E's conduct and found him guilty. The judge, who disallowed introduction of the veteran's diary, records from the Vet Center, and most of the testimony of the defense psychiatrist, was equally pragmatic and sentenced him to 10 years in a federal penitentiary. Mr. E's PTSD remains untreated.

TEN
SUMMARY AND CONCLUSION

HISTORICAL PERSPECTIVE – TRAUMA AND STRESS

The effects of trauma upon humans must have been observed since their origin. However, until recent times, the psychophysiological manifestations of trauma have not been well appreciated or understood. Wars have afforded clinicians of modern times the opportunity to study and observe large groups of men who have been subjected to the trauma of battle. It had been noted by earlier clinicians that long after the battle was over a number of soldiers with no evidence of physical injury continued to suffer from abnormalities which were especially evident in their cardiovascular system. Appellations such as "Irritable Heart," "Soldier's Heart," "Effort Syndrome," and "Neurocirculatory Asthenia" evolved to describe the phenomena, which were later noted in the general population among persons who had been subjected to civilian trauma. The symptoms of chest pain, palpitations, tachycardia, headaches, gastrointestinal upset, worry and fatigue found in a "nervous" person with no evidence of organic disease came to be known as "Neurasthenia." In 1895 Sigmund Freud suggested that anxiety was the common denominator underlying the syndrome of neurasthenia and proposed a unified theory and the term "Anxiety Neurosis" to more adequately explain the cluster of symptoms. Subsequently, the psychological manifestations of trauma were viewed within the context of a Neurosis and the term "Traumatic Neurosis" came into popular usage. Inconsistencies emerged, however, when the psychoanalytic theory of Neurosis was used to explain both lifelong neurotic behavior and symptoms precipitated by a trauma. Some clinicians, adhering to the psychoanalytic theory of Neurosis, attempted to force fact into theory. Traumatic Neurosis was defined as the reaction of a healthy individual to an overwhelming stress; Compensation or Triggered Neurosis designated those individuals who had a latent illness "triggered" or precipitated by the trauma. Little clarification emerged over the years, and the term "Traumatic Neurosis" was never incorporated as a diagnostic entity into the *DSM* of the APA (1980).

Meanwhile, in other quarters, the psychophysiological and neuroendocrine aspects of trauma (environmental emergency situations) were being studied by Cannon (1929; fight-or-flight response) and Selye (1946; 1950; 1956; the alarm reaction). Both investigators studied an organism's reaction to noxious or life-threatening environmental stimuli, and the symptoms they observed were strikingly similar to the clinical conditions "Irritable Heart," "Soldier's Heart," and "Effort Syndrome." The concept of stress, first introduced by Selye, was used to explain an organism's response to environmental trauma, and it became an accepted medical term. Although stress and anxiety involve the same psychophysiological systems, unification was impeded by the different theoretical orientations of stress research and psychoanalysis. Even today, the two terms cannot be freely interchanged, for in the minds of many clinicians, researchers, and even the public, stress is associated with environmentally induced events, whereas anxiety reflects an intrapsychic process.

Behaviorists have a natural kinship with stress researchers because both share a scientific orientation based on laboratory experimentation. Classic conditioning experiments by Pavlov (1927) that were refined by Wolpe (1948) demonstrated the relationship of pathologic anxiety, conditioning, and learning. Wolpe (1948) demonstrated that animals traumatized by an electrical shock exhibit signs of fearfulness (anxiety) and quickly become conditioned to elements of the situation in which the trauma took place, e.g., the experimental room, the cage, and the people involved in the experiment. The stimulus-response conditioning model can be analogized to trauma-anxiety with subsequent conditioned phobic behavior exhibited by human subjects who have been involved in a traumatic incident. Importantly, such a conceptualization allowed specific therapeutic interventions to be developed by behavior therapists over the last thirty years.

In 1980 the APA for the first time included the clinical entity PTSD in its *DSM*. Eschewing the term "Traumatic Neurosis" in favor of the atheoretical diagnosis of PTSD, the manual points out that psychoanalytic, social learning, cognitive, behavioral, and biological models have all attempted to explain the development of the various neurotic disorders. Rather than endorse any theoretical conceptualization, the framers of the manual decided to eliminate the diagnostic category of "Neurosis" and substitute instead the term "Anxiety Disorders," under which PTSD is listed. For the first time there was official acceptance by the psychiatric community that a mental disorder can develop following exposure to a traumatic incident.

TRAUMA AND PATHOLOGIC ANXIETY

The severity of the trauma and the degree of physical injury incurred do not necessarily correlate with the genesis and severity of a PTSD. Rather, the essential feature associated with the onset and maintenance of a PTSD is pathologic anxiety. Anxiety is always pathologic when the autonomic nervous system discharges: so intensively that it renders an individual incapable of speech, movement, or thought; unpredictably and frequently in an attacklike manner; or regularly for long periods of time. The effect of a trauma upon a person's autonomic nervous system determines whether or not a PTSD develops. The sources for the production and maintenance of pathologic anxiety are the Three E's — environmental, encephalic, or endogenous events. The Three E's can be easily identified by the administration of an ASP.

The Traumatic Principle is: Any environmental stimulus, whether it produces physical injury or not, if perceived as dangerous can be regarded as a trauma and precipitate a PTSD. The stimulus (trauma) is always an environmental event that impacts on one or more of the five sensory pathways to the brain, stimulating the sympathetic nervous system and resulting in pathologic anxiety. The environmental stimulus (trauma) may be of short duration and may occur only once, as in the case of an accident, or intermittently and be of longer duration, as in wars, imprisonment, or systematic torture.

When pathologic anxiety persists beyond 4 to 6 weeks, one must look toward encephalic events as the main factor in the sustentation of symptoms. Visual images and thoughts related to the original trauma have been recorded in the mind and these memories can be played back like a tape cassette in a video recorder. When these video tapes of the mind are played back, the autonomic nervous system is stimulated and pathologic anxiety results. Invariably, persons who develop a PTSD have vivid imaginations and become morbidly preoccupied with their trauma. Visual images that project dangerousness together with speculations that a more devastating outcome could have resulted from the trauma occupy the minds. The sights, sounds, and even the smells associated with the trauma are re-created in the mind together with self-statements as, "I could have been paralyzed, blinded, maimed, or killed." Persistence in the encephalic habit of thinking and visualizing scenes directly or indirectly related to the trauma is one of the more important factors contributing to the chronicity of PTSD. As time passes, disruptive, anxiety-evoking thoughts have reference to physical disability, inability to work, financial problems, marital conflicts, sexual dysfunction, disintegration of social relatonships, lack of enjoyment in life, and a contrasting of pretraumatic and post-traumatic behavior.

Endogenous sensations, afferently perceived as evidence of organic damage, stimulate pathologic anxiety. When pain or other uncomfortable physiological sensations persist in spite of treatment and negative examinations, patients can develop the erroneous idea that there is something physically wrong with them. Overreaction is pathological but not without substance, because the source of uncomfortable endogenous sensations may result from: residual soft tissue damage to muscles and ligaments resulting from the original trauma, which cannot be detected by objective examination; motor tension; or visceral symptoms resulting from pathologic anxiety. In all cases, pathologic anxiety either accentuates or initiates the uncomfortable somatic symptoms. Negative physical and laboratory examinations fail to quell the patient's complaints and suspicion of organic disease because the symptoms persist without adequate explanation.

Retraumatization — reliving the trauma by talk, thought, or visualization — perpetuates pathologic symptomatology. When patients encephalically re-create the frightening aspects of their trauma, pathologic anxiety is generated; the patients unwittingly sensitize themselves to various situational components of the trauma. Even questions by doctors, lawyers, or friends can evoke pathologic anxiety because patients relive the trauma when they begin to relate the history. Environmental stimuli similar to or resembling those present at the scene of the trauma can also stimulate encephalic activity whereby the trauma is visualized and the patient retraumatized.

Pain or other physical discomfort associated with the trauma can also stimulate encephalic activity, reminding the patient of the trauma and thus increasing pathologic anxiety. In turn, the physiological effects of anxiety intensify pain and create additional discomfort, and these increased endogenous sensations are encephalically perceived as evidence of serious physical injury. This cycle, the Spiral Effect, explains how pathologic anxiety can be intensified in lieu of any observable environmental event. If the Spiral Effect is not explained to the patient or goes unchecked, it will revivify the trauma and sustain the idea of organic pathology.

PREDISPOSITION AND CLINICAL COURSE

The hypothesis offered in this book is that persons who are pathologically anxious appear predisposed to the development of a PTSD. Although patients may or may not have received treatment for an Anxiety Disorder prior to the trauma, histories usually reveal evidence of pathologic anxiety at Levels 2 or 3, and, more often than not, family histories will reveal one or both parents who are "nervous" and who have exhibited the signs and symptoms of an Anxiety Disorder. Since there is a paucity of statistical studies regarding genetic and environmental factors related specifically to PTSD, data from studies involving other Anxiety Disorders might be relevant. Family and twin studies strongly suggest a genetic predisposition for an Anxiety Disorder; however, the hereditary evidence is not as strong as it is for schizophrenia. Nevertheless, it is not too rash to assume that in the future, more evidence will be gathered to support the contention that genetic factors strongly influence nervous system functioning, predisposing a person to an Anxiety Disorder including PTSD. Obviously, more studies will be necessary to sort out the genetic and environmental factors related to PTSD.

Clinical Course of PTSD

For clearer understanding, PTSD can be divided into three stages. During Stage I — response to trauma — environmental stimuli impact on one or more of the five senses, activating the autonomic nervous system and producing symptoms of anxiety. For most people the symptoms dissipate rather quickly, and within 4 to 6 weeks the trauma is forgotten and does not intrude upon everyday life. On the other hand, persons whose pretraumatic anxiety is at Level 2 or 3 respond pathologically. Their symptoms are more intense and do not abate, and they become patients who are morbidly preoccupied with the trauma and obsess at length about a close call with death. The trauma becomes the focal point of patients' existence during Stage II — Acute PTSD. Retraumatization occurs many times each day, as patients relive their trauma in imagination and talk inordinately about it with others. The mind's eye turns inward and the perception of endogenous sensations, interpreted erroneously, sets in motion the Spiral Effect. Retraumatization and the Spiral Effect together intensify and sustain pathologic anxiety, thus maintaining a PTSD. If the Acute PTSD is not treated successfully, pathologic anxiety is followed by frustration, anger, and irritability. The presence of a phobia or phobic anxiety restricts movement and increases stress. An inability to work may result in financial hardship, and disintegrating family relationships may lead to marital dissatisfaction and sexual dysfunction. As life-style and status take a downhill course, a retributive attitude solidifies, and a visit to an attorney may result in a personal injury lawsuit or another form of legal action.

According to the *DSM-III* (1980), when the symptoms of a PTSD persist for longer than 6 months, the condition becomes chronic. Actually, there is no sharp distinction between Stage II (acute) and Stage III (chronic) PTSD. However, as time passes, the patient's emphasis and orientation gradually change from preoccupation with the original trauma to obsessive concern with disability attributable to the trauma. Anxiety symptoms become chronic, similar in many respects to a Generalized Anxiety Disorder. Depression, secondary to chronic anxiety and disability, commonly manifests itself during Stage III, and sometimes suicidal ideas emerge and coalesce into half-hearted gestures and infrequently to death. Changes during Stage III, from employed to unemployed, physically active to dormant, good natured to grouchy, fun loving to depressed, solvent to in debt, self-sufficient to dependent, and potent to impotent reflect but some of the unpleasant changes in life-style and status noted by patients. During Stage III patients become notoriously resistant to treatment and begin to believe that they are incurable and chronically disabled, and have reached the end stage of their illness. At some point during Stage III, litigation reaches a conclusion (if a lawsuit had been initiated). Depositions and courtroom appearances may cause a surge of anxiety, and patients may become more restless, irritable, and agitated. At the conclusion of the legal action, even if the suit had been concluded successfully, patients seldom have a quick remission of symptoms. The "greenback poultice" is mostly myth, and patients still require vigorous treatment following litigation if they are ever to return to a productive life.

Delayed PTSD

The onset of symptoms in a Delayed PTSD, according to the *DSM-III* (1980), is at least 6 months after the trauma. This definition suggests that the original trauma remained latent or dormant for a period of time only to emerge later as a full-blown clinical entity. Implicit in the concept of Delayed PTSD is that the impact of the original trauma may mysteriously erupt into consciousness many months or even years after being incurred. Although this notion of a delayed response to trauma may fit well into psychodynamic concepts of conflict, repression, and defense mechanisms, it does not mesh well with clinical observations. At least three possibilities exist to explain what has been called a Delayed PTSD: (1) Some persons experience a pathologic reaction to trauma, but their PTSD remains unreported, undiagnosed, and untreated. Upon learning that their symptoms are pathologic (usually from persons who have been similarly traumatized), these patients report their symptoms to a physician, and a diagnosis of PTSD is made long after the original trauma. Vietnam-era veterans are notable examples of persons in this group. (2) Persons marginally coping with a Chronic PTSD may be exposed to environmental stressors unrelated to the original trauma, and the intensification of anxiety may take on the coloring of the original trauma. Patients and clinicians mistakenly point to the original trauma as the source of pathologic anxiety. Actually, current environmental stressors are responsible for the resurgence of symptoms. Recognition of this has important therapeutic significance, because treatment should be directed toward the resolution of existing problems rather than the rehashing of memories of a trauma long past. (3) A person may experience two totally unrelated traumas at two different periods of time and develop a PTSD following each trauma. Like the person who breaks the same arm twice, the second PTSD can produce symptoms similar to the first and even reawaken memories associated with the first trauma.

When persons display anxiety symptoms long after the time of the traumatic incident, it is appropriate to delve into but not dwell on any relationship between the past trauma and current symptoms. One can discover an untreated Chronic PTSD, symptoms of pathologic anxiety not directly related to a PTSD, or, if another trauma has occurred, a second PTSD unrelated to the first. The diagnostic label "Delayed PTSD" seems a poor choice because of the implication that all subsequent anxiety symptoms are directly related to the original trauma.

SIGNS AND SYMPTOMS

In PTSD what appears to be a potpourri of symptoms is really a complex and well-organized set of pathologic behaviors interlaced with multiple issues occurring at different periods of time. In Chapter four, Tables 4-1, 4-2, and 4-4 present the characteristics, signs, and symptoms occurring during Stages I, II, and III, respectively. Pathologic anxiety initiated and maintained by one or a combination of the Three E's lies at the core of PTSD. The stage of the disorder and hence the time at which an evaluation is done determine which set of symptoms is clinically more manifest. The SIC (Chapter four) helps patients and clinicians sort out symptoms. For each item in the SIC, patients are asked, on a scale from one (not at all) to five (practically all of the time), to mark the frequency with which they experienced symptoms before and after the accident or traumatic event. The SIC contains items related to anxiety, somatic symptoms, sleeping patterns, choleric mood, interest in sex, marital problems, interest in family, social/recreational activities, depression, memory, and concentration. An analysis of the SIC and the ASP (Chapter two) together with the patient's history and a mental status examination give the clinician ample information upon which to base a diagnosis and, if indicated, a treatment plan.

DIFFERENTIAL DIAGNOSIS

Somatic complaints (loss of or alteration in physical functioning) suggesting a physical disorder, pain, and preoccupation with a fear or belief of serious disease are characteristics of Somatoform Disorder, which may be confused with PTSD. A phobia, Generalized Anxiety Disorder, and depression, separate disorders in the *DSM-III* (1980), can be part of the clinical picture in PTSD. PTSD patients, especially if litigation is pending, may exaggerate or embellish their symptoms. However, the core of their disorder remains and must be differentiated from deliberate falsification. Fabrication, feigning, or overt lying, as occurs in the cases of Factitious Disorder, Antisocial Personality Disorder, and Malingering, is infrequent. The onset and history of a well-documented traumatic event followed by the progression of symptoms typical of PTSD clearly differentiate PTSD from other mental disorders. Organic factors and Substance Use Disorder must, of course, be taken into consideration and evaluated by appropriate examinations, tests, and laboratory procedures.

TREATMENT

PTSD is a multifaceted disorder involving not only post-traumatic stress, but also disordered family relationships, problems of physical disability, an inability to work, disruption of social/recreational life, worker's compensation claims, personal injury litigation, criminal behavior, impaired interpersonal relationships, and detrimental health habits. Since personal, interpersonal, and social factors interact pathologically in PTSD, the formulation of a viable treatment regimen requires the inclusion of a broad spectrum of approaches.

Specific treatment for PTSD involves a correct conceptualization of the disorder with an accurate analysis of the sources of pathologic anxiety. Since pathologic anxiety emanates from one or a combination of the Three E's — environmental, encephalic, or endogenous events — therapeutic interventions must change or modify their pathologic impact. At the beginning of treatment, attention should be directed to lowering the patient's level of personal discomfort. Explanation-education, training in relaxation, encephalic reconditioning, and medication afford the patient immediate relief and should be implemented as soon as possible.

PTSD invariably impacts upon all members of a family. Therefore, wisdom dictates that a family conference be convened to: enlist the family member's cooperation; gather additional information about the patient; make a determination of the family member's role in the furtherance of symptoms; and teach concepts regarding the reinforcement of positive behavior. Family conferences constitute one of the more important aspects of treatment, especially if the patient is married. A disabled breadwinner or homemaker plays havoc with family life. Therapeutic interventions can help reinstate marital equilibrium and harmony.

Unnecessary and self-defeating outbursts of anger can be moderated or eliminated when patients learn techniques of assertive behavior. Often patients develop a retributive attitude, and anger spurs rancor toward those believed responsible for their disability. Teaching assertiveness mitigates personal discomfort and directs patients toward more appropriate self-serving behavior. Nonassertiveness, a lack of social skills, or indecisiveness leading to procrastination can be combated by employing assertive techniques consisting of behavior rehearsal, modeling, instructions, feedback, and encephalic reconditioning. Anxiety diminishes when patients act assertively.

Unsolved problems are a source of anxiety for PTSD patients, who often develop tunnel vision and are unable to see alternatives to their dilemmas. Through problem-solving discussions, the clinician can present information and opinions that widen the patient's vision, making it easier to envisage and decide upon solutions. The clinician can provide sound counsel or refer the patient to an appropriate social service agency when questions arise concerning: the legal process, money management, health and human resources, social security procedures, vocational rehabilitation, worker's compensation, educational institutions, and law enforcement agencies. Letters, phone calls, or advice from the clinician often remove bureaucratic barriers and break the impasse to a viable remedy. Successful people in all walks of life consult experts for guidance and consultation. The clinician can provide this service, directly or indirectly, for the PTSD patient.

When the patient has a phobia or experiences phobic anxiety, systematic desensitization (exposure treatment) is indicated. After a hierarchy involving the phobic theme has been constructed, imaginal or in vivo desensitization proceeds as described in Chapter six. It is important to recognize and treat phobias that have developed following exposure to a traumatic incident. The procedure of systematic desensitization, if assiduously applied, almost always results in the alleviation of phobic behavior. Prolonged exposure or flooding has been found to be particularly useful in the treatment of Vietnam veterans.

In the absence of objective data to the contrary, patients must be persuaded about the value of exercise and dissuaded from the erroneous idea that they are physically disabled. If pain or physical discomfort is present, the source can usually be traced to: chronic anxiety and increased motor tension; minor residual injury related to the original trauma; and muscular aches and pains caused by poor muscle tone. With the approval of an orthopedic surgeon, a supervised program of gradated exercise should be recommended. The prescription to engage in regular exercise carries with it the implicit messages "There is nothing seriously wrong with you" and "You are capable of improving your physical health." When patients begin to derive the benefits from exercise, enhanced strength and endurance reinforce the idea of physical soundness.

Self-assessment, recording the occurrence and frequency of selected symptoms, helps to control and to regulate targeted behavior and is a way of evaluating the outcome of treatment. The Self-Assessment Form can assist patients to organize and record data concerning the occurrence and source of pathologic anxiety as well as selected target behaviors. In addition, the form allows patients to record and comment on the effectiveness of therapeutic interventions. At the conclusion of each day, the patient is asked to make a global rating of progress based on a scale from zero (no progress) to ten (excellent progress). Recording events facilitates self-analysis and self-management of pathologic behavior and associated symptoms. The information also furnishes the clinician with data concerning the patient's progress upon which an adjustment of the therapeutic regimen depends.

Treatment conducted in groups has the advantage of economy in terms of time and money. PTSD patients do poorly in psychodynamically based groups that are primarily insight oriented. "Rap group therapy," popularized with Vietnam-era veterans, likewise has limited value and can be detrimental because veterans have a tendency to repeatedly relive their war experiences, allowing for retraumatization. Many of the treatment approaches outlined in this book can be conducted in a group setting, but individual sessions, especially at the beginning of treatment, are necessary. When patients are in group treatment, they must have easy access to a therapist on an individual basis.

Patients who experience chronic anxiety, physical discomfort, and depression derive little pleasure from social/recreational activities. PTSD is a desocializing condition, and patients soon become withdrawn and isolated from family and friends, diminishing potentially pleasing interactions with others. During the later stages of treatment, discussions concerning social/recreational activities are best conducted in family conferences. The involvement of the spouse increases the patient's compliance, and the pleasure derived from the activity reinforces a repeat performance. The patient's progress measured by enjoyment in social/recreational activities is a good index of improvement.

The ability to work is often impaired when patients develop a PTSD. Somatic symptoms, anxiety, depression, and a phobia of the work premises all interfere with the patient's ability to function and perform tasks associated with work. During the course of treatment, the clinician must exercise judgment when recommending a resumption of employment, for a premature decision that a patient return to work may meet with resistance and noncompliance. Although work has a high priority in treatment, this recommendation must be titrated with symptomatic improvement. Issues of worker's compensation and personal injury litigation may influence and complicate reemployment, but the "greenback poultice" is usually insufficient balm to motivate patients back to the workplace. Chronic unemployment is also correlated with chronic depression and emotional instability. Patients who are disabled and unemployed because of a chronic psychiatric disorder must be treated before they can be expected to obtain and retain a job.

A patient's response to treatment is usually slow, and the clinician can become impatient and irritable, often overlooking the tortoiselike but steady progress that has occurred. Between appointments patients often store up all complaints and heap them on the clinician at the beginning of the session. Patients also have a tendency to ignore positive gains, perhaps feeling that when one goes to a doctor only symptoms and "bad things" should be mentioned. Several actions can be taken to minimize the onslaught of negativism brought to each therapy session by patients who could not, by any stretch of the imagination, be doing that badly. The pessimistic patient who seems always to walk under a "black cloud" should be required to fill out a daily Self-Assessment Form supplemented by a log of all activities from the time of awakening to retiring. Unless particularly relevant, the clinician should ignore all negative comments and verbally reinforce positive gains made by the patient. It is also a good idea to periodically administer the SIC, which will usually disclose improvements in the profile of the patient's symptoms and behavior. The SIC can be scored and the results shown to patients. These techniques place therapy in proper perspective, usually buoying up the spirits of patient and clinician. When patients concentrate only on major items and large issues in absolute disparaging terms, e.g., pain versus no pain, unemployment versus work, symptoms versus no symptoms, the totality of treatment effects is distorted and an accurate assessment of therapy is thwarted. Some attention to the patient's grievances must be paid by the clinician, but detachment and a lack of interest, irritation with expressions of anger, and overconcern with an attitude of alarm must be avoided because they are antitherapeutic. Chronic patients who are complainers can best be controlled when they are placed in group treatment. A group has the effect of moderating disagreeable behavior and focusing attention on coping skills and problem solving. Chronic patients, particularly those who have abandoned all hope, can be a challenging and fulfilling experience for clinicians who should periodically remind themselves that many others have failed to effectively treat this difficult group of patients.

PREVENTION

The treatment concepts and strategies described in Chapter six are applicable to primary, secondary, and tertiary prevention of PTSD. Whether used to educate persons to prevent or lessen the emotional impact of trauma (primary prevention), to intervene promptly following a trauma (secondary prevention), or to decrease or eliminate impairment and hence chronicity (tertiary prevention), morbidity is reduced. Prevention, often ignored in the behavioral sciences, is important and particularly applicable in modifying a person's psychological response to trauma.

LEGAL ISSUES

PTSD is of interest to lawyers and mental health professionals during personal injury suits, worker's compensation disputes, and criminal cases when the insanity defense is raised. Lawyers need to know the basis upon which mental health professionals formulate conclusions and should become familiar with the elements that constitute a thorough forensic evaluation. Mental health professionals who participate in legal proceedings should also be familiar with the legal concepts underlying tort, worker's compensation, and the criminal law as they relate to the evaluation of a patient and testimony in court.

Tort and PTSD

In a personal injury suit, the tort action generally claims that a trauma has caused damages that have resulted from the negligence or intentional action of the defendant. In the past the courts have been reluctant to accept mental consequences of a trauma as a compensable entity. It is now clearly established that a clinical disorder, PTSD, can result from a trauma, and that such a trauma need not be accompanied by any observable physical defect. In 1980 the APA officially recognized PTSD and included it in its 1980 edition of the *DSM*. A tort action based solely on a PTSD is quite appropriate and medically justifiable.

Worker's Compensation

Worker's compensation is an insurance system to supply security to injured workers to meet minimal needs during a period of disability. It differs from conventional damage suits in two important respects:

fault on the part of either employer or employee is eliminated; and compensation is substituted for damages and payable according to a definite schedule based on the type of injury sustained by the worker. The history of compensation for injured workers demonstrates a long, uphill struggle, but all of the United States have adopted worker's compensation statutes that entitle employees who are injured on the job to receive compensation until they are able to return to work. Workers who are suffering from PTSD should be entitled to such benefits.

Criminal Responsibility

In 1843 the M'Naughten (Right and Wrong) Rule was formulated and has dominated the judicial scene concerning the issue of criminal responsibility and the insanity defense. Cognition (understanding, knowing) is the key element in the M'Naughten Rule:

> "To establish a defense on the ground of insanity, it must be clearly proven that at the time of committing of the act, the party accused was laboring under such a defect of reason, from disease of the mind, as not to know the nature and quality of the act he was doing, or, if he did know it . . . he did not know he was doing what was wrong" (Guttmacher and Weihofen 1952; Davidson 1965).

Since M'Naughten the Irresistible Impulse Test, the Durham Rule, and the Currens Test have been proposed, but the ALI Model Penal Code has become the accepted standard in the federal system and has also been adopted by about one-half of the states. Utilizing variations of the M'Naughten Rule and the Irresistible Impulse Test, the ALI Standard incorporates elements of cognition, volition, and capacity to control behavior (Slovenko 1963):

> "A person is not responsible for criminal conduct if at the time of such conduct, as a result of mental disease or defect, he lacks substantial capacity either to appreciate the criminality of his conduct or to conform his conduct to the requirements of law."

APA Statement on the Insanity Defense

Following the Hinckley verdict, attention was focused on the wording of the insanity defense, post-trial mechanisms for containing the "insane acquittees," and the effect of abolishing the insanity defense. The APA's position paper of 1983 as approved by the Board of Trustees is that "the insanity defense should be retained in some form" and "retention of the insanity defense is essential to the moral integrity of the criminal law." The APA's Insanity Defense Workgroup disapproved of the "guilty but not mentally ill" verdict that has been adopted into law by some states either to supplement or to take the place of traditional insanity defenses. In answer to the question of if the legal standards now in use concerning the insanity defense should be modified, the APA group suggested that the more important question is whether or not judges will allow psychiatrists to testify concerning the broad range of mental functioning that would be relevant for the jury's deliberation. The APA was reluctant to take a position on the question of if the burden of proof should always rest on the prosecution, stating that "this matter clearly requires further empirical study." The fourth question asked by the APA workgroup was if psychiatric testimony should be limited to statements of mental condition. The APA is not opposed to legislatures restricting psychiatric testimony on the "ultimate issues" such as whether the defendant is "sane," "insane," or "responsible" or not. It is adamant that psychiatrists be permitted to testify about the defendant's psychiatric diagnosis, mental state, and motivation at the time of the alleged criminal act, so as to permit the judge and jury to reach the ultimate conclusion about which "they and only they" are expert. One would have difficulty in agreeing that the jury members are experts at reaching the ultimate conclusion, but, of course, judges and jury make the final determination of guilty or not guilty by reason of insanity. The answer to this question by the APA seems a public relations statement designed to smooth over the controversy of opposing opinions of expert witnesses that receive wide publicity. The critical, most important question was asked last: "What should be done with defendants following not guilty by reason of insanity verdicts?" The APA Workgroup suggested that special legislation be designed for those persons charged with violent offenses who have been found not guilty by reason of insanity and that a special board be constituted to include psychiatrists and other professionals representing the criminal justice system. The board would have jurisdiction over the release of insanity acquittees and should have the authority to reconfine. Whether federal and state governments would expend the necessary funds to implement these post-trial recommendations remains to be seen.

Criminal Behavior and PTSD

Ordinarily, persons with PTSD are in contact with reality and do not display any symptoms of psychosis such as hallucinations or delusions. Occasionally, when anxiety is very high, patients develop transient dissociative reactions with episodes of depersonalization and/or derealization. Most of the time these feelings of unreality only frighten patients but, in some instances, may result in erratic behavior that may be criminal. The question of criminal responsibility, therefore, is pertinent as it relates to any criminal act occurring during a dissociative reaction.

According to the *DSM-III* (1980), "The symptoms of depersonalization involve an alteration in the perception or experience of the self so that the usual sense of one's own reality is temporarily lost or changed." During these periods of unreality, PTSD patients may feel that they are going insane or out of control and begin to act strangely. The onset occurs quickly; however, gradually the feelings of unreality diminish in intensity and disappear altogether. Patients report that they had been "stunned" or "in shock." In the *DSM-III* (1980), the predisposing factors for depersonalization, a form of dissociative disorder, are listed: "fatigue, recovery from substance intoxication, hypnosis, meditation, physical pain, anxiety, depression, and severe stress such as military combat or an automobile accident." It is evident that many of these predisposing factors are to be found in Chronic PTSD patients.

The Criminal Process and PTSD

When the insanity defense is raised in a criminal process, the law provides different procedures for the pretrial, trial, and post-trial stages of criminal procedure, and different issues confront lawyers, mental health professionals and the court.

Pretrial Stage

When the insanity defense is raised by the defendant's attorney, a sanity commission consisting of two or more physicians (commonly psychiatrists) is usually convened to determine the accused's present mental capacity to proceed. The mental examination attempts to answer two questions: Does the defendant understand the proceedings against him or her? Can the defendant cooperate and communicate with his or her attorney during the preparation of the case? Unless suffering from PTSD and experiencing a dissociative reaction (episode of depersonalization or derealization) at the time of the pretrial psychiatric evaluation, the accused is likely to be found mentally competent to stand trial. After a judicial hearing it can be expected that most defendants diagnosed as having PTSD will be remanded for trial.

The Trial Stage

The question concerning criminal responsibility to be addressed during the trial stage is if, at the time of the alleged criminal conduct, as a result of mental disease or defect, the defendant lacked substantial capacity either to appreciate the criminality of the conduct or to conform the conduct to the requirements of the law. PTSD is certainly a mental disease or defect. During a dissociative reaction, persons do lack such substantial capacity either to appreciate the criminality of their conduct or to conform their conduct to the requirements of the law. Also, PTSD is a clinical entity that does not include abnormalities of behavior manifested by repeated criminal or otherwise antisocial conduct. It would therefore seem evident that PTSD would be an acceptable defense in a criminal trial utilizing the ALI Standard.

The defense attorney must establish that a trauma had taken place, and the expert witness should detail the psychological effects of the trauma upon the defendant and how they culminated in a PTSD. The expert witness explains PTSD, emphasizing that a dissociative reaction interferes with the perception of reality. Next, a connection or link must be established between the patient's PTSD and mental state at the time of the alleged criminal act. Any similarity between the traumatic scene and the scene of the crime helps to explain a flashback, or dissociative episode during which an irrational criminal act may have been committed. Finally, the expert witness concludes by offering an opinion of the defendant's mental state at the time of the alleged criminal conduct in accordance with the court's rules regulating criminal responsibility.

Post-Trial Stage

The undercurrent covertly permeating all aspects of the trial is the disposition of the defendant adjudicated not guilty by reason of insanity. In most instances the acquitted person is committed to a mental hospital for further evaluation and, if necessary, treatment. In the past it has been found that this is not a satisfactory arrangement, because lines of responsibility for the insanity acquittee are blurred and the mechanisms for release, supervision, and reconfinement are not well established. The APA recognizing the importance of the post-trial stage, recommended that special legislation should constitute a board to include psychiatrists and other professionals representing the criminal justice system with the authority to confine, release, and reconfine insanity acquittees. This should be adopted by the federal system and by all states.

A challenge confronts the court and mental health professionals who have the responsibility of supervising and treating PTSD insanity acquittees. Hospital treatment may not be required. However, in lieu of alternatives, it can be expected that most PTSD acquittees will be committed to a maximum security hospital for further observation. Even though PTSD is not a severe psychiatric disorder, certain precautions, especially in the case of acquittees who have committed violent acts, should be taken regarding confinement, release, supervision, and treatment. The involvement of a multidisciplinary board to review all cases at designated intervals ensures that the best interests of the individual and society are served. Such a system can provide better supervision than most probation and parole agencies and better ongoing treatment than most mental health clinics. PTSD may serve as the impetus for reform within the criminal justice system for a long-neglected group – the insanity acquittees.

Psychiatric Evaluation

Whether used during civil or criminal proceedings or solely for treatment purposes, a psychiatric evaluation must take into consideration the patient's pretraumatic history, response to the trauma, and adaptation following the trauma. Particularly for forensic purposes, clinicians should obtain data from sources other than the identified patient.

The pretraumatic history should record: educational background, all employment, and service in the military, antisocial behavior, previous litigation, medical and psychiatric treatment, the use of alcohol and drugs (including prescription and nonprescription agents), family and marital chronicles. The traumatic incident must be described in great detail and the patient's perceptions and reactions noted. The patient's self-talk and visual images just before impact are especially important. The presence of all symptoms at the time of the trauma, whether caused by intense stimulation of the autonomic nervous system or physical injury or both, should be recorded. Symptoms of severe autonomic reaction at the time of the trauma, the sine qua non of the genesis of PTSD, should be confirmed by the patient and documented if possible by onlookers. An evaluation of the post-traumatic period includes the patient's immediate reaction and the response to the trauma during the first several weeks. All medical treatment received post-traumatically should be reviewed prior to a mental status examination. The ASP and SIC are useful in determining the effect of the trauma upon the patient. Interviews with other persons and a review of all available records are considered before a final diagnosis is made and a conclusive opinion rendered. For personal injury cases, the temporal relationship between the trauma, psychiatric disorder, and the degree of disability is important. The length, and hence the cost of future treatment are compensable and therefore prognosis is an important consideration in personal injury suits.

In worker's compensation cases, the relatedness of the trauma to the psychiatric disorder and the current ability to work is an important issue. If the person involved in a work-related accident is disabled, an opinion regarding prognosis with recommendations related to treatment and rehabilitation is given.

When the insanity defense is used in criminal trials, the matter of criminal responsibility revolves around the defendant's state of mind at the time of the commission of the alleged criminal act. First, it must be demonstrated that a trauma culminated in a PTSD. Second, an additional link must be established to show that the PTSD negated criminal responsibility.

Forensic Issues during the Trial

In the author's experience, a concise, well-written psychiatric report usually precludes an appearance in court. In civil cases depositions are sometimes requested when either the plaintiff or defense attorney requires additional information or clarification of the mental health professional's report. If arbitration does not lead to settlement of the civil suit, the mental health professional is subpoenaed to testify as an expert witness at trial.

In criminal cases a well-reasoned psychiatric or psychological report can assist all parties during pretrial discussions when posttrial issues are arbitrated. Mental health professionals can participate during these informal hearings in the judge's chambers in which issues of PTSD, criminal conduct, treatment, and prognosis are discussed. If the case goes to trial, the mental health professional testifies as an expert witness to explain PTSD or its absence and renders an opinion regarding criminal responsibility.

Civil Law

The attorney for the plaintiff will utilize expert testimony first to educate the judge and jury about PTSD and second to establish the relationship between the trauma and the PTSD. The degree of disability imposed by the PTSD and requirements for future treatment are issues for which the plaintiff can be compensated and are of vital importance.

After the mental health professional's qualifications as an expert are presented, the plaintiff's attorney is likely to ask such questions as: "Upon what examinations, tests, review of records, etc. have you based your conclusions?" "Please state the results of your findings." "What is a PTSD?" "What is the relationship of the plaintiff's PTSD to the trauma?" "How is a PTSD treated?" "How long will the plaintiff require treatment?" "Does the plaintiff's PTSD prevent him or her from working?" "How has the trauma and subsequent PTSD affected the plaintiff's life?" "Do you feel that the patient is malingering?"

The objective of the defense attorney is then to portray the plaintiff as a malingerer or to demonstrate that if any psychiatric disorder exists, it was present before the traumatic incident. During cross-examination of the plaintiff's expert witness, a challenge of the credentials of the plaintiff's expert witness may be expected, and the following are likely to be raised: "Upon what do you base your diagnosis?" "Isn't it true that all or most of your testimony merely restates what the plaintiff has told you?" "What is Malingering?" "How do you know that the plaintiff is not a malingerer?" "Are some persons predisposed to PTSD?" When the plaintiff has a past history of treatment for a mental disorder, it can be expected that the defense attorney will ask a series of questions attempting to demonstrate that any mental disorder that the patient currently has was present before the traumatic incident. "What is a normal person's response to trauma?" The defense may ask a series of questions aimed at uncovering the bias of the expert witness. "When testifying as an expert in the past, what percentage of the time did you testify in favor of the plaintiff and what percentage in favor of the defense?" "During the last several years, how many clients have you examined for the plaintiff's attorney?" "What is your fee for testifying as an expert witness and who is paying your fee?" Finally, the defense attorney may ask a series of questions related to psychiatry, mental disorders, and PTSD that are intended to demonstrate to the judge and jury that psychiatry is unscientific, imprecise, and just short of "witchcraft."

Criminal Law

As an insanity defense, PTSD is relatively new, and the case law is limited. Defenses based on PTSD have been advanced in cases ranging from murder, attempted murder, assault including rape, and weapon offenses to nonviolent crimes such as burglary, robbery, drug conspiracies, and tax fraud. The first two cases in which PTSD was used successfully as an insanity defense involved violent crimes — State versus Heads (1981) and People versus Wood (1982).

PTSD may result following a sexual assault. Expert testimony was allowed concerning the presence of a Rape Trauma Syndrome, another name for PTSD, in one case (State versus Marks 1982) and upheld by the State Supreme Court. In another case with an opposite outcome (Minnesota versus Saldana 1982), the State Supreme Court overturned the conviction of a defendant accused of rape because an expert witness testified that the complainant suffered from a Rape Trauma Syndrome (PTSD). As data concerning

PTSD accrue and judges become better informed, it can be expected that PTSD will be a viable defense in criminal trials. It will not be surprising if some criminal defendants who have been raped in the past plead insanity due to Rape Trauma Syndrome (PTSD).

Battered women who kill abusing spouses may attempt to plead insanity, diminished responsibility, or self-defense based on PTSD to explain their actions. Paradoxically, many view PTSD sufferers such as Vietnam-era veterans as dangerous and hence claim that homicide in self-defense against the PTSD sufferer would be justifiable. The vicissitudes of PTSD and the law seem bound only by the imagination of attorneys, but common sense and the restraint of a judge and jury usually prevail and determine the limits of PTSD and the criminal law.

PTSD in the Insanity Defense — The Defendant's Position

The dilemma facing the defendant's attorney is that of an obviously guilty client and a crime usually discordant with the life history of the defendant prior to a trauma. The attorney will attempt to prove that a trauma took place and was responsible for the production in the client of an officially recognized psychiatric disorder — PTSD. Furthermore, the attorney desires to establish that the PTSD rendered the client criminally irresponsible at the time of the alleged commission of the crime. The manner in which PTSD is presented in a criminal trial is much the same as in a personal injury suit. However, some important differences exist. Any similarities between the traumatic incident experienced by the defendant (accident, rape, combat experiences, etc.) and the circumstances of the alleged act should be highlighted. The concept of a flashback or automatism must be explained to the fact finders along with the definition and description of a dissociative reaction. First, the connection between the defendant's trauma and PTSD must be established. Second, a dissociative state, characteristic of PTSD, must be linked to the defendant's state of mind at the time of the alleged criminal act. At the conclusion of testimony, if the ALI Test prevails, the mental health professional must answer the question "Does the defendant, as a result of mental disease or defect, lack substantial capacity either to appreciate the criminality of his or her conduct or to conform his or her conduct to the requirements of law?" If the defendant experienced a trauma, developed a PTSD, and experienced a dissociative reaction at the time of the alleged criminal conduct, the answer to the above question is "yes."

The Prosecutor's Position

The prosecutor will attempt to denigrate the testimony of the defendant's expert as "intellectual balderdash" designed to excuse an obviously guilty defendant from the penalty usually imposed on all law breakers, and will present his or her own expert to support this position. Whenever possible the prosecutor will introduce and emphasize detrimental information indicating that the defendant is a reprobate, deserving punishment, not acquittal on the grounds of insanity. If the expert witness is verbose, tending toward polysyllabic explanation, the prosecutor's job is made easier, for all that is required is to let the expert babble on. A common tactic of prosecutors that can nullify the impact of the expert testimony is to facetiously challenge certain conclusions in the hope that this will anger the mental health professional. Clever prosecutors will make the most out of unflattering characteristics of the expert witness, such as pomposity, grandiosity, dogmatism, and an unwillingness to concede even small or inconsequential points of view. Prosecutors are on the alert for any inconsistencies or inaccuracies in testimony. Seemingly inconsequential statements, although not directly related to the major issue at hand, may be seized upon to undermine the expert's testimony. If a mistake has been made, it is better for the mental health professional to admit it, apologize, and calmly correct it. The best protection against embarrassing confrontations in the courtroom is thorough preparation.

The Future of Law and the Behavioral Sciences

It can be expected that as technology continues to advance in the future, the biochemical and physiological processes of the brain will be correlated with specific behavior and treatment will become more refined. This utopian view is not as far-fetched as it may seem, when one considers the current advances in psychopharmacology, the appearance of biochemical tests that correlate chemical substances with clinical syndromes, and the development of sophisticated instruments like the computed axial tomographic, positron emission tomographic, and nuclear magnetic resonance scans, and it can be expected that more progress will be made in these areas. Although it is premature to introduce some of these procedures in court, their admissibility in the not-too-distant future is almost a certainty.

In the case of PTSD, there can be no doubt that objective tests will be developed to quantify pathologic anxiety and identify brain structures associated with dissociative reactions. The days when expert witnesses render opinions based solely on subjective data are rapidly passing. In the future when discussing the psychological reactions to trauma, experts in both civil and criminal cases will be more likely to be scientists trained in biochemistry, physiology, and computer technology. At the present time, PTSD, unlike many psychiatric disorders, offers lawyers and mental health professionals the opportunity to gather evidence external to the person who experiences symptoms and integrate this data during the presentation of the case in court. The emergence of PTSD in the courtroom ushers in a new frontier for the law and the behavioral sciences.

REFERENCES

Agras, W. S., Leitenberg, H., Barlow, D. H., and Thomson, L. E. 1969. Instructions and Reinforcement in the Modification of Neurotic Behavior. *Am. J. Psychiatry*, 125, pp. 1435-1439.

Alberti, R. E., and Emmons, M. L. 1978. *Your Perfect Right* (third edition). San Luis Obispo, Impact.

American Psychiatric Association Statement on the Insanity Defense. 1983. *Am. J. Psychiatry*, 140, p. 681.

Asher, R. 1951. Munchhausen's Syndrome. *Lancet*, 1, pp. 339-341.

Auerbach, D. B. 1982. The Ganser Syndrome. In *Extraordinary Disorders of Human Behavior*, edited by C. T. Friedmann and R. A. Faguet. New York, Plenum, pp. 29-46.

Bain, J. S. 1928. *Thought Control in Everyday Life*. New York, Funk and Wagnalls.

Beck, A. T. 1976. *Cognitive Therapy and the Emotional Disorders*. New York, International Universities.

Bonnie, R. J. 1982. A Model Statute on the Insanity Defense. Institute of Law, Psychiatry, and Public Policy, University of Virginia, Charlottesville, Virginia.

Bonnie, R. J. 1983. The Moral Basis of the Insanity Defense. *Am. Bar. Assoc. J.*, 9, pp. 194-197.

Bradbury Workman's Compensation (third edition). 1917. chap. 2, article A.

Brend, W. A. 1939. *Traumatic Mental Disorders in Courts of Law*. London, William Heinemann.

Brende, J. O. 1981. Combined Individual and Group Therapy for Vietnam Veterans. *Int. J. Group Psychother.*, 31, pp. 367-378.

Brill, N. Q., and Beebe, G. W. 1951. Follow-up Study of Psychoneurosis. *Am. J. Psychiatry*, 108, pp. 417-425.

Bromberg, W. 1979. *The Uses of Psychiatry in the Law: A Clinical View of Forensic Psychiatry*. Westport, Quorum Books.

Brown, W. A., Johnston, R., and Mayfield, D. 1979. The 24-Hour Dexamethasone Suppression Test in a Clinical Setting: Relationship to Diagnosis, Symptoms, and Response to Treatment. *Am. J. Psychiatry*, 136, pp. 543-547.

Burgess, A. W. 1983. Rape Trauma Syndrome. *Behav. Sci. Law*, 1, pp. 97-114.

Burris, B. T. 1983. Symposium on Post-Traumatic Stress Disorder. American Psychiatric Association Convention, New York.

Cannon, W. B. 1929. *Bodily Changes in Pain, Hunger, Fear, and Rage: An Account of Recent Researches into the Function of Emotional Excitement* (second edition). New York, Appleton-Century-Crofts.

Caplan, G. 1961. *An Approach to Community Mental Health*. New York, Grune and Stratton.

Caplan, G. 1964. *Principles of Preventive Psychiatry*. New York, Basic Books.

Cheek, D. B., and LaCron, L. M. 1968. *Clinical Hypnotherapy*. New York, Grune and Stratton.

Cloninger, C. R., Martin, R. L., Clayton, P., and Guze, S. B. 1981. A Blind Follow-Up and Family Study of Anxiety Neurosis: Preliminary Analysis of the St. Louis 500. In *Anxiety: New Research and Changing Concepts*, edited by D. Klein and J. Rabkin, New York, Raven Press, pp. 137-154.

Cohen, M. E., Badal, D. W., Kilpatrick, A., Reed, E. W., and White, P. D. 1951. The High Familial Prevalence of Neurocirculatory Asthenia (Anxiety Neurosis, Effort Syndrome). *Am. J. Hum. Genet.*, 3, pp. 126-158.

Cohen, R. R. L. 1970. *Traumatic Neurosis in Personal Injury Cases*. Washington D.C., Trial Lawyer's Service.

Crowe, R. R., Pauls, D. L., Slyman, D. J., and Noyes, R. 1980. A Family Study of Anxiety Neurosis. *Arch. Gen. Psychiatry*, 37, pp. 77-79.

Curran, J. B., and Gilbert, F. S. 1975. A Test of the Relative Effectiveness of a Systematic Desensitization Program and an Interpersonal Skills Training Program with Date-Anxious Subjects. *Behav. Ther.*, 6, pp. 510-521.

DaCosta, J. M. 1871. On Irritable Heart: A Clinical Study of a Form of Functional Cardiac Disorder and Its Consequences. *Am. J. Med. Sci.*, 61, pp. 17-52.

Dalessio, D. J. 1978. Hyperventilation, the Vapors, Effort Syndrome, Neurasthenia. *JAMA*, 239, pp. 1401-1402.

Davidson, H. 1965. *Forensic Psychiatry* (second edition). New York, Ronald Press.

Dawley, H. H., and Wenrich, W. W. 1976. *Achieving Assertive Behavior*. California, Bricks/Cole.

Diagnostic and Statistical Manual of Mental Disorders (second edition). 1968. Washington D.C., American Psychiatric Association.

Diagnostic and Statistical Manual of Mental Disorders (third edition). 1980. Washington D.C., American Psychiatric Association.

Diamond, B. L. 1956. Isaac Ray and the Trial of Daniel M'Naughten. *Am. J. Psychiatry*, 112, p. 651.

Dunner, F. 1983. An Evaluation of the Clinical Efficacy of Alpraxolam (Xanax) in Vietnam Veterans with PTSD. Presented at the Second National Conference on the Treatment of Post-Traumatic Stress Disorder (PTSD), Chicago.

Durham v. United States, 214 F 2D862 (D.C. Cir. 1954).

Employer's Liability and Workman's Compensation Commission Report (SEN DOC #338) I. 1912. pp. 97-99.

Erlinder, C. P. 1983a. Post-Traumatic Stress Disorder, Vietnam Veterans and the Law: A Challenge to Effective Representation. *Behav. Sci. Law*, 1, pp. 25-30.

Erlinder, C. P. 1983b. Legal Problems and PTSD: Building a Common Perspective. Presented at the Second National Conference on the Treatment of Post-Traumatic Stress Disorder (PTSD), Chicago.

Fairbank, J. A., and Keane, T. M. 1982. Flooding for Combat-Related Stress Disorders: Assessment of Anxiety Reduction across Traumatic Memories. *Behav. Ther.*, 13, pp. 499-510.

Feindler, E. L., and Fremouw, W. J. 1983. Stress Inoculation Training for Adolescent Anger Problems. In *Stress Reduction and Prevention*, edited by D. Meichenbaum and M. E. Jaremko, New York, Plenum, pp. 451-485.

Figley, C. R. 1978. *Stress Disorders Among Vietnam Veterans*. New York, Bruner/Mazel.

Fisher, E. B., Levenkron, J. C., Lowe, M. R., Loro, A. D., and Green, L. 1982. Self-Initiated Self-Control in Risk Reduction. In *Adherence, Compliance and Generalization in Behavioral Medicine*, edited by R. Stuart, New York, Bruner/Mazel.

Fischer, V., Boyle, J. M., and Bucuvalas, M. 1980. *Myths and Realities: A Study of Attitudes towards Vietnam Era Veterans*. Washington D.C., Louis Harris.

Ford, C. V. 1982. Munchhausen Syndrome. In *Extraordinary Disorders of Human Behavior*, edited by C. T. Friedmann and R. A. Faguet. New York, Plenum, pp. 15-27.

Frank, J. 1961. *Persuasion and Healing*. Baltimore, Johns Hopkins.

Frank, J. 1978. *Effective Ingredients of Successful Psychotherapy*. New York, Bruner/Mazel.

Freidin, R. B. 1980. Primary Care Multi-Dimensional Model. A Framework for Formulating Health Problems in a Primary Care Setting. *Gen. Hosp. Psychiatry*, 2, pp. 10-19.

Freud, S. 1962. On the Grounds for Detaching a Particular Syndrome for Neurasthenia under the Description "Anxiety Neurosis." In *Standard Edition of the Complete Psychological Works of Sigmund Freud* vol. 3, p. 90. London, Hogarth Press.

Friedman, M. J. 1981. Post-Vietnam Syndrome: Recognition and Management. *Psychosomatics*, 22, pp. 931-943.

Gallant, D. M., and Simpson, G. M. 1976. *Depression: Behavioral, Biochemical, Diagnostic and Treatment Concepts*. New York, Spectrum.

Ganser, S. J. M. 1898. Uber Einen Eigenartigen Hysterischen Dammerzustand. *Arch. Psychiatr. Nervenkr.* 38, p. 633.

Glass, R. M., Allan, A. T., Uhlenhuth, E. H., Kimball, C. P., and Borinstein, D. I.

1978. Psychiatric Screening in a Medical Clinic: An Evaluation of a Self-Report Inventory. *Arch. Gen. Psychiatry*, 35, pp. 1189-1195.

Glueck, S. 1962. *Law and Psychiatry: Cold War or Entente Cordiale?* Baltimore, Johns Hopkins.

Golden, S., and MacDonald, J. E. 1955. The Ganser State. *J. Ment. Sci.*, 101, pp. 267-280.

Goldstein, A., Kaizer, S., and Whitby, O. 1969. Psychotropic Effects of Caffeine in Man. IV. Quantitative and Qualitative Differences Associated with Habituation to Coffee. *Clin. Pharmacol. Ther.*, 10, pp. 489-497.

Goodwin, J. 1980. The Etiology of Combat-Related Post-Traumatic Stress Disorders. In *Post-Traumatic Stress Disorder of the Vietnamese Veterans*, edited by T. Williams. Cincinnati, Disabled American Veterans.

Gottschalk, L. S. 1974. Self-Induced Visual Imagery, Affect Arousal and Autonomic Correlates. *Psychosomatics*, 4, pp. 166-169.

Greden, J. F. 1979. Coffee, Tea, and You. *Sciences*, 19, pp. 6-11.

Grinker, R., and Spiegel, J. P. 1945. *Men Under Stress*. Philadelphia, Blakiston.

Guttmacher, M., and Weihofen, H. 1952. *Psychiatry and the Law*. New York, Norton.

Heath, R. G., Franklin, D. E., and Shraberg, D. 1979. Gross Pathology of the Cerebellum in Patients Diagnosed and Treated as Functional Psychiatric Disorders. *J. Nerv. Ment. Dis.*, 167, pp. 585-591.

Heath, R. G., Franklin, D. E., Walker, C. F., and Keating, J. W. 1982. Cerebellar Vermal Atrophy in Psychiatric Patients. *Biol. Psychiatry*, 17, pp. 569-583.

Hogben, G. O., and Cornfield, R. B. 1981. Treatment of Traumatic War Neurosis with Phenalzine. *Arch. Gen. Psychiatry*, 38, pp. 440-445.

Holland, B. C., and Ward, R. S. 1966. Homeostasis and Psychosomatic Medicine. In *American Handbook of Psychiatry, Vol. III*, edited by S. Arieti. New York, Basic Books. pp. 344-361.

Hollister, L. E., Greenblatt, D. J., Rickels, I., and Ayd, F. J. 1980. A Symposium: Benzodiazepines 1980, Current Update. *Psychosomatics (Suppl.)*, 21, pp. 4-32.

Horowitz, M. J., Wilner, N., Kaltreider, N., and Alvarez, W. 1980. Signs and Symptoms of Post-Traumatic Stress Disorder. *Arch. Gen. Psychiatry*, 37, pp. 85-92.

Jack, 1980. The Vietnam Connection: Charles Head Verdict. *Criminal Defense*, 9, p. 7.

Jacobsen, E. 1974. *Progressive Relaxation: A Physiological and Clinical Investigation of Muscular States and Their Significance in Psychology and Medical Practice* (third edition). Chicago, University of Chicago.

Jones, M. C. 1924. A Laboratory Study of Fear. The Case of Peter. *J. Gen. Psychol.*, 31, p. 308.

Kaiser, L. 1968. *The Traumatic Neurosis*. Philadelphia, Lippincott.

Kardiner, A., and Spiegel, H. 1947. *War Stress and Neurotic Illness*. New York, Hoeber:Harper.

Keane, T. M., and Fairbank, J. A. 1983. Survey Analysis of Combat-Related Stress Disorders in Vietnam Veterans. *Am. J. Psychiatry*, 140, pp. 348-350.

Keane, T., Fairbanks, J., Cadell, J., Zimering, R., and Russell, S. 1983. Progress in the Behavioral Assessment and Treatment of PTSD in Vietnam Veterans. Presented at the Second National Conference on the Treatment of Post-Traumatic Stress Disorder (PTSD), Chicago.

Keane, T. M., and Kaloupek, D. G. 1982. Brief Reports: Imaginal Flooding in the Treatment of a Post-Traumatic Stress Disorder. *J. Consult. Clin. Psychol.*, 50, pp. 138-140.

Klinger, E. 1970. *Structure and Function of Fantasy*. New York, John Wiley.

Kolb, L. C., and Mutalipassi, L. R. 1982. The Conditioned Emotional Response: A Subclass of the Chronic and Delayed Post-Traumatic Stress Disorder. *Psychiatr. Ann.*, 12, pp. 979-987.

Kosbad, F. P. 1974. Imagery Techniques in Psychiatry. *Arch. Gen. Psychiatry*, 31, pp. 283-290.

Kroger, W. S., and Fezler, W. D. 1976. *Hypnosis and Behavior Modification: Imagery Conditioning*. Philadelphia, Lippincott.

Larson, A. 1972. *The Law of Workman's Compensation, Vol. I*. New York, Mathew Bender.

Lewis, T. 1919. *The Soldier's Heart and the Effort Syndrome*. New York, Hoeber.

Lewy, E. 1941. Compensation for War Neurosis. *War Med.*, 1, p. 887.

Linn, L. 1975. Other Psychiatric Emergencies. In *Comprehensive Textbook of Psychiatry*, edited by A. M. Freedman, H. I. Kaplan, and B. J. Sadock. Baltimore, Williams and Wilkins, pp. 2003-2009.

Lipkin, J. O., Scurfield, R. M., and Blank, A. S. 1983. Post-Traumatic Stress Disorder in Vietnam Veterans: Assessment in a Forensic Setting. *Behav. Sci. Law*, 1, pp. 51-68.

Ludwig, A. M. 1979. Anxiety and Substance Abuse. *Psychiatr. Ann.*, 9, pp. 499-503.

Mace, E. B., O'Brien, C., Mintz, J., Ream, N., and Meyers, A. L. 1978. Adjustment among Vietnam Veteran Drug Users Two Years Post-Service. In *Stress Disorders Among Vietnam Veterans*, edited by C. R. Figley. New York, Bruner/Mazel, pp. 71-128.

Mahoney, M. J. 1971. The Self-Management of Covert Behavior: A Case Study. *Behav. Ther.*, 2, pp. 575-578.

Mahoney, M. J., and Arnoff, D. B. 1979. Self-Management in Behavioral Medicine: Theory and Practice. In *Behavioral Medicine: Theory and Practice*, edited by O. F. Pomerlau and J. P. Brady. Baltimore, Williams and Wilkins, pp. 75-96.

Malone, W. S. 1951. *Louisiana Workman's Compensation Law and Practice*. St. Paul, West Publishing.

Malone, W. S. 1970. Ruminations on the Role of Fault in the History of the Common Law of Torts. *Louisiana Law Rev.*, 31, p. 1.

Malone, W. S., and Johnson, H. S. 1980. *Louisiana Civil Code Treatacy, Vol. 13, Worker's Compensation Law and Practice* (second edition). St. Paul, West Publishing.

Manchester, W. 1980. *Goodbye Darkness: A Memoir of the Pacific War*. Boston, Little, Brown.

Marks, I. 1981. *Cure and Care of Neuroses*. New York, Wiley.

Marks, I., and Lader, M. 1973. Anxiety States (Anxiety Neurosis): A Review. *J. Nerv. Ment. Dis.*, 156, pp. 3-18.

Masters, W. H., and Johnson, V. E. 1970. *Human Sexual Inadequacy*. Boston, Little, Brown and Co.

Mavissakalian, M., and Barlow, D. H. 1981. *Phobia*. New York, Guilford.

McCabe, B., and Tsuang, M. T. 1982. Dietary Consideration in Inhibitor Regimens. *J. Clin. Psychiatry*, 43, pp. 178-181.

McCalb, J., opinion of, in Atchison v. May, 201 La. 1003, 1001, 10 SO 2D785-738. 1942. (Noted in *Louisiana Law Rev.*, 5, p. 358).

McInnes, R. G. 1937. Observations on Heredity in Neurosis. *Proc. R. Soc. Med.*, 30, pp. 895-904.

McLean, A. 1975. Occupational (Industrial) Psychiatry. In *Comprehensive Textbook of Psychiatry* (second edition), edited by A. M. Freedman, H. I. Kaplan, and B. J. Sadock. Baltimore, Williams and Wilkins, pp. 2368-2375.

Meichenbaum, D. D. 1977. *Cognitive-Behavior Modification: An Integrated Approach*. New York, Plenum.

Meichenbaum, D., and Cameron, R. 1983. Stress Inoculation Training: Towards a General Paradigm for Training Coping Skills. In *Stress Reduction and Prevention*, edited by D. Meichenbaum and M. E. Jaremko. New York, Plenum, pp. 115-154.

Mielke, D. H., and Winstead, D. K. 1981. The Problem of Drug Dependence. Proceedings of the Symposium Anxiety: The Therapeutic Dilemma. *Psychiatr. Ann.*, 11, pp. 15-18.

Minnesota v. Saldana, 324 NW 2d 227, 1982 (Minnesota).

Modlin, H. 1967. The Post-Accident Anxiety Syndrome: Psychosocial Aspects. *Am. J. Psychiatry*, 123, pp. 1008-1012.

Noyes, R., Clancy, J., Crowe, R., Hoenk, P. R., and Slyman, D. J. 1978a. The Familial Prevalence of Anxiety Neurosis. *Arch. Gen. Psychiatry*, 35, pp. 1057-1059.

Noyes, R., Clancy, J., Hoenk, P. R., and Slyman, D. J. 1978b. The Prognosis of Anxiety Neurosis. *Arch. Gen. Psychiatry*, 37, pp. 173-178.

Oppenheimer, B. S. 1918. Report on Neurocirculatory Asthenia and Its Management. *Milit. Surg.*, 42, pp. 7-11.

Pasewark, R. A. 1981. Insanity Plea: A Review of the Research Literature. *J. Psychiatr. Law*, 9, pp. 357-401.

Paul, G. L. 1968. Two Year Follow-Up of Systematic Desensitization In Therapy Groups. *J. Abnorm. Psychol.*, 73, pp. 119-130.

Pavlov, I. P. 1927. *Conditioned Reflexes*. New York, Liveright.

People v. Wood, 80-7410 (Cir. Ct. Cook County, Ill., May 5, 1982).

Quitkin, F. M., Rifkin, A., Kaplan, J., and Klein, D. F. 1972. Phobic Anxiety Syndrome Complicated by Drug Dependence and Addiction. *Arch. Gen. Psychiatry*, 27, pp. 159-162.

Raifman, L. J. 1983. Problems of Diagnosis and Legal Causation in Courtroom Use of Post-Traumatic Stress Disorder. *Behav. Sci. Law*, 1, pp. 115-130.

Rapoport, J., Elkins, R., Zahn, T. P., Buchsbaum, M. S., Weingartner, H., and Kopin, I. J. 1981. Acute Effects of Caffeine on Normal Prepubertal Boys. In *Anxiety: New Research and Changing Concepts*, edited by D. Klein and J. Rabkin. New York, Raven Press, pp. 355-365.

Ray, I. 1962. *A Treatise on the Medical Jurisprudence of Insanity*. Cambridge, Harvard U. Press.

Robinson, D. S., Nies, A., Ravaris, C. L., Ives, J. O., and Bartlett, D. 1978. Clinical Pharmacology of Phenalzine. *Arch. Gen. Psychiatry*, 35, pp. 629-635.

Robitscher, J. B. 1966. *Pursuit of Agreement – Psychiatry and the Law*. Philadelphia, Lippincott.

Rosenheim, E., and Elizur, A. 1977. Group Therapy for Traumatic Neuroses. *Curr. Psychiatr. Ther.*, 17, pp. 143-148.

Rosenthal, T. L., and Bandura, A. 1978. Psychological Modeling: Theory and Practice. In *Handbook of Psychotherapy and Behavior Change: An*

Empirical Analysis, edited by S. L. Garfield and A. E. Bergin, New York, Wiley, pp. 621-658.

Rosner, R. 1982. *Clinical Issues in American Psychiatry and the Law*. Springfield, Charles C Thomas.

Round Table Meeting. Neurosis and Trauma. APA Convention, Atlantic City, N.J., 1960.

Sachse, H. R., and Scrignar, C. B. 1968. The Evolution of a Law and Psychiatry Program. *J. Legal Ed.*, 21, pp. 192-195.

Schultz, J. H., and Luther, W. 1969. *Autogenic Therapy (Vol. I)*. New York, Grune and Stratton.

Scrignar, C. B. 1967a. The Physician and the Law. Determination of Mental Competency to Stand Trial. *JAMA*, 201, pp. 343-346.

Scrignar, C. B. 1967b. Tranquilizers and the Psychotic Defendant. *Am. Bar Assoc. J.*, 533, pp. 43-45.

Scrignar, C. B. 1971. Maximum Security Hospitals: Where the People Are. *Newsletter Am. Acad. Psychiatr. Law*, 2, pp. 4-22.

Scrignar, C. B. 1974. Exposure Time as the Main Hierarchy Variable. *J. Behav. Ther. Exp. Psychiatry*, 5, pp. 153-155.

Scrignar, C. B. 1980. Mandatory Weight Control Program for 550 Police Officers Choosing Either Behavior Modification or "Will Power." *Obesity Bariatric Med.*, 9, pp. 88-92.

Scrignar, C. B. 1983. *Stress Strategies: The Treatment of the Anxiety Disorders*. Basel, S. Karger.

Scrignar, C. B., and Sachse, H. R. 1966. Tulane University School of Law – School of Medicine Training Program in Forensic Psychiatry. *Bull. Tulane Univ. Med. Faculty*, 25, pp. 311-315.

Scrignar, C. B., and Sachse, H. R. 1969. A Community and Action-Oriented Training Program in Law and Psychiatry. *J. Med. Ed.*, 44, pp. 52-56.

Scrignar, C. B., Swanson, W. C., and Bloom, W. A. 1973. Use of Systematic Desensitization in the Treatment of Airplane Phobic Patients. *Behav. Res.*

Ther., 2, pp. 129-131.

Selye, H. 1946. The General Adaptation Syndrome and the Diseases of Adaptation. *J. Clin. Endocrinol.*, 6, pp. 117-130.

Selye, H. 1950. *The Physiology and Pathology of Exposure to Stress*. Montreal, Acta Inc.

Selye, H. 1956. *The Stress of Life*. New York, McGraw-Hill.

Server, M. 1972. Teaching the Nonverbal Components of Assertive Training. *J. Behav. Ther. Exp. Psychiatry*, 3, pp. 179-183.

Shader, R. I., Greenblatt, D. J., and Ciraulo, D. A. 1981. Benzodiazepine Treatment of Specific Anxiety States. *Psychiatr. Ann.*, 11, pp. 30-40.

Shapiro, D. 1977. A Monologue on Biofeedback and Psychophysiology. *Psychophysiology*, 14, pp. 213-227.

Shields, J. 1962. *Monozygotic Twins Brought Up Apart and Together*. London, Oxford University.

Sierles, F. S., Chen, J. J., McFarland, R. E., and Taylor, M. A. 1983. Post-Traumatic Stress Disorder and Concurrent Psychiatric Illness: A Preliminary Report. *Am. J. Psychiatry*, 140, pp. 117-179.

Silving, H. 1967. *Essays on Mental Incapacity and Criminal Conduct*. Springfield, Charles C Thomas.

Skinner, B. F. 1938. *The Behavior of Organisms*. New York, Appleton-Century-Crofts.

Slater, E. 1943. The Neurotic Constitution. *J. Neurol. Psychiatry*, 6, pp. 1-16.

Slater, E., and Shields, J. 1969. Genetical Aspects of Anxiety. *Br. J. Psychiatry*, 3, pp. 62-71.

Slovenko, R. 1963. Psychiatry, Criminal Law, and the Role of the Psychiatrist. *Duke Law J.*, 3, pp. 395-426.

Slovenko, R. 1973. *Psychiatry and Law*. Boston, Little, Brown and Co.

Sparr, L., and Pankratz, L. 1983. Factitious Post-Traumatic Stress Disorder.

Am. J. Psychiatry, 140, pp. 1016-1019.

Spiegel, D. 1981. Vietnam Grief Work Using Hypnosis. *Am. J. Clin. Hypn.*, 24, pp. 33-40.

Spiro, H. R. 1968. Chronic Factitious Illness: Munchhausen's Syndrome. *Arch. Gen. Psychiatry*, 18, pp. 569-579.

Sprehe, D. J. 1982. Follow-up of Five Hundred and Ten (510) Consecutive Worker's Compensation Cases with Significant Psychiatric Disability. Presented at the 8th International Congress of Law and Psychiatry, Quebec, Canada.

State v. Heads, no. 106 126 (1st Jud. Dis. Ct. Caddo Parish) October 10, 1981.

State v. Jones 50 N.H. 369 (1871).

State v. Marks, 647 P2d 1292, Kansas, 1982.

State v. Pike 49 N.H. 399 (1869).

Stuart, R. B. 1975. *Treatment Contract*. Illinois, Research Press.

Stuart, R. B. 1980. *Helping Couples Change*. New York, Guilford.

Stuart, R. B., and Davis, B. 1982. *Slim Change in a Fat World: Behavioral Control of Obesity*. Chicago, Research.

Supplemental Studies for the National Commission on Workman's Compensation Laws. I(14). 1973.

Taylor, J. G. 1963. A Behavioral Interpretation of Obsessive-Compulsive Neurosis. *Behav. Res. Ther.*, 1, pp. 237-244.

Torgersen, S. 1978. The Contribution of Twin Studies to Psychiatric Nosology. In *Twin Research, Part A: Psychology and Methodology*, edited by W. E. Nance. New York, Alan R. Liss, pp. 125-130.

Trimble, M. R. 1981. *Post-Traumatic Neurosis: From Railway Spine to the Whiplash*. Chichester, John Wiley.

U.S. v. Currens, 290 Fed 2D751 (1961).

Valliant, G. E. 1981. Natural History of Male Psychological Health X: Work as a Predictor of Positive Mental Health. *Am. J. Psychiatry*, 125, pp. 1435-1439.

Volle, F. O. 1975. *Mental Evaluation of the Disability Claimant*. Springfield, Charles C Thomas.

Walker, J. I. 1981a. The Psychological Problems of Vietnam Veterans. *JAMA*, 246, pp. 781-782.

Walker, J. I. 1981b. Vietnam Combat Veterans with Legal Difficulties: A Psychiatric Problem. *Am. J. Psychiatry*, 138, pp. 1385-1395.

Walker, J. I., and Nash, J. L. 1981. Group Therapy in the Treatment of Vietnam Combat Veterans. *Int. J. Group Psychother.*, 31, pp. 379-388.

Wallace, R. K. 1970. Physiological Effects of Transcendental Meditation. *Science*, 167, pp. 1751-1754.

Washington v. United States, 390F. 2D862 (D.C. Cir. 1967).

Watson, J. B., and Rayner, P. 1920. Conditioned Emotional Reactions. *J. Exp. Psychol.*, 3, p. 1.

Weston, D. W. 1975. Development of Community Psychiatry Concepts. In *Comprehensive Textbook of Psychiatry*, edited by A. M. Freedman, H. I. Kaplan, and B. J. Sadock. Baltimore, Williams and Wilkins, pp. 2310-2323.

Wheeler, E. O., White, P. D., Reed, E., and Cohen, M. E. 1948. Familial Incidence of Neurocirculatory Asthenia ("Anxiety Neurosis," "Effort Syndrome"). *J. Clin. Invest.*, 27, p. 562.

Wilson, J. P. 1980. *Forgotten Warrior Project*. Cincinnati, Disabled American Veterans.

Wolpe, J. 1948. An Approach to the Problem of Neurosis Based on the Conditioned Response. M.D. Thesis, University of the Witerwatersrand.

Wolpe, J. 1958. *Psychotherapy by Reciprocal Inhibition*. Stanford, Stanford University.

Wolpe, J. 1978. Cognition and Causation in Human Behavior and Its Therapy. *Am. Psychol.*, 33, pp. 437-446.

Wolpe, J. 1982. *The Practice of Behavior Therapy* (third edition). New York, Pergamon.

Wooley, C. F. 1976. Where are the Diseases of Yesteryear? DaCosta's Syndrome, Soldier's Heart, the Effort Syndrome, Neurocirculatory Asthenia, and the Mitral Valve Prolapse Syndrome. *Circulation*, 53, pp. 749-751.

Wooley, C. F. 1982. Jacob Mendez DaCosta: Medical Teacher, Clinician, and Clinical Investigator. *Am. J. Cardiol.*, 50, pp. 1145-1148.

Yamagami, T. 1971. The Treatment of an Obsession by Thought-Stopping. *J. Behav. Ther. Exp. Psychiatry*, 2, pp. 133-135.

Ziskin, J. 1981. *Coping with Psychiatric and Psychological Testimony* (third edition). Venice, Law and Psychiatry Press.

Zunzunegui, V. 1982. Data Findings in the Examination of Torture Victims. Symposium on Torture, Medical Practice, and Medical Ethics, American Association for the Advancement of Science, Washington D.C.

Zusman, J., and Simon, J. 1983. Differences in Repeated Psychiatric Examinations of Litigants to a Lawsuit. *Am. J. Psychiatry*, 140, pp. 1300-1304.

INDEX

abreaction: under hypnosis, 112-13; in intravenous administration, 113

accidents: encephalic events, 36; endogenous sensations, 36; environmental event, 35; and PTSD development, 15-17. *See also specific accident case history*

acute PTSD stage, 44-48; abreaction under hypnosis, 112; anxiety in, 61, 64, 68, 88, 90; and litigation, 65, 68-69; nightmares in, 64-65, 102; retraumatization in, 64; sleep disturbance in, 64-65, 102; spiral effect in, 68; symptoms, 61, 64-65, 68-69, 101-2; treatment during, 101-2

aggressive behavior, and assertive behavior, comparison of, 124-26

Agras, W. S., 121

airplane crash, case history: family conference, 190-91; family history, 187; history of illness, 185-86; past history, 186; problem-solving sessions, 191; treatment, 118-20, 187-92

alarm reaction, 6

Alberti, R. E., 124

alcohol/drug abuse: in chronic PTSD stage, 72, 114; PTSD patients and, 96-97. *See also* substance use disorder

ALI test, 144-45, 152-54, 237

alprazolam, 114

American Journal of Medical Sciences, 2

American Psychiatric Association, 5, 145-48, 155, 237-39

antidepressants, 115

antisocial personality disorder: diagnostic criteria, 93, 96; and PTSD, 92

anxiety: in acute PTSD stage, 61, 64, 68; in chronic PTSD stage, 69, 74; nomenclature revision, 8-10; phobic, 118; in PTSD patients, 80-81; and stress, 7; and trauma, 8

anxiety disorder, 9; family incidence, 40-41; prevalence of, 40; and PTSD predisposition, 41-43; twin studies, 41. *See also* generalized anxiety disorder

anxiety neurosis, *see* neurosis

assertive behavior: comparison with aggressive behavior, 124-26; treatment of, 123-26, 232

Ativan, *see* lorazepam

audio cassette, use of: in behavioral rehearsal, 125; in encephalic reconditioning treatment, 111; in hypnosis treatment, 108, 191-92; in relaxation treatment, 107, 203

Auerbach, D. B., 84

automobile accident, case history: family history, 202-3; history of illness, 200-2; past history, 202; treatment, 203-6

Bain, J. S., 110

Barlow, D. H., 118, 121

Beck, A. T., 109, 113, 198

behavioral rehearsal, 125-26

benzodiazepines, 114

Brend, W. A., 39, 54

Brende, J. O., 130

Brill, N. Q., 39

Bromberg, W., 49, 85, 142

Brown, W. A., 174

Burgess, A. W., 209

Burris, B. T., 115

Cameron, R., 109, 114

Cannon, Walter B., 6

Caplan, G., 175

case histories: airplane crash, 185-92; automobile accident, 200-6; environmental trauma, 28-30, 35; oil

rig accident, 192-200; rape, 206-11; Vietnam veterans and criminal conduct, 211-21
catastrophe victims, delayed PTSD in, 54
Cheek, D. B., 105
chronic PTSD stage, 48-51; abreaction under hypnosis, 112-13; alcohol/drug abuse, 72; anxiety in, 69, 88, 90; exercise and, 128; and group therapy, 130; among hypochondriacal patients, 82; and litigation, 50-51, 69, 73; medication, 114-15; nightmares in, 72, 74; sleep disturbance in, 72, 74; symptoms, 69, 72-74, 102; tertiary prevention, 181-82, 184; treatment, 102-3
clonazepam, 115
cognition therapy, 113
Cohen, M. E., 4, 39, 40, 85
combat neurosis, 4
combat veterans, see Vietnam veterans
conversion disorder, 78, 80-81
Cornfield, R. B., 115
Council on Research and Development, Committee on Anxiety and Dissociative Disorders, 8-9
criminal conduct, Vietnam-era veterans and, 211-21
criminal process, 151-55, 239-41
criminal responsibility: ALI test, 144-45, 152-54, 237; Durham rule, 143-44, 237; irresistible impulse test, 142-43, 237; M'Naughton rule, 142-43, 237
Crowe, R. R., 40, 41
Curran, J. B., 126

DaCosta, J. M., 2-3
DaCosta's Syndrome, 3
Dalmane, 117
Dawley, H. H., 124
delayed PTSD, 51-55, 229-30; case study, 52-53; in catastrophe victims, 54; diagnosis, 52, 54; in Vietnam veterans, 54-55

depression: during chronic PTSD stage, 72-73, 74; dysthmic disorder, 90, 92; medication, 115; PTSD and, 90, 92; treatment, 113
desensitization process, see systematic desensitization
Desyrel, see Trazadone HCl
diagnosis of PTSD, 75-97, 231; antisocial personality disorder, 93, 96; conversion disorder, 78, 80-81; dysthmic disorder, 90, 92; factitions disorder, 83-85; generalized anxiety disorder, 88, 90; hypochondriasis, 81-82; malingerers, 85-87; and psychiatric disorder, 77; psychogenic pain disorder, 81; simple phobia, 88; somatization disorder, 78; substance use disorder, 96-97
Diamond, B. L., 142
diazepam, 114, 190, 210
dissociative reaction: depersonalization/derealization, 149-51, 239; and PTSD, 149-51, 239
drug/alcohol abuse, see alcohol/drug abuse
Dunner, F., 114
Durham rule, 143-44, 237
dysthmic disorder, 90, 92

Effort Syndrome, 3, 4
Elizur, A., 130
emergency situations, 6
Emmons, M. L., 124
encephalic events: case history, 28-30, 36; role in PTSD development, 23-24, 232; spiral effect in, 27-28, 38, 109; treatment and, 103
encephalic reconditioning treatment, 109-14; abreaction following hypnosis, 112-13; airplane crash patients, 189; assertive behavior and, 125; automobile accident patients, 203; cognition therapy, 113-14; definition, 109; depression, 113; hypnosis and, 112; oil rig accident patients, 197; positive encephalic

practice, 110-11; positive reinforcing statements, 111
endogenous events: spiral effect in, 27-28, 38; and treatment, 103, 232
environmental stimulus, see environmental trauma
environmental trauma: case history, 28-30, 35; chemical substances, 19-20; criminal assaults, 17-19; industrial trauma, 16-17; minimal, 21-22; PTSD development and, 15-23; rescuers at disaster site, 20-21; as source of pathological anxiety, 15-23; treatment and, 103; vehicular trauma, 15-16
Erlinder, C. P., 162, 168
exercise in treatment, 127-29, 233

factitious disorder, 83-85
Fairbank, J. A., 55
family conferences: for airplane crash patients, 190-91; marital therapy, 123, 190-91; for oil rig accident patients, 197, 199; in treatment, 122-23, 233
Fezler, W. D., 105, 109
Figley, C. R., 55
Fischer, V. Boyle, 55
flight-or-fight response, 6
flurazepam, 117
Ford, C. V., 84
Fremouw, W. J., 125
Freud, Sigmund, 3
Friedman, M. J., 55

Gallant, D. M., 115
Ganser, S. J. M., 84
Ganser's Syndrome, 84
General Adaptation Syndrome, 6
generalized anxiety disorder: in chronic PTSD stage, 48; diagnostic criteria, 88, 90
Gilbert, F. S., 126
Glueck, S., 142, 143
Golden, S., 84
Goodbye Darkness: A Memoir of the Pacific War, 54
Goodwin, J., 55
Gottschalk, L. S., 109
Greden, J. F., 130
Grinker, R., 4
group treatment, 130-31, 234
Guttmacher, M., 142, 144

Halcion, 118
Hogben, G. O., 115
Holland, B. C., 85
Hollister, L. E., 114
homeostasis response, 6
Horowitz, M. J., 61
hypnosis, 107-9, 188; encephalic reconditioning and, 112; and treatment of pain, 108
hypochondriasis, 81-82

Inderal, 115
industrial accidents: primary prevention of PTSD, 176-77; and PTSD development, 42-43; secondary prevention of PTSD, 178, 180. See also oil rig accident case
injury, and PTSD development, 16-17
injury litigation, see litigation
insanity defense: APA statement, 145-48, 155, 237-39; criminal responsibility tests, 142-45; defense position, 165-68, 243-44; murder cases, 168-69; plaintiff position, 162-65, 243; prosecutor position, 172-73, 246; psychiatric evaluation, 155-61; and PTSD, 151-55, 161-74, 245-46; rape cases, 169-70
insomnia, see sleep disturbance
irresistible impulse test, 142-43, 237
irritable heart, 3, 4

Jacobsen, E., 105
Jones, M. C., 7

Kaiser, L., 4
Kaloupek, D. G., 118
Kardimer, A., 4, 138

Keane, T. M., 55, 118
Klinger, E., 109
Kolb, L. C., 51, 113, 115
Kosbad, F. P., 109
Kroger, W. S., 105, 109

LaCron, L. M., 105
Larson, A., 140
legal action, *see* litigation
Lewis, T., 3, 4
Lewy, E., 39, 54
Linn, L., 61
litigation: during acute PTSD stage, 65, 68-69; during chronic PTSD stage, 50-51, 69, 73; among conversion disorder patients, 80-81; among PTSD patients, 80-81
Little Albert experiment, 7
lorazepam, 114
Ludiomil, 115
Ludwig, A. M., 114
Luther, W., 105

MacDonald, J. E., 84
Mace, E. B., 92
Mahoney, M. J., 110
malingering: diagnostic criteria, 85-87; and insanity defense, 165-68, 244
Malone, W. S., 138, 140
Manchester, W., 54
maprotiline HCl, 115
Marks, I., 121, 125, 130
Mavissakalian, M., 118
McCalb, J., 141
McInnes, R. G., 40
McLean, A., 176
medication, 114-15, 117-18; for airplane crash patients, 190; antidepressants, 115, 203; for automobile accident patients, 203-4; for oil rig accident patients, 199; in sleep disturbance, 117-18, 203-4
Meichenbaum, D. D., 109, 113
Mielke, D. H., 114
Mitral Valve Prolapse Syndrome, 3
M'Naughton rule, 142-43, 237
Modlin, H., 5

monoamine oxidase inhibitor, 115
Mutalipassi, L. R., 51, 113, 115

Nardil, 115
Nash, J. L., 130
neurocirculatory asthenia, 3
neurosis: development of, 4; war veterans and, 4. *See also* traumatic neurosis; triggered neurosis
nightmares: in acute PTSD stage, 64-65; in chronic PTSD stage, 72, 74
Noyes, R., 40
nutrition, in treatment, 127-28, 130

oil rig accident case history: family history, 195; history of illness, 193-94; past history, 195; treatment, 195-200
Oppenheimer, B. S., 3
Organic Brain Syndrome, 76

pain: hypnosis treatment, 108; among PTSD patients, 81
Pankratz, L., 85
Pasewark, R. A., 148
passive relaxation technique, 106
pathologic anxiety, 13-14; acute PTSD stage and, 61, 68; case history, 28-30, 35-37; encephalic events, 23-24, 36, 37-38, 226, 232; endogenous events, 24-26, 36-38, 226, 232; environmental trauma, 15-23, 35, 37, 225; phobic patients and, 88; sources of, 14-26; treatment, 103
Paul, G. L., 118
Pavlov, I. P., 7
personality, antisocial, *see* antisocial personality disorder
phenalzine sulfate, 115
phobia: acute PTSD stage and, 102; diagnostic criteria, 88
phobic treatment: construction of hierarchy, 119; imaginal desensitization, 120-21; in vivo desensitization, 121-22; systematic desensitization, 118-19, 189-90, 233

physical injury, *see* injury
PMR, *see* progressive muscle relaxation
Post Accident Anxiety Syndrome, 5
post-traumatic stress disorder, *see* PTSD; PTSD development
predisposition, 41-43, 55-56, 227
prevention, of PTSD: primary, 175, 176-77; secondary, 177-78, 180-81; tertiary, 181-82, 184; types of, 175, 235-36
primary prevention, 175, 176-77; defined, 175
progressive muscle relaxation: airplane crash patients, 188-89; automobile accident patients, 203; difference between hypnosis and, 108-9. *See also* passive relaxation
propanolol HCl, 115
pseudodementia, 84
pseudopsychosis, 84
psychiatric evaluation: history of trauma, 158-59, 242; mental status examination, 160-61, 242; posttraumatic history, 159-60, 242; pretraumatic history, 156-58, 242
psychogenic pain disorder, 81
psychophysiology: effects of war, 4; traumatic aspects, 6
psychosis, trauma and, 76-77
PTSD: and ALI test, 152-54; antisocial personality disorder, differentiation from, 93, 96; as clinical disorder, 139-40; and criminal process, 151-55, 239-41; depression and, 90, 92; diagnosis of, 75-97, 231; and dissociative reaction, 149-51, 239; encephalic reconditioning, 109-14; factitious disorder, differentiation from, 83-85; hypochondriasis, differentiation from, 81-82; hypnosis treatment, 107-9, 112; and insanity defense, 151-55, 161-74, 245-46; malingering, differentiation from, 85-87; medication, 114-15, 117-18; and murder, 168-69; psychiatric evaluation, 155-61, 241-42; psychogenic pain disorder, differentiation from, 81; and rape, 169-70, 244-45; relaxation treatment, 105-9; simple phobia, differentiation from, 88; somatization disorder, differentiation from, 78; substance use disorder and, 92, 96-97; symptoms, 58, 60-61, 64-65, 68-69, 72-74, 230-31; and tort, 137-38, 236; and worker's compensation, 141, 236-37
PTSD development: case histories, 28-30, 35-37; chemical substances, 19-20; clinical course, 43-56, 58, 60-61, 64-65, 68-69, 72-74, 228-30; in criminal assaults, 17-19; delayed PTSD, 51-55, 229-30; encephalic events and, 23-24, 36, 37-38, 226; endogenous events and, 24-26, 36-38, 226; environmental trauma and, 15-23; minimal environmental trauma and, 21-22, predisposition toward, 41-43, 55-56, 227; in rescuers at a disaster site, 20-21

Quitkin, F. M., 114

Raifman, L. J., 161
rape case history: family history, 208; history of illness, 206-7; past history, 207-8; treatment, 208-11
Rapoport, J., 130
relaxation training, 105-9; airplane crash patients, 188; oil rig accident patients, 197, 198; passive relaxation, 106; progressive muscle relaxation, 105-7; techniques, 105. *See also* hypnosis
Restoril, *see* temazepam
retraumatization, 26, 226-27; during acute PTSD stage, 64, 68; explanation during treatment, 103, 105; in insanity defense, 163
Robinson, D. S., 115
Robitscher, J. B., 5, 39, 85, 143
Rosenheim, E., 130

Rosenthal, T. L., 121
Rosner, R., 85

Schultz, J. H., 105
Scrignar, C. B., 126, 130, 154, 191
secondary prevention, 177-78, 180-81; defined, 175
Selye, H., 6
Server, M., 125
Shader, R. I., 114
Shapiro, D., 105
Shields, J., 41
Sierles, F. S., 92, 139, 151
Silving, H., 143
Simon, J., 77, 85
simple phobia, *see* phobia
Simpson, G. M., 115
Skinner, B. F., 7
Slater, E., 39, 41
sleep disturbance: in acute PTSD stage, 64-65; in chronic PTSD stage, 72; medication, 115, 117-18, 203-4; treatment, 117
Slovenko, R., 4, 85, 144
Soldier's Heart, 3
soldiers' symptoms, 4
somatization disorder, 78
somatoform disorders, 77-78; conversion disorder, 78, 81; hypochondriasis, 81-82; psychogenic pain disorder, 81; somatization disorder, 78
Sparr, L., 85
Spiegel, D., 4, 138
Spiegel, J. P., 113
Spiral Effect, 27-28, 38; in acute PTSD stage, 68; explanation during treatment, 103, 105; in insanity defense, 163
Sprehe, D. J., 50
stages of PTSD: acute PTSD stage, 44-48, 61, 64-65, 68-69, 88, 90, 228; chronic PTSD stage, 48-51, 69, 72-74, 88, 90, 228-29; response to trauma stage, 43, 58, 60-61, 228
stress: and anxiety, 7; behavioral perspective, 7-8

Stuart, R. B., 123, 130, 191
substance use disorder: defined, 96; diagnostic criteria, 96-97; Vietnam veterans and, 92
symptoms, 230-31: acute PTSD stage, 61, 64-65, 68-69, 101-2; antisocial personality disorder, 93, 96; chronic PTSD state, 69, 72-74; conversion disorder, 78, 80-81; dysthmic disorder, 90, 92; factitious disorder, 83-85; generalized anxiety disorder, 88, 90; hypochondriasis, 81-82; psychogenic pain disorder, 81; response to trauma stage, 58, 60-61; simple phobia, 88; somatization disorder, 78; substance use disorder, 96-97
systematic desensitization, in phobic treatment, 118-19, 189-90, 205, 233

Taylor, J. G., 110
temazepam, 118; for oil rig accident patients, 199
tertiary prevention, 181-82, 184; defined, 175
Torgersen, S., 41
tort and PTSD, 137-38, 236
trauma: delayed response to, 51-55; environmental, 1; nature of, 12; and psychological reactions, 2; psychophysiological aspects of, 6; psychosis and, 76-77; relationship to anxiety, 8; response to, 43, 58, 60-61. *See also* war trauma
traumatic neurosis, 1, 4-5; animal experimentation, 7-8
traumatic principle, 22-23, 225
Traumatic War Neurosis, 4; and Nardil use, 115
trazadone HCl, 115, 203
treatment of PTSD: abreaction, 112-13; acute PTSD stage, 101-2; airplane crash case, 187-92; assertiveness training, 123-26, 232; chronic PTSD stage, 102-3; clinicians attitude, 100; cognition

therapy, 113-14; depression, 113; encephalic reconditioning, 109-14, 197, 203, 209; exercise, 127-29, 191-92, 233; explanation and education, 100-3, 105, 187-88, 196-97, 203; family conferences, 122-23, 190-91, 197, 205, 232; goal of, 99; group treatment, 130-31, 234; hypnosis, 107-9; marital therapy, 123, 190-91; medication, 114-15, 117-18, 190, 199, 203-4; nutrition, 127-28, 130, 191-92; oil rig accident patients, 195-200; pathologic anxiety and, 103, 231-32; patients' responses, 234-35; phobic anxiety, 118-22, 233; problem solving, 126, 191, 232-33; rape victims, 208-11; self-assessment, 131-33, 233, self-hypnosis, 107-9; and social/recreational activities, 135-36, 234; termination of, 136; training in relaxation, 105-9, 188, 197, 203; and work activities, 133-35, 234
triggered neurosis, 5
Trimble, M. R., 76, 85

Valium, *see* diazepam
Valliant, G. E., 50
vehicular trauma, 15-16
Vietnam veterans: antisocial personality disorder, 92, 93; case history of, 211-21; delayed PTSD in, 54-55, 229; hostage incident, 217-19; rap group therapy, 130, 234; substance use disorder, 92; treatment of phobic anxiety, 119
Volle, F. O., 156

Walker, J. I., 55, 92, 130
Wallace, R. K., 105
war trauma, 2-4; and psychological sequel, 2; in World War II veterans, 3, 4
Ward, R. S., 85
Watson, J. B., 7
Wenrich, W. W., 124
Weston, D. W., 175
Wheeler, E. O., 41
Wilson, J. P., 55, 92
Winstead, D. K., 114
Wolpe, J., 7-8, 114, 118, 120, 121, 125
worker's compensation: defined, 139-40; history, 140-41; objectives of, 141; and PTSD, 141, 236-37

Xanax, *see* alprazolam

Yamagami, T., 110

Ziskin, J., 173
Zunzunegui, V., 138
Zusman, J., 77, 85

ABOUT THE AUTHOR

C. B. Scrignar, M.D., received his training in medicine and psychiatry at Tulane University School of Medicine in New Orleans following which he joined the faculty in 1964. As director of social psychiatry, he guided programs combating juvenile delinquency and drug abuse, and consulted at prisons and a maximum security hospital. For over a decade he codirected the Tulane University School of Law – School of Medicine Training Program in Law and Psychiatry and was appointed an adjunct professor of law and psychiatry at Tulane Law School. By appointment of the governor, he has served as chairman of the Louisiana Narcotics Rehabilitation Commission and was appointed by the mayor of New Orleans as chairman of the Action Task Force on Juvenile Delinquency Prevention.

He has written extensively about forensic psychiatry, stress and anxiety disorders, drug addiction, human sexuality, crime and delinquency, behavior therapy, and hypnosis. In 1981, his writing received recognition with a Milton H. Erickson Award of Scientific Excellence for writing in Hypnosis. His first book, *Stress Strategies: The Treatment of the Anxiety Disorders*, was published by S. Karger in 1983.

Currently, Dr. Scrignar is in the private practice of psychiatry and is a clinical professor of psychiatry at Tulane University School of Medicine and an adjunct professor at Xavier University. He also lectures at Tulane University Schools of Law and Social Work.